ETHICS IN CARIBBEAN ARCHAEOLOGY

UNIVERSITY PRESS OF FLORIDA

Florida A&M University, Tallahassee
Florida Atlantic University, Boca Raton
Florida Gulf Coast University, Ft. Myers
Florida International University, Miami
Florida State University, Tallahassee
New College of Florida, Sarasota
University of Central Florida, Orlando
University of Florida, Gainesville
University of North Florida, Jacksonville
University of South Florida, Tampa
University of West Florida, Pensacola

Ethics in Caribbean Archaeology

Past, Present, and Future

Edited by
Felicia J. Fricke,
Eduardo Herrera Malatesta,
and Maaike S. de Waal

UNIVERSITY PRESS OF FLORIDA

Gainesville/Tallahassee/Tampa/Boca Raton
Pensacola/Orlando/Miami/Jacksonville/Ft. Myers/Sarasota

Published in the United States of America

31 30 29 28 27 26   6 5 4 3 2 1

DOI: https://doi.org/10.5744/9780813079509

Library of Congress Cataloging-in-Publication Data
Names: Fricke, Felicia editor | Herrera Malatesta, Eduardo editor | Waal, Maaike S. de editor
Title: Ethics in Caribbean archaeology : past, present, and future / edited by Felicia J. Fricke, Eduardo Herrera Malatesta, Maaike S. de Waal.
Description: Gainesville : University Press of Florida, 2026. | Includes bibliographical references and index.
Identifiers: LCCN 2025027402 (print) | LCCN 2025027403 (ebook) | ISBN 9780813079509 hardback | ISBN 9780813081281 paperback | ISBN 9780813075129 ebook | ISBN 9780813074207 pdf
Subjects: LCSH: Archaeology—Moral and ethical aspects—Caribbean Area | Archaeologists—Professional ethics—Caribbean Area | Indians of the West Indies—Antiquities | Caribbean Area—Antiquities
Classification: LCC CC175 .E836 2026 (print) | LCC CC175 (ebook) | DDC 972.9—dc23/eng/20250919
LC record available at https://lccn.loc.gov/2025027402
LC ebook record available at https://lccn.loc.gov/2025027403

The University Press of Florida is the scholarly publishing agency for the State University System of Florida, comprising Florida A&M University, Florida Atlantic University, Florida Gulf Coast University, Florida International University, Florida State University, New College of Florida, University of Central Florida, University of Florida, University of North Florida, University of South Florida, and University of West Florida.

University Press of Florida
PO Box 140239
Gainesville, FL 32614
floridapress.org

GPSR EU Authorized Representative: Mare Nostrum Group B.V., Doelen 72, 4831 GR Breda, The Netherlands, gpsr@mare-nostrum.co.uk

CONTENTS

FIGURES

TABLES

ACKNOWLEDGMENTS

The editors of this volume would like to thank Mary Puckett, our acquisitions editor at the University Press of Florida, for her help and encouragement throughout the development of this volume. We would also like to thank those who funded, administered, and presented at the workshop in Leiden (The Netherlands) in November 2023, where we brought chapter authors together to discuss the ethical issues they came across during their work; Henriette Jensenius and Maria Krebbers at the Lorentz Center; Alfredo González-Ruibal for an inspiring keynote speech; and the University of Copenhagen's Centre for Modern European Studies (CEMES). We would also like to thank those who contributed to the open-access fee, allowing this volume to be read in PDF format anywhere in the world: the Max Planck Institute for Evolutionary Anthropology; the Wenner-Gren Foundation; Marie Skłodowska-Curie Action (HORIZON-MSCA-2021-PF-01-01, grant agreement no. 101062882); and the In the Same Sea history project funded by the European Research Council (ERC) under the European Union's Horizon 2020 research and innovation programme (grant agreement no. erc-2019-cog 863671), PI Gunvor Simonsen. Thanks also to the Racialized Motherhood history project funded by the Danmarks Frie Forskningsfond (Grant ID 10.46540/2063-00035B). Finally, we would like to thank all the chapter authors, whose insights have been so stimulating. We learned a lot during the process of developing this volume and we are excited to continue learning from our colleagues, stakeholders, and friends in the field of Caribbean archaeological ethics.

Introduction

Sparking the Fire for an Ethically Committed Discipline

Felicia J. Fricke, Eduardo Herrera Malatesta, and Maaike S. de Waal

For decades, there has been a latent interest in doing Caribbean archaeology "right" and in decolonizing the discipline (see, for example, González-Tennant 2014; Pagán-Jiménez and Rodríguez Ramos 2008; and Rivera-Collazo 2011), but since 2019 this has solidified into a more radical movement toward ethics. This shift (as in the wider discipline) is primarily coming from local and early career scholars (González Ruibal 2019; Ostapkowicz and Hanna 2021; Wade 2019). Yet, it is surprising that this is the first edited volume to be written on ethics in Caribbean archaeology. Here, we bring together 28 of the region's thinkers at the cutting edge of Caribbean archaeological ethics and ask: Where has the discipline been? Where is it now? And most importantly, where is it going?

Although different authors in this volume may have different approaches and different definitions of ethics, we consider that ethics comprises how to systematize, defend, and recommend parameters of what is right and wrong behavior in a given context (Colley 2015; Floridi and Taddeo 2016). For example, Pierce and Henry (1996) identified three main influences on people's ethical decisions: the individual's own personal code of ethics (also known as morals), any informal code of conduct that exists in the context, and exposure to formal codes of ethics. While their paper is almost 30 years old, its conclusions are still valid, particularly in contexts such as the Caribbean, where there is a combination of largely unethical "traditional" approaches, there are limited or absent legal regulations regarding archaeological work, and the majority of researchers involved are not originally from the region itself.

In archaeology as a wider profession, ethics debates have been happening since the 1930s (Colley 2015), and many associations, groups, and organizations have created professional codes to direct appropriate actions, behaviors, and quality of research. One specialist area that has had a lot of attention in recent years has been that of human osteology or biological anthropology (see, for example, de la Cova et al. 2024; Mickleburgh et al. 2022; and Sholts 2024). However, the advancement of such codes has often not kept pace with technological and other developments, for example in digital archaeology (see Herrera Malatesta, this volume), biomolecular analysis (see Nägele, Benn Torres, and Nieves-Colón, this volume; and Nilsson Stutz 2022), open science (Palmisano and Titolo 2024), and with respect to archaeological contributions to climate change (see Fricke, Giovas, Hanna, Shorter, and Victorina, this volume). Although a few archaeological organizations do have codes of ethics that aim to tackle fast developing technologies, such as the Society of American Archaeology (Dennis 2020) and the Computer Applications and Quantitative Methods in Archaeology (CAA) (Brughmans et al. 2018), the lack of appropriate ethical codes worldwide has left "digital archaeology operating in an ethical limbo, wherein practitioners have clear expectations of how the conventional . . . archaeological aspects of their work should be considered in terms of ethics, but are largely left to their own devices as regards ethical decision-making" (Dennis 2020: 210). This quote might well have been written about Caribbean archaeology, which has often been considered a field of free reign by archaeologists, particularly those from outside the region.

Improvement will of course necessitate consideration of how researchers can be held accountable for ethical misconduct or malpractices in the future. This is difficult. As Dennis (2020) rightly argues, it is often unclear "how this is to be accomplished, what metrics should be used to measure effectiveness, and mostly [sic] importantly what should happen if the archaeologist fails to 'practice and promote stewardship'" (Dennis 2020: 211). The fact is that codes of ethics are guidelines based on peer consensus and do not provide a legally binding set of rules. Moreover, while a code of ethics serves to regulate and suggest "good" behavior, it is important to consider that what is good for one group might not be for another. A code of ethics is set by the standards and cultural patterns of its producers and rarely is consultation with external communities considered (Curtoni 2015). For example, current heritage movements led by local leaders and communities are fighting to gain access to heritage sites and to narrative creation (kok 2022). For centuries, scholars have been the gatekeepers of the past, often forgetting the rights and perspectives of local communities, particularly when those communities are non-elite groups, such as African diasporic and Indigenous communities (see White, this volume). Shepherd (2015: 11), debating the extent of the language of ethics, has asked, "How do we develop a conversation around questions of care, accountability, and responsible or 'right' action in the world, outside of the framework of a professionalized discourse on ethics?" Together with other authors who have raised critiques about codes of ethics and the discussion of ethics in general, Shepherd argues that archaeological ethics is an epistemological project that perpetuates the coloniality of archaeology. This is because the knowledge produced within these debates originates from professional archaeologists and not from affected local communities. In this sense, ethics debates should not aim to just talk with local communities but integrate them within knowledge production. As long as terms such as "science" versus "tradition" and "knowledge" versus "local beliefs" are placed against each other, ethics debates will continue to be asymmetrical and perpetuate hegemonic archaeological discourses (Herrera Malatesta and Jean 2023). Including many voices in the archaeological narrative creation is not just important; it is at bottom an ethical issue.

The Insular Caribbean

Indeed, there are many voices in the region (Jean and Herrera Malatesta 2024). The insular Caribbean (Figure 0.1) is an archipelago made up of more than 700 islands, varying wildly in their social, economic, political, and environmental characteristics. In terms of their governance, they exist on a spectrum from completely independent countries (e.g., Barbados, Cuba), to independent entities remaining under the aegis of the colonial power (e.g., Aruba, Curaçao, Sint Maarten), to comprehensively colonized territories (e.g., the US Virgin Islands, Guadeloupe, Puerto Rico). Even within each of these categories, there is a lot of variation. That the governance practiced in the Caribbean is often exploitative and oppressive is reflected in the fact that of the 17 territories currently on the United Nations list of "Non-Self-Governing Territories," six are in the Caribbean (Turks and Caicos, the Cayman Islands, the US Virgin Islands, the British Virgin Islands, Anguilla, and Montserrat) (United Nations 2020). Additionally, several Caribbean nations are listed as "Small Island Developing States," known to "face unique social, economic and environmental vulnerabilities" (United Nations 2014). These circumstances all lead to a great diversity of heritage management systems.

Geographically, the insular Caribbean includes tectonically uplifted reef bed formations, such as Aruba and Anguilla, and volcanic islands, such as

Figure 0.1. The insular Caribbean, the region under discussion. Map by Eduardo Herrera Malatesta using Natural Earth public domain data, scale 1:10m.

Sint Maarten / Saint Martin and Martinique (Haviser 2001; Wilson 2007). These islands are populated by genetically and culturally diverse societies, consisting of the descendants of Indigenous people, European colonizers, African enslaved people, and indentured laborers from China and India (Palmié and Scarano 2013). More recently, the region's popularity with holidaymakers has encouraged the development of expatriate communities of wealthy Europeans and North Americans who choose to spend their retirement in the sunshine. Indeed, tourism has had a profound impact on the region as a whole and, importantly for this volume, on the region's archaeological heritage. The development of coastline resorts has led not only to the immediate destruction of archaeology at the construction site but also to widespread mangrove deforestation, which exacerbates the destruction of archaeological sites through erosion (Hofman et al. 2021). This is in addition to the increased coastal erosion occurring as a result of more frequent and stronger hurricanes caused by climate change (Stancioff et al. 2018). These trends mean that much Caribbean archaeology is under threat today in a way that it never has been before. The ethical turn in Caribbean archaeology is therefore more urgent than ever.

Brief History of Caribbean Archaeology

Broadly, archaeological research in the Caribbean can be divided into four stages. The first was led by explorers and naturalists who started reporting on Indigenous material culture in the late nineteenth and early twentieth centuries (e.g., De Booy 1915; Fewkes 1891; Schomburgk 1854). A second stage, initiated by professional archaeologists from the United States, ran from the early twentieth century until around the 1980s. This period was initially characterized by researchers following the culture-historical theoretical framework and focused mostly on the examination of single archaeological sites to construct culture histories (e.g., Cruxent and Rouse 1958; De Josselin de Jong 1947; Krieger 1929, 1931; Rouse 1939). Later, researchers following the historical materialist and Marxist theoretical frameworks sought to deepen archaeological interpretations of past people but continued working with single sites (e.g., Sanoja and Vargas Arenas 1974; Veloz Maggiolo, Ortega, and Caba Fuentes 1981). From the 1980s, a third stage saw increasing interest in regional archaeology and large-scale excavations. Even though previous research considered the analysis of large regions or even the entire Caribbean, these works were based on "single site" methodologies and not on regional perspectives (e.g., Versteeg and Rostain 1997; Versteeg and Schinkel 1992). This third period followed the new methodological developments of the processual school in archaeology and its aim of reconstructing past landscapes using detailed and large-scale databases (e.g., Binford 1964; Dunnell 1971; Kowalewski 1990).

The fourth stage, which we currently inhabit, relates to the use of new methods such as digital tools and computational analysis (see Herrera Malatesta, this volume) and biomolecular methods (see, for example, Nägele, Benn Torres, and Nieves-Colón, this volume). Chronologically, it overlaps with the previous stage, but it can be considered to have begun in the late 1990s and to have become established in the 2000s. This stage refers not simply to the use of digital technologies (e.g., computers, cameras), but rather to the use of digital tools for the identification or analysis of archaeological data (e.g., remote sensing) and the use of statistical and mathematical methods for the understanding of past patterns (Ullah 2018). Some examples from the Caribbean are studies in geophysics technologies and photogrammetry (e.g., Ulloa Hung and Sonnemann 2017; Whiting, McFarland, and Hackenberger 2001); GIS modeling, including visibility analysis (e.g., Brughmans et al. 2018; Torres and Rodríguez Ramos 2008); landscape modeling (e.g., Giovas et al. 2020; Stancioff 2018); critical cartographic modeling (e.g., Dunnavant, Wernke, and Kohut 2023; Hauser 2022); mobility analysis (e.g., Cooper 2010; Slayton 2018); predictive modeling (e.g., Ejstrud 2008; Hanna and Giovas 2022); 3D modeling (González-Quevedo et al. 2021; Landon and Seales 2005); spatial analysis (Altes 2013; Herrera Malatesta, Ulloa Hung, and Hofman 2023); network analysis (Hofman et al. 2019; Mol 2014); and Cultural Resource Management (e.g., Farmer 2008; Stancioff et al. 2018). Biomolecular contributions have included, for example, those in ancient DNA (e.g., Benn Torres 2016; Schroeder et al. 2015), isotopic analysis (e.g., Ebert et al. 2024; Laffoon et al. 2017), and proteomics (e.g., Harvey et al. 2019). Even this list does not represent the true breadth of work currently happening in the region. Important theoretical advances have included, for example, decolonial approaches (e.g., Pagán-Jiménez and Rodríguez Ramos 2008; and Rivera-Collazo 2011) and slow archaeology (e.g., Flewellen et al. 2022), while interdisciplinary studies are also increasing (e.g., Antczak and Hofman 2019; Cunningham 2023; Espersen 2016; Fricke 2020; Martin 2023; Reilly 2019; Zahedi 2025). Caribbean archaeology has been growing exponentially in recent decades, and this brings the need to reflect on how archaeologists will cope with the rapidly developing considerations of ethics in new stages of the discipline.

Coalition for Caribbean Archaeological Heritage

In the course of putting together this volume, it was important to us as editors that chapter authors were able to engage with one another in a mutually beneficial way. To this end, we organized a week-long hybrid workshop hosted by the Lorentz Center (Leiden, the Netherlands) in November 2023. During this workshop, we gave chapter authors the opportunity to meet each other, share their ethical challenges and solutions, and debate ideas with each other in a safe environment. While the workshop was helpful in developing the volume, it came to be a lot more than that. By the end of the week, workshop attendees had put together the outlines of an agenda for the ethical advancement of archaeology in the Caribbean region, including the concrete goals of putting together a network of Caribbean archaeologists supporting ethical work and developing an educational certificate in Caribbean archaeology to get more Caribbean people into the discipline (Herrera Malatesta et al., forthcoming). The success of this workshop and the urgency of addressing these goals led us to organize a second workshop, this time held at the University of Copenhagen in March 2024. Here, we expanded the participation to more Caribbean researchers beyond the authors of this book. During four days, a group of in-person and online participants worked toward making these goals a reality. We left this second workshop with concrete outputs, including a website to support the network, which is now named the Coalition for Caribbean Archaeological Heritage.[1] The coalition is a decentralized community of (primarily early career and Caribbean) scholars that will support the ethical development of the archaeological and heritage disciplines well into the future, together with local communities, museums, and local government agencies.

Chapter Summaries

In the following chapters, we learn from various people working in Caribbean archaeology and heritage. They bring their individual perspectives not only as archaeologists but also as activists, historians, museum curators, students, scholars, professors, independent researchers, and commercial employees. They are diverse in their national identities, coming from across the Caribbean (Barbados, Bonaire, Curaçao, Grenada, Haiti, Jamaica, Puerto Rico, Trinidad and Tobago, Venezuela) as well as from the wider Americas (Canada, Mexico, the United States) and Europe (Germany, Greece, the Netherlands, the United Kingdom). We have encouraged each author or group of authors to approach the topic of ethics in Caribbean archaeology in their own way, to define their own terms of engagement (such as "morals" or "ethics"; see Fink 2020), and to contribute what they think is most important to the discussion. Not all of us agree with each other or approach the subject in the same way, but for progress to be made in this area, complete agreement on terminology or approach is not always necessary (see, for example, Burns 2024 and Yin 2024 on use of language). Here, it is simply important to listen and learn from one another. We aimed to create a safe space for expressing important ethical concerns, whether we agreed with them or not.

An important landmark in the movement toward more ethical archaeological practice in the Caribbean was the unanimous ratification of a new code of ethics for the International Association for Caribbean Archaeology (IACA) in 2022. In Chapter 1, Fricke, Giovas, Hanna, Shorter, and Victorina describe the thorny process of developing such a code, the strengths and opportunities afforded by the document, and the areas where there is still room for improvement. Covering the topics of fieldwork, human remains, looting, curation, environmental impact, harassment, and strategies for holding perpetrators to account, they stress that such codes are supposed to be living documents that respond to developments in ethical and archaeological thought.

The most recognizable activity that archaeologists perform is that of fieldwork, a key locus for ethical challenges. The following few chapters present case studies from across the Eastern Caribbean, where the heritage of small islands is particularly affected by a lack of personnel, resources, and expertise, and where environmental threats may be more severe (Fricke and Hoerman 2023). White's presentation of community engagement practices in fieldwork on Saint Croix in the US Virgin Islands (Chapter 2) exposes an interesting debate about how heritage practitioners of African descent on this island are creating new ways to engage with the materiality of the past and the stories associated with it. White uses the simile of homegrown organic food production to highlight how people in Saint Croix are engaging with the challenging colonial past and reframing it into historical narratives that enhance Black history in the Caribbean. Looking beyond the standard representation of the past that over-focuses on the white colonizers is, based on White's perspective, an ethical issue that can only be solved by giving power to voices that have been unheard for centuries.

Taking discussions of recent heritage practices on Sint Eustatius as a starting point, kok (Chapter 3) investigates the relationship between ethics and cooperation with the local community. Rather than stemming from a formal research project, this chapter is an activist account representing personal opinions. It asks what might happen if heritage management and heritage protection are not approached only by looking at professional codes of ethics, but also by active community engagement. Similarly, in Chapter 4, Antczak, Ammerlaan, Morris, and Rodríguez Velásquez provide concrete examples of heritage strategies at various sites on the islands of Bonaire and Trinidad, and in the Venezuelan Caribbean. They stress the importance for archaeologists to actively and sensitively address and engage with Indigenous narratives and multivocality, to make sure that Indigenous and local people are engaged in setting research priorities and values, even before projects start.

After excavation, archaeologists may perform specialist analyses in the laboratory, away from the field and often entirely outside the Caribbean itself. This presents its own problems, from destruction of precious archaeological materials without community consent, to the (sometimes permanent) removal of archaeological remains from their island. On this topic, Seferidou, Chiappa, Brito-Pacheco, and Marengo Camacho (Chapter 5) provide a diachronic analysis of human bioarchaeological publications using Caribbean remains, focusing on whether they report community engagement and community consent. Their chapter encourages us to think about how the authors of academic articles in the field of human osteology or biological anthropology should be expected to cover this topic in the future.

In Chapter 6, Cunningham discusses the ancestral remains at Rupert's Valley on Saint Helena, an island geographically separated from the Caribbean but very much historically intertwined with it, and facing many of the same challenges. Rupert's Valley has been the focus of sustained archaeological research, as well as increasing public scrutiny and international attention, each presenting ethical issues. Cunningham describes the complexities associated with themes such as local community identities, and the roles of external activists and researchers.

Subsequently, Nägele, Benn Torres, and Nieves-Colón (Chapter 7) provide a comprehensive overview of the challenges facing ethical work in archaeogenomics, a discipline that has historically extracted vast amounts of data from the region without offering much in return. The authors argue that after decades of development in this field to study past migrations and relations across the Caribbean, we are at an excellent moment in history to assess the ethical implications of extracting genomes from human remains, as well as to evaluate the impact that this type of research has on the narratives archaeologists create about the past and pass along to local communities, governments, and other researchers. The contributors warn about the dangers of omitting the legacy of colonialism from scientific practices, as colonial perspectives have already permeated Caribbean archaeology for decades. Their chapter discusses the multilayered ethical challenges current and future researchers in archaeogenomics face and will face while providing guidelines for best practices.

Museums and curation must also be considered, to discuss what happens when projects end, or when archaeologists work with legacy data collected by others for (in some cases) different purposes. Both Martin and Jean (Chapter 8) and de Waal, Reilly, Bancroft, and Farmer (Chapter 9) focus on ethical issues and severe practical problems relating to storage and conservation of collections, gathered by international archaeologists, in local Caribbean heritage institutions, and the need to return collections that are kept outside the islands of origin. These contributions also highlight logistical challenges related to the care of returned collections. Where Martin and Jean stress the importance of post-excavation obligations for foreign researchers in order to guarantee solid storage of local and returned collections in the contexts of Haiti, Grenada, and Carriacou, de Waal, Reilly, Bancroft, and Farmer also emphasize the importance of the formulation of clear sets of demands by local heritage institutions before (international) archaeology projects can even start to be developed in Barbados and beyond.

In Chapter 10, Herrera Malatesta focuses on the topic of Caribbean digital archaeology, first highlighting challenges and often unforeseen side effects relating to the use of digital data and the creation of models. Then, he focuses on how Caribbean colonial history has impacted or could potentially impact digital database creation and representations. Third, he discusses the potential for digital neocolonialism and the importance of the involvement and accurate representation of Indigenous and local communities in Caribbean digital archaeology. Finally, he presents an overview of ethical issues and outlines best practices and recommendations.

We close the volume with a valuable and insightful critical reflection by Pagán-Jiménez and Rodríguez Ramos, who underline the complex nature of and diverse approaches toward ethics in Caribbean archaeology. They provide keywords that will help us move toward a more ethical future in our discipline: acknowledgment, deference, awareness, politics, and action.

With the contributions outlined above, we present an important selection of ethical issues that are pertinent in Caribbean archaeology today. However, we acknowledge that we will need to constantly adjust our approaches as ethical challenges change according to present and future technological, archaeological, environmental, social, economic, and political developments (Richardson 2018). While this volume is not, and cannot be, comprehensive, we very much hope that it is a useful and important entry point into the field. It is the first edited volume on ethics in Caribbean archaeology, and we all hope that it will spark the fire for an ethically committed discipline in years to come.

Note

1 The website can be found at www.cocah.net.

References Cited

Altes, Christopher F. 2013. "An Archaeology of Spatiality in the Caribbean." In *The Oxford Handbook of Caribbean Archaeology,* edited by William F. Keegan, Corinne L. Hofman, and Reniel Rodríguez Ramos, 296–302. Oxford: Oxford University Press.

Antczak, Andrzej T., and Corinne L. Hofman. 2019. "Dearchaizing the Caribbean Archaic." In *Early Settlers of the Insular Caribbean: Dearchaizing the Archaic,* edited by Corrine L. Hofman and Andrzej T. Antczak, 29–42. Leiden: Sidestone Press.

Benn Torres, Jada. 2016. "Genetic Anthropology and Archaeology: Inter-disciplinary Approaches to Human History in the Caribbean." *PaleoAmerica* 2(1): 1–5.

Binford, Lewis R. 1964. "A Consideration of Archaeological Research Design." *American Antiquity* 29(4): 425–441.

Brughmans, Thomas, Hugh Corley, L. Meghan Dennis, Kate Ellenberger, Penelope Foreman, César González-Pérez, Vivian S. James, Rachel Opitz, Hanna Marie Pageau, Sara Perry, Lorna-Jane Richardson, Doug Rocks-Macqueen, and Arianna Traviglia. 2018. "Ethics Policy of the Computer Applications and Quantitative Methods in Archaeology (CAA)." Computer Applications and Quantitative Methods in Archaeology (CAA). https://caa-international.org/about/policies/ethics-policy/ (accessed June 28, 2024).

Brughmans, Thomas, Maaike S. de Waal, Corinne L. Hofman, and Ulrik Brandes. (2018). "Exploring Transformations in Caribbean Indigenous Social Networks through Visibility Studies: The Case of Late Pre-Colonial Landscapes in East-Guadeloupe (French West Indies)." *Journal of Archaeological Method and Theory* 25(2): 475–519.

Burns, James Robert. 2024. "'Slaves' and 'Slave Owners' or 'Enslaved People' and 'Enslavers'?" *Transactions of the Royal Historical Society* 2: 371–388.

Colley, Sarah. 2015. "Ethics and Digital Heritage." In *The Ethics of Cultural Heritage,* edited by Tracy Ireland and John Schofield, 13–32. New York: Springer. https://doi.org/10.1007/978-1-4939-1649-8_2.

Cooper, Jago. 2010. "Modelling Mobility and Exchange in Pre-Columbian Cuba: GIS Led Approaches to Identifying Pathways and Reconstructing Journeys from the Archaeological Record." *Journal of Caribbean Archaeology* 9(3): 122–137.

Cruxent, José Maria, and Irving Rouse. 1982 [1958–1959]. *Arqueología Cronológica de Venezuela.* Caracas: Ernesto Armitano Editor.

Cunningham, Andreana. 2023. "Reframing Diaspora: Southeastern African Contributions to Biosocial Variation in Atlantic Afro-Descendant Groups." PhD dissertation, University of Florida, Gainesville.

Curtoni, Rafael Pedro. 2015. "Against Global Archaeological Ethics: Critical Views from South America." In *Ethics and Archaeological Praxis,* edited by Cristóbal Gnecco and Dorothy Lippert, 41–47. New York: Springer. https://doi.org/10.1007/978-1-4939-1646-7_4.

De Booy, T. D. 1915. "Pottery from Certain Caves in Eastern Santo Domingo, West Indies." *American Anthropologist* 17(1): 69–97.

De Josselin de Jong, Jan Petrus Benjamin. 1947. "Archaeological Material from Saba and St Eustatius, Lesser Antilles." Leiden: Rijksmuseum voor Volkenkunde.

De la Cova, Carlina, Courtney A. Hofman, Kathryn Marklein, Sabrina Sholts, Rachel Watkins, Paige Magrogan, and Molly Kathleen Zuckerman. 2024. "Ethical Futures in Biological Anthropology: Research, Teaching, Community Engagement, and Curation Involving Deceased Individuals." *American Journal of Biological Anthropology* 185: e24980.

Dennis, L. Meghan. 2020. "Digital Archaeological Ethics: Successes and Failures in Disciplinary Attention." *Journal of Computer Applications in Archaeology* 3(1): 210–218. https://doi.org/10.5334/jcaa.24.

Dunnavant, Justin P., Steven A. Wernke, and Lauren E. Kohut, 2023. "Counter-Mapping Maroon Cartographies: GIS and Anticolonial Modeling in St. Croix." *ACME: An International Journal for Critical Geographies* 22(5): 1294–1319. https://doi.org/10.7202/1107310ar.

Dunnell, Robert C. 1971. *Systematics in Prehistory.* New Jersey: Blackburn Press.

Ebert, Claire E., Sean W. Hixon, Richard J. George, Sofia I. Pacheco-Fores, Juan Manuel Palomo, Ashely E. Sharpe, Óscar R. Solís-Torres, J. Britt Davis, Ricardo Fernandes, and Douglas J. Kennett. 2024. "The Caribbean and Mesoamerica Biogeochemical Isotope Overview (CAMBIO)." *Scientific Data* 11: 394.

Ejstrud, Bo. 2008. "Maroons and Landscapes." *Journal of Caribbean Archaeology* 8: 1–14. https://www.floridamuseum.ufl.edu/jca.

Espersen, Ryan. 2016. "'Better than We': Landscapes and Materialities of Race, Class, and Gender in Pre-Emancipation Colonial Saba, Dutch Caribbean." PhD dissertation, Leiden University.

Farmer, Kevin. 2008. "Forward Planning: The Utilization of GIS in the Management of Archaeological Resources in Barbados." In *Archaeology and Geoinformatics: Case Studies from the Caribbean,* edited by Basil A. Reid, 74–86. Tuscaloosa: University of Alabama Press.

Fewkes, J. Walter. 1891. "On Zemes from Santo Domingo." *American Anthropologist* 4(2): 167–176.

Fink, Hand. 2020 "Against Ethical Exceptionalism—Through Critical Reflection on the History of Use of the Terms 'Ethics' and 'Morals' in Philosophy." *SATS* 21(2): 85–100.

Flewellen, Ayana Omilade, Alicia Odewale, Justin Dunnavant, Alexandra Jones, and William White III. 2022. "Creating Community and Engaging Community: The Foundations of the Estate Little Princess Archaeology Project in St. Croix, United States Virgin Islands." *International Journal of Historical Archaeology* 26: 147–176.

Floridi, Luciano, and Mariarosaria Taddeo. 2016. "What Is Data Ethics?" *Philosophical Transactions of the Royal Society A: Mathematical, Physical and Engineering Sciences* 374(2083): 20160360.

Fricke, Felicia, and Rachel Hoerman. 2023. "Archaeology and Social Justice in Island Worlds." *World Archaeology* 54(3): 484–489.

Fricke, Felicia J. 2020. *Slaafgemaakt: Rethinking Enslavement in the Dutch Caribbean.* Chicago: Common Ground Research Networks.

Giovas, Christina M., Michiel Kappers, Kelsey M. Lowe, and Laura Termes. 2020. "The Carriacou Ecodynamics Archaeology Project: First Results of Geophysical Survey and Landscape Archaeology at the Sabazan Site, The Grenadines." *Journal of Island and Coastal Archaeology* 15(3): 421–435. https://doi.org/10.1080/15564894.2019.1642969

González-Quevedo, Esteban Rubén Grau, Silvia Teresita Hernández Godoy, Racso Fernández Ortega, Ulises Miguel González Herrera, Jorge Garcell Domínguez, Alexis Morales Prada, Adolfo José López Belando, Mirjana Roksandic, and Yadira Chinique de Armas. 2021. "The Use of 3D Photogrammetry in the Analysis, Visualization, and Dissemination of the Indigenous Archaeological Heritage of the Greater Antilles." *Open Archaeology* 7(1): 435–453. https://doi.org/doi:10.1515/opar -2020-0144.

González-Ruibal, Alfredo. 2019. "Ethical Issues in Indigenous Archaeology: Problems with Difference and Collaboration." *Canadian Journal of Bioethics* 2(3): 34–43.

González-Tennant, Edward. 2014. "The 'Color' of Heritage: Decolonizing Collaborative Archaeology in the Caribbean." *Journal of African Diaspora Archaeology and Heritage* 3(1): 26–50.

Hanna, Jonathan A., and Christina M. Giovas. 2022. "An Islandscape IFD: Using the Ideal Free Distribution to Predict Pre-Columbian Settlements from Grenada to St. Vincent, Eastern Caribbean." *Environmental Archaeology* 27(4): 402–419. https://doi.org/10.1080/14614103.2019.1689895.

Harvey, Virginia L., Michelle J. LeFebvre, Susan D. deFrance, Casper Toftgaard, Konstantina Drosou, Andrew C. Kitchener, and Michael Buckley. 2019. "Preserved Collagen Reveals Species Identity in Archaeological Marine Turtle Bones from Caribbean and Florida Sites." *Royal Society of Open Science* 6: 191137.

Hauser, Mark W. 2022. "The Work of Boundaries: Critical Cartographies and the Archaeological Record of the Relatively Recent Past." *Annual Review of Anthropology* 51: 509–526.

Haviser, Jay B. 2001. "Historical Archaeology in the Netherlands Antilles and Aruba." In *Island Lives: Historical Archaeologies of the Caribbean,* edited by Paul Farnsworth, 60–81. Tuscaloosa: University of Alabama Press.

Herrera Malatesta, Eduardo, Felicia J. Fricke, Maaike de Waal, Eleni Seferidou, Andreana Cunningham, Kathrin Nägele, Amy Victorina, et al. 2025. "Rethinking Caribbean Archaeology: Towards an Ethical Position for a Truly Decolonial Practice." *Peer Community Journal* 5, article no. e125. https://doi.org/10.24072/pcjournal.648.

Herrera Malatesta, Eduardo, Jorge Ulloa Hung, and Corinne L. Hofman. 2023. "Looking at the Big Picture: Using Spatial Statistical Analyses to Study Indigenous Settlement Patterns in the North-Western Dominican Republic." *Journal of Computer Applications in Archaeology* 6(1): 16–28. https://doi.org/10.5334/jcaa.83.

Herrera Malatesta, Eduardo, and Joseph Sony Jean. 2023. "Colonization, Indigenous Resilience, and Social Justice in Caribbean Archaeology." In *The Oxford Handbook of Global Indigenous Archaeologies,* edited by Claire Smith, C21P1–C21P102. Oxford: Oxford University Press.

Hofman, Corinne L., Lewis Borck, Emma R. Slayton, and Menno Hoogland. 2019. "Archaic Age Voyaging, Networks, and Resource Mobility around the Caribbean Sea." In *Early Settlers of the Insular Caribbean: Dearchaizing the Archaic,* edited by Corinne L. Hofman and Andrzej T. Antczak, 245–261. Leiden: Sidestone Press.

Hofman, Corinne L., C. Eloise Stancioff, Andrea Richards, Irvince Nanichi Auguiste, Augustine Sutherland, and Menno L. Hoogland. 2021. "Resilient Caribbean Communities: A Long-Term Perspective on Sustainability and Social Adaptability to Natural Hazards in the Lesser Antilles." *Sustainability* 13(17): 9807.

Jean, Joseph Sony, and Eduardo Herrera Malatesta, eds. 2024. *Local Voices, Global Debates: The Uses of Archaeological Heritage in the Caribbean.* Leiden: Brill.

kok, marjolijn. 2022. "A Future That Does Not Forget: Collaborative Archaeology in the Colonial Context of Sint Eustatius (Dutch Caribbean)." BAT-Report 1. Rotterdam: Bureau Archeologie en Toekomst.

Kowalewski, Stephen A. 1990. "Merits from Full-Coverage Survey: Examples from the Valley of Oaxaca, Mexico." In *The Archaeology of Regions: A Case for Full-Coverage Survey,* edited by Suzanne K. Fish and Stephen A. Kowalewski, 33–85. Washington, DC: Smithsonian Institution Press.

Krieger, Herbert W. 1929. *Archeological and Historical Investigations in Samaná, Dominican Republic.* Volume 147. Washington, DC: Smithsonian Institution.

Krieger, Herbert W. 1931. *Aboriginal Indian Pottery of the Dominican Republic.* Volume 156. Washington, DC: Smithsonian Institution.

Laffoon, Jason E., Till F. Sonnemann, Termeh Shafie, Corinne L. Hofman, Ulrik Brandes, and Gareth R. Davies. 2017. "Investigating Human Geographic Origins Using Dual-Isotope (87Sr/86Sr, δ18O) Assignment Approaches." *PLoS One* 12(2): e0172562.

Landon, George V., and W. Brent Seales. 2005. "Building and Visualizing 3D Textured Models for Caribbean Petroglyphs." 21st Congress of the International Association for Caribbean Archaeology, University of the West Indies, Trinidad and Tobago.

Martin, John Angus. 2023. "We Navel-String Bury Here: Landscape History, Representation and Identity in the Grenada Islandscape." PhD dissertation, Leiden University.

Mickleburgh, Hayley, Willem A. Baetsen, Anne Dijkstra, Ellen Edens, Norbert Eeltink, Felicia J. Fricke, Lina de Jonge, Lisette M. Kootker, Rachel Schats, Sarah Schrader, and Eleni Seferidou. 2022. "NVFA Ethical Guidelines on Human Remains." Leiden: Nederlandse Vereniging voor Fysische Antropologie (NVFA).

Mol, Angus. 2014. "The Connected Caribbean: A Socio-Material Network Approach to Patterns of Homogeneity and Diversity in the Pre-Colonial Period." PhD dissertation, Leiden University. Leiden: Sidestone Press.

Nilsson Stutz, Liv. 2022. "Rewards, Prestige, Power: Interdisciplinary Archaeology in the Era of the Neoliberal University." *Forum Kritische Archäologie* 11: 40–52.

Ostapkowicz, Joanna, and Jonathan A. Hanna (eds) 2021. *Real, Recent, or Replica: Precolumbian Caribbean Heritage as Art, Commodity, and Inspiration.* Tuscaloosa: University of Alabama Press.

Pagán-Jiménez, Jaime, and Reniel Rodríguez Ramos. 2008. "Toward the Liberation of Archaeological Praxis in a 'Postcolonial Colony': The Case of Puerto Rico." In *Archaeology and the Postcolonial Critique,* edited by Uzma Rizvi and Matthew Liebmann, 53–71. New York: AltaMira Press.

Palmié, Stephan, and Francisco A. Scarano, eds. 2013. *The Caribbean: A History of the Region and Its Peoples.* Chicago: University of Chicago Press.

Palmisano, Alessio, and Andrea Titole, 2024. "The Good, the Bad, and the Ugly: Evaluating Open Science Practices in Archaeology." *Archeologia e Calcolatori* 35(2): 75–84.

Pierce, Margaret Anne, and John W. Henry. 1996. "Computer Ethics: The Role of Personal, Informal, and Formal Codes." *Journal of Business Ethics* 15(4): 425–437. http://www.jstor.org/stable/25072766.

Reilly, Matthew C. 2019. *Archaeology below the Cliff: Race, Class, and Redlegs in Barbadian Sugar Society.* Tuscaloosa: University of Alabama Press.

Richardson, Lorna-Jane. 2018. "Ethical Challenges in Digital Public Archaeology." *Journal of Computer Applications in Archaeology* 1(1): 64–73.

Rivera-Collazo, Isabel C. 2011. "The Ghost of Caliban: Island Archaeology, Insular Archaeologists, and the Caribbean." In *Islands at the Crossroads: Migration, Seafaring, and Interaction in the Caribbean,* edited by L. Antonio Curet and Mark W. Hauser, 22–40. Tuscaloosa: University of Alabama Press.

Rouse, Irving. 1939. *Prehistory in Haiti: A Study in Method.* New Haven: Yale University Press.

Sanoja, Mario, and Iraida Vargas Arenas. 1974. *Antiguas formaciones y modos de producción venezolanos.* Caracas: Monte Avila Editores.

Schomburgk, Robert. 1854. "Ethnological Researches in Santo Domingo." *Journal of the Ethnological Society of London* 3: 115–122.

Schroeder, Hannes, María C. Ávila-Arcos, Anna-Sapfo Malaspinas, G. David Poznik, Marcela Sandoval-Velasco, Meredith L. Carpenter, José Víctor Moreno-Mayar, Martin Sikora, Philip L. F. Johnson, and Morten Erik Allentoft, et al. 2015. "Genome-Wide Ancestry of 17th-Century Enslaved Africans from the Caribbean." *PNAS* 112(12): 3669–3673.

Shepherd, Nick. 2015. "Undisciplining Archaeological Ethics." In *After Ethics: Ancestral Voices and Post-Disciplinary Worlds in Archaeology,* edited by Alejandro Haber and Nick Shepherd, 11–25. New York: Springer.

Sholts, Sabrina B. 2024. "'To Honor and Remember': An Ethical Awakening to African American Remains in Museums." *American Journal of Biological Anthropology* 186: e24943.

Slayton, Emma R. 2018. "Seascape Corridors: Modeling Routes to Connect Communities Across the Caribbean Sea." PhD dissertation, Leiden University. Leiden: Sidestone Press.

Stancioff, C. Eloise. 2018. "Landscape, Land-Change & Well-Being in the Lesser Antilles. Case Studies from the Coastal Villages of St. Kitts and the Kalinago Territory, Dominica." PhD dissertation, Leiden University. Leiden: Sidestone Press.

Stancioff, C. Eloise, Julijan Vermeer, Anirban Mukhopadhyay, Samantha De Ruiter, G. Brown, and Corinne L. Hofman. 2018. "Predicting Coastal Erosion in St. Kitts: Collaborating for Nature and Culture." *Ocean & Coastal Management* 156: 156–169. https:/doi.org/10.1016/j.ocecoaman.2017.09.015.

Torres, Joshua M., and Reniel Rodríguez Ramos. 2008. "The Caribbean: A Continent Divided by Water." In *Archaeology and Geoinformatics: Case Studies from the Caribbean,* edited by Basil A. Reid, 13–29. Tuscaloosa: University of Alabama Press.

Ullah, Isaac I. 2018. "What Is 'Computational Archaeology?'" https://isaacullah.github
.io/What-is-Computational-Archaeology/ (accessed June 28, 2024).

Ulloa Hung, Jorge, and Sonnemann, Till F. 2017. "Exploraciones arqueológicas en la
Fortaleza de Santo Tomás de Jánico. Nuevos aportes a su comprensión histórica."
Ciencia y Sociedad, 42(3): 11–27.

United Nations. 2014. "About Small Island Developing States." https://www.un.org/
ohrlls/content/about-small-island-developing-states (accessed June 28, 2024).

United Nations. 2020. "Non-Self-Governing Territories." https://www.un.org/dppa/
decolonization/en/nsgt (accessed April 19, 2024).

Veloz Maggiolo, Marcio, Elpidio Ortega, and Angel Caba Fuentes, Angel. 1981. *Los
modos de vida Meillacoides y sus posibles origenes: Un estudio interpretativo.* Santo
Domingo: Museo del Hombre Dominicano.

Versteeg, Aad H., and Stéphen Rostain, eds. 1997. *The Archaeology of Aruba: The Tanki
Flip Site.* Amsterdam: Archaeological Museum Aruba.

Versteeg, Aad H., and Kees Schinkel. 1992. *The Archaeology of St. Eustatius: The Golden
Rock Site.* Publications of the St. Eustatius Historical Foundation 2. Publications of
the Foundation for Scientific Research in the Caribbean Region, 131.

Wade, Lizzie. 2019. "#MeToo Controversy Erupts at Archaeology Meeting." *Science*
364(6437): 219–220.

Whiting, Brian M., Douglas P. McFarland, and Steven Hackenberger. 2001. "Three-
Dimensional GPR Study of a Prehistoric Site in Barbados, West Indies." *Journal of
Applied Geophysics* 47(3): 217–226. https://doi.org/10.1016/S0926-9851(01)00066-0.

Wilson, Samuel M. 2007. *The Archaeology of the Caribbean.* Cambridge: Cambridge
University Press.

Yin, Karen. 2024. *The Conscious Style Guide: A Flexible Approach to Language that
Includes, Respects, and Empowers.* Minneapolis: Scribe.

Zahedi, Pardis. 2025. "Elements of Community: An Exploration of Postcolonial
Heritage, Identity, and Memory in St. Croix, US Virgin Islands." PhD dissertation,
Aarhus University.

1

Developing a New Code of Ethics for the International Association for Caribbean Archaeology (IACA)

Challenges and Opportunities

Felicia J. Fricke, Christina M. Giovas,
Jonathan A. Hanna, John Shorter,
and Amy A. Victorina

The first International Congress for the Study of Pre-Columbian Cultures in the Lesser Antilles, organized by Révérend Père Pinchon and Jacques Petitjean Roget, was held in Martinique in 1961, and included attendees from Guadeloupe, Saint Lucia, Barbados, Tobago, Suriname, and the United States (Geijskes 1961; International Association for Caribbean Archaeology [IACA] n.d.; Nicholson and Harris n.d.). It was officially founded as an association in France the following year,[1] and in 1983 it changed its name to the International Association for Caribbean Archaeology (IACA)[2] to include the Greater Antilles, the mainland, and colonial time periods (Nicholson and Harris n.d.). This trilingual association aims to provide a network for professional and amateur archaeologists working in the Caribbean region in order to improve scholarship through communication (International Association for Caribbean Archaeology [IACA] n.d.). Since the beginning, the association's small membership (usually around 125 people) and informal atmosphere have been excellent for fostering connections in the field (Geijskes 1961) but have also meant that until recently the organization lacked initiatives to codify any evolving ethical concerns and formal structures for addressing ethical violations by its members.

Following concerns that emerged at the Society for American Archaeology meeting in 2019 (Wade 2019), archaeological organizations around the world were forced to consider whether their own policies on harassment, abuse, and ethical violations were robust enough to deal with similar problems at their own events. At IACA, it was clear that any code of ethics used by its members had to take into account the specific context and requirements of such a politically diverse, multilingual, and geographically extensive region. The existing IACA code of ethics (developed by E. Kofi Agorsah, Reg Murphy, and James Petersen and edited by Mary Hill Harris) had remained in draft form since 2005 and was never formally ratified by the membership. This draft code was short and, reflecting its temporal context, only covered issues such as fieldwork process and general legal compliance (Agorsah, Murphy, and Petersen 2005). It consisted of Part A (with five clauses briefly outlining the required compliances on professional standards, legal compliance, local permissions, dissemination, and looting) and Part B (process of intervention) and ran fewer than 700 words, omitting issues that have emerged as prominent concerns within the discipline and the association in the past two decades (for example, diversity, equity, and inclusion policies and accountability processes) (Agorsah, Murphy, and Petersen 2005). Between 2019 and 2022, a five-member IACA working group (Felicia J. Fricke, Christina M. Giovas, Jonathan A. Hanna, Tibisay Sankatsing Nava, and Amy A. Victorina) developed through a consultative process a new code of ethics that would guide archaeologists working in the Caribbean. The code was ratified in a unanimous vote of the general membership at the IACA Congress in Cuba in June 2022. It is now openly accessible and available in three languages (English, French, and Spanish) on the IACA website (see Cunningham et al. 2022a, 2022b). This chapter describes the process of code development and the challenges and opportunities encountered, and reflects on future directions for ethics documents in the Caribbean.

Developing the Code

When work on the new code of ethics began, it immediately became clear that it would be impossible to ratify a document that included recommendations about specific best practices. Archaeological methods and norms are developing at such a rate that any document containing reference to certain methods would quickly become outdated. The working group, therefore, chose to separate the basic rules of ethical practice (defined as "archaeological and academic practice that is fair, moral, truthful, and honest"; Cunningham et al. 2022a: 2) from best practice (current standards of methodological quality). This distinction required the working group to develop an ethics brain—a term that we use to describe a habit of thinking through problems in relation to their potential harm in a broad sense. We found this quite challenging in practical application, as archaeological professionals often equate ethics and best practices with one another. Notwithstanding, the working group developed two documents: first, a code of ethics that is binding for any member of IACA, and second, a best practice guide for professional guidance. Both documents will require future updating, as appropriate, to remain current and relevant. To minimize the updating needed in the future, the working group strove to write a code of ethics that was both specific enough to require ethical conduct at all times and flexible enough to encompass the diversity of the Caribbean region, where there are many different cultural and legal contexts for archaeologists to take into account. In leaving space to accommodate many different legal contexts, the development of this code of ethics did not warrant consultation with lawyers. It is not a legally binding document but a social agreement between IACA members.

The IACA Ethics Working Group was proposed by Fricke, approved by the board, and initially composed of the five members, including an IACA director (Giovas), and the IACA student representative (Sankatsing Nava), who made their interest known in 2019. The wider IACA membership was given subsequent opportunities to be involved, but no further volunteers joined the group. Between 2019 and 2021, the working group met regularly, to discuss and revise iterative drafts of the code of ethics and best practice guide, with each of the five original working group members responsible for producing first drafts of sections that related most closely to their own expertise. Following this, Andreana Cunningham and John Shorter were invited in 2022 to assist with the preparation of the final versions. English-language documents were submitted to the IACA board in January 2021 and to the IACA membership in September 2021, each time with a three-month window for readers to submit comments. Marianny Aguasvivas and Gérard Richard then translated the documents into Spanish and French respectively. Documents in English, French, and Spanish were distributed to the membership for final comments in April 2022, with a one-month commenting period. Feedback was incorporated by the working group into the final version, distributed in June 2022 and approved by the membership at the IACA Congress in July 2022.

In the text that follows, working group members describe the challenges and opportunities encountered during this process. These sections follow the structure of the "IACA Code of Ethics" and "IACA Best Practice Guide" documents, with sections addressing fieldwork, human remains, looting and antiquities, curation and archiving, public engagement, environmental impact and sustainability, publication, harassment and discrimination, and the process of intervention. They are followed by a critical reflection.

Fieldwork

Fieldwork provides a lot of information, which is collected using different practical methods. For each of these methods, whether employing excavation, survey, remote sensing, or other techniques, archaeologists must adhere to certain procedures and ethical standards to ensure the integrity of their work. To craft a code of ethics tailored to support IACA members in the field while addressing contemporary ethical challenges, the working group thoughtfully considered the overarching direction they intended to take with their recommendations in the best practice guide document (Cunningham et al. 2022a).

During the document's formulation, the working group grappled with the heterogeneous nature of the Caribbean region, seeking to encompass varied archaeological practices and integrate them into a single framework. Our objective was to craft a comprehensive code of ethics that mirrors the richness of archaeological practices and processes across the region. Furthermore, while tailored to the membership of IACA, we wanted this document to transcend its confines and be accessible to other groups within the broader heritage community.

To craft a comprehensive code of ethics for fieldwork spanning the entire region, the working group conducted a thorough survey of the literature. Drawing upon a wealth of resources, we meticulously reviewed IACA's previous code of ethics (Agorsah, Murphy, and Petersen 2005), alongside codes of conduct and practice from esteemed organizations such as Stichting Infrastructuur Kwaliteitsborging Bodembeheer (2018), the Society for American Archaeology (1996), and the European Association of Archaeologists (2022). Integrating this collective wisdom with our own experiences working in the Caribbean, we aimed to produce a document that would complement its predecessor and bring it up to date with the current state of archaeology in the region. While the previous code had addressed fieldwork and legal requirements, our focus extended to more detailed considerations of conduct, providing members with a robust framework from which to draw invaluable insights. For example, article 1.1, "Ascertain if there are local procedures and (international) treaties and include them in the research," and article 1.2, which states, "Acquire research permits (if applicable, each island has its own protocol) as well as permission of private landowners, community groups that have a connection to the heritage, etc.," encourage permit applicants to do some form of outreach together with government agencies, heritage organizations, or communities, as applicants are required to submit a project plan along with the permit application (Agorsah, Murphy, and Petersen 2005).

Human Remains

The discipline of human osteology (also known as human osteoarchaeology or biological anthropology) in the Caribbean benefits from the fact that organizations in other geographical regions have been assiduous in producing codes of ethics for their members, due to the sensitive nature of any interaction with human remains. The "IACA Code of Ethics" was therefore able to draw on existing codes such as those by the British Association for Biological Anthropology and Osteoarchaeology (BABAO) (Redfern and Jones 2019) and the American Association of Biological Anthropologists (AABA), formerly the American Association of Physical Anthropologists (AAPA) (Peacock et al. 2003) for inspiration. While much of the development was thus straightforward, in the Caribbean there are additional issues that the working group needed to consider.

First, the often neocolonial and extractive nature of archaeological projects in the Caribbean, particularly on small islands that are still occupied by colonial powers (Fricke and Hoerman 2023), makes the excavation, curation, and analysis of human remains an issue that requires extreme sensitivity to local, descendant, and Indigenous wishes (Haviser et al. 2022). In some cases, this may mean that human osteologists are not wanted at all. Where archaeologists are able to study human remains in the Caribbean, and the study does not conflict with existing laws, community goals should be the first priority (Fricke and Hoerman 2023).

Second, the Caribbean generally lacks local expertise in human osteology or bioarchaeology. Osteologists often live abroad and are not immediately available for rescue excavation, for example, in the event of coastal erosion, which is becoming increasingly severe due to global warming (Douglass and Cooper 2020). It was, therefore, important to specify in the code that archaeologists on the ground should (at the very least) consult with a qualified osteologist before excavating human remains and that osteological analyses not be carried out by nonspecialists except in an educational setting under professional supervision. This is not to say that members of the public should be prevented from excavating human remains—far from it; we believe it should be a priority for archaeologists and osteologists to encourage and support stakeholders in the excavation, study, curation, and possibly reburial of human remains, with appropriate guidance from a qualified professional.

Third, Caribbean heritage institutions often lack the physical and capital resources to house human remains in climate-controlled environments, leading to their rapid deterioration (Mickleburgh 2015). However, in the context of ethics and where legislation permits, it may be more important for human remains to remain within the community where they were excavated rather than curated strictly according to archaeological best practices. This is in line with prevailing attitudes on the repatriation of human remains to their countries of origin (Janes 2021).

Finally, particularly complicated was the issue of how to treat isolated human body parts (such as teeth and hair) that can become detached from an individual prior to their death. This was something that the working group discussed at length. In some cases, for example, local, descendant, and Indigenous communities may consider these body parts to be ancestral remains of equal importance to those that are found fully articulated in cemetery settings. We also reflected on the status of such body parts in medical ethics (Goold 2014). In the end, the wording of this section of the "IACA Code of Ethics" does not distinguish between detached body parts and other human remains, but the "IACA Best Practice Guide" advises that decisions in this area are made on a case-by-case basis (Cunningham et al. 2022a).

Looting and Antiquities

Like human remains, looted objects (removed from their context without archaeological documentation) present unique ethical challenges. Most members of the International Association for Caribbean Archaeology presume the organization requires its members to follow disciplinary principles (and international conventions) that aim to prevent looting from occurring and prohibit the trafficking of cultural materials. As mentioned, the code of ethics previously drafted by IACA members (Agorsah, Murphy, and Petersen 2005) stated exactly this but was never officially adopted by the organization.

Meanwhile, IACA's statutes maintained only that "cultural heritage of the French Caribbean is safeguarded, preserved, and valued" (International

Association for Caribbean Archaeology [IACA] 2003). It said nothing about the illegal antiquities market, and its employment of the ambiguous term "valued" ignored the problem of commercialization. Perhaps surprising to its current members, IACA has a checkered history in this regard. Local dealers have been permitted to present papers at the congress, looted ceramics have been taken as conference souvenirs, tours of private collections have validated the activities of those funding the illicit market, and excavations have been conducted illegally by conference attendees. While most members today are professional and/or academic archaeologists who are unaware of this history and eschew such activities, every congress to date has included papers that engaged in analyses of looted artifacts without any mention of the ethical dilemma (sometimes even failing to mention that the objects were from an illegal or unethical private collection).

That said, this is not surprising considering the extent of the Caribbean's looting problem. Indeed, Caribbean nations born from independence move-ments in the 1960s have often excluded themselves from the protection of heritage matters predating their birth, focusing instead on intangible heritage, such as traditional dances, foods, songs, and so forth (Cummins 2006). Thus, all the islands have suffered from theft and destruction of cultural materials at one time or another. Within the past 50 years alone, petroglyphs have been chiseled from boulders and sold on the private market; colonial ruins have been stripped of cannons; historic waterwheels and large copper pots have been sold as scrap metal; and precolonial sites have been pillaged until nothing was left (Hanna 2021; Ostapkowicz and Hanna 2021; Siegel and Righter 2011). The Caribbean also has a long history of neo-Amerindian art (new creations inspired by Indigenous iconography) marketed as artifacts, not least the extraordinary, decades-long Los Paredones scandal in the Do-minican Republic (Ostapkowicz 2021).[3] These challenges are attributed in part to the commercialization of cultural material in the antiquities market.

Thus, aside from the general rules stated in our code of ethics, in our best practices document we sought to expand and discuss some of the most pressing issues, including why researchers should avoid engaging looted artifacts in their research. For instance, a local museum may have only a few examples of a desired type of object, whereas a nearby private collection may have copious examples. While we may not know what site or context the private collection came from, we know they are authentic—is that not enough to warrant their inclusion in a study? No, we argue it is not enough. The study of private collections legitimizes their mode of acquisition, thereby condoning looting and the destruction of archaeological sites. To stem such destruction, we must be careful about how our behaviors (as experts) affect the local situation.

That said, there are exceptions. For example, many museums in the Caribbean have considerable quantities of unprovenienced artifacts that should be studied. These objects are not being sold, nor have most ever been on the market. They are usually salvage artifacts given by well-meaning donors who did not know what to record. A visiting archaeologist may therefore be one of the few people with the ideal skillset to pull together the available clues and reconstruct the lost provenience information for such objects. Counterintuitively then, archaeologists can have an ethical duty to study certain kinds of unprovenienced objects where such critical information could still be recovered by an expert.

Curation and Archiving

At the end of an archaeological excavation, what happens to the collected materials? Curation and archiving are necessary to complete the archaeological process and make the collected information accessible. The terms "curation" and "archiving" cover a wide range of activities that follow fieldwork in the archaeological process (Victorina and Kraan 2019). In general, there are three fundamental areas of focus that the relevant parties (government agencies, researchers, cultural heritage organizations, etc.) involved in a project should consider in the planning phase of a project. The first area of focus is processing the fieldwork records and administering the materials collected. The second is the storage of this information and establishing how it will be curated for posterity. And finally, the third is what the project produces. These are digital and analog products such as the final report, photographs, drawings, and publications (Stichting Infrastructuur Kwaliteitsborging Bodembeheer 2018; Victorina and Kraan 2019).

In formulating appropriate behavior in respect to this part of the archaeological process, the working group recognized that the underlying issue is financial. Processing and storage require financial commitment. There are several things to consider when thinking about the cost of processing. The parties involved should consider the requirements for storage of digital and analog information; storage materials such as bags, labels, and storage boxes; and an appropriate storage location to house the collections (Cunningham et al. 2022b). Caribbean islands have many pressing issues to deal with, so funding for cultural heritage needs is not always available. Fieldwork continues to produce more material that needs to be processed and stored. After a project is completed, funding is still needed for maintenance and to make the information accessible (e.g., to communities, researchers, etc.).

Having members of the IACA Ethics Working Group working on the islands has provided the group with practical, up-to-date experience. There is a clear distinction between seasonal researchers and those who reside on the islands. The latter group is naturally concerned with a variety of local issues that go beyond archaeology and the scope of seasonal projects. Local organizations often manage multiple projects and issues concurrently. In response, the working group explored ways to overcome financial constraints. Among various options, the discussion centered on revisiting older collections (Giovas et al. 2023) and implementing in situ conservation (Council of Europe 1992). Revisiting old collections, which are often overlooked, can inspire new approaches. The suggestion to encourage in situ conservation, whenever possible, is an effective strategy for reducing the workload of organizations. This approach eases financial burdens and recognizes the ever-evolving nature of archaeological methods and standards. By keeping sites intact, researchers can also explore new avenues of investigation, such as noninvasive survey techniques, without compromising the integrity of the archaeological record.

As such, the goal was to outline important points about the curation and archiving of archaeological projects that IACA members should consider as they prepare for current and future projects.

Public Engagement

By involving the public in the research process, archaeologists can generate mutual benefit through genuine dialogue, participation, and equitable collaboration. This not only leads to a more productive and respectful relationship between researchers and the communities they work with but also fosters a greater understanding and appreciation of the cultural heritage of the region (e.g., Hofman and Haviser 2015). For these reasons, we felt public engagement was an essential section to include in our code of ethics.

The funding for and evaluation of public engagement should be planned in parallel with the research project to ensure time and resources are allocated to meet the community's needs and maximize the project's societal impact. Archaeologists have a responsibility to inform the public about the purpose and results of their work, to make research results accessible to descendant communities, and to provide summaries of their findings in simplified language for non-archaeologists.

Engagement with descendant communities is particularly important, and researchers should prioritize the involvement of these communities and seek their consent when planning project activities. But descendants are also only one stakeholder community, and archaeologists must strive to address the views of *all* relevant stakeholders in their research design. Researchers can engage with the public by holding public meetings or presentations, by creating accessible hands-on educational materials and exhibits, by partnering with local schools and community organizations, and by using social media and other online platforms to connect with the public and share their work. More inclusive approaches can, for example, incorporate citizen science initiatives and coauthorship, among other collaborative strategies (National Trust for Historic Preservation and African American Cultural Heritage Action Fund 2018). By taking the time and effort to build trust and mutual understanding between themselves and the public, archaeologists can instill a sustainable cycle that ensures Caribbean heritage is safeguarded and valued.

Environmental Impact and Sustainability

Section 6 addressing environmental ethics is the shortest of the IACA code, reflecting the issue's limited treatment in the literature and existing professional codes. Here, "environment" refers simply to the "surroundings of an organism including the physical and chemical environment, and other organisms with which it comes into contact" (Ecological Society of America [ESA] 2023). Section 6 was conceived in the wake of the 2019 United Nations Climate Action Summit and the global climate strikes to confront and address the ecological impact of archaeological practice. Development began with a survey of academic and professional treatment of archaeological environmental ethics, including the ethical codes of major professional bodies (e.g., World Archaeological Congress, Society for American Archaeology, European Association of Archaeologists, and Register of Professional Archaeologists). Following Shaw's (2017) approach, our survey identified three ethical dimensions, which ultimately informed Section 6 and IACA's best practice guide: (1) legal compliance; (2) the ecological effects of archaeological practices, particularly field and laboratory activities; and (3) archaeology's "positionality" (Shaw 2017) with respect to environmental action and justice.

Legal compliance is captured in the ethical directives of archaeological organizations to follow environmental laws. Such directives are typically oblique, subsumed under covering statements to operate within a nation's legal and regulatory frameworks (e.g., European Association for Archaeologists [EAA] 2022: 1c.ii), and while they are widespread, their context makes it clear that they were formulated largely with heritage and cultural resource legislation in mind. IACA's code departs from these in its explicit reference to "environmental laws," and, more significantly, in its purposeful acknowledgment of "environmental and biosecurity" permitting as an aspect of this compliance (IACA Article 6.1). The latter permitting is a concern especially for environmental archaeologists, who may conduct research in ecologically sensitive areas and export/import biological samples and soils for analysis to institutions abroad. By explicitly naming these considerations, the code draws attention to the wider legal and interdisciplinary framework in which archaeologists operate and the obligations that arise from this.

Section 6 was intended to prompt critical assessment of archaeology's "ecological footprint" (Wackernagel and Rees 1996), that is, the natural resources consumed in the course of professional practice or otherwise needed to deal with pollution and waste. Aspects of the discipline—air travel to field locations,[4] heavy reliance on fossil-fuel-derived plastics for curation and fieldwork, and use of hazardous chemicals for conservation and archaeometric applications—are resource-intensive compared to other social sciences and humanities. Some archaeologists have noted this issue (Dalglish 2012; Shaw 2017), but detailed discussion, survey, or quantification of these impacts is absent, forestalling the development of meaningful solutions. A notable exception occurs with the 2021 Kiel Statement on Archaeology and Climate Change, wherein the European Association of Archaeologists (EAA) pledged to work toward net-zero emissions, limiting global temperature increase to 1.5°C, and to supporting the United Nations climate change goals.

Since complete elimination of the negative consequences of archaeological practice for Earth's biophysical systems is likely impossible, emphasis should be on reduction. Article 6.2 of the code captures this principle as an ethical "duty of care to minimize" ecological impacts. A similar guideline was adopted under Section 4 of the "EAA Principles" a few months after ratification of the IACA code. The section states archaeologists "have a moral and ethical responsibility . . . to address climate change in all aspects of their work, regardless of statutory requirements" (Article 4.a), and are encouraged to reduce greenhouse gas emissions and waste in their activities and to develop carbon management plans at an organizational level (Article 4b.1). Derived from the Kiel statement, the EAA Section 4 principles are focused on climate change. The IACA code is more expansive and includes considerations for disruption to wildlife and alteration of the landscape and biophysical processes. Both documents reflect an emerging concern with how the discipline of archaeology conducts itself within a larger community of actors. More compellingly, these documents represent a shift from the purely anthropocentric ethical frameworks that have traditionally informed archaeological practice to bio- and eco-centric frameworks and an expansion of archaeology's perceived moral community.

The final dimension concerns how archaeologists engage with questions of human-environment relationships in their own research. Some argue that archaeology's capacity for diachronic understanding of socio-ecological dynamics obliges practitioners to apply insights to contemporary environmental issues and policy or even to pursue research explicitly targeting the development of modern environmental sustainability solutions (Riede, Andersen, and Price 2017; Shaw 2017). The IACA code and "EAA Principles," Section 4, reflect the discipline's confrontation with climate change (Dawson et al. 2017; Rockman 2011), the Anthropocene concept (Braje et al. 2014), and the emergence of applied zooarchaeology, which articulates zooarchaeological knowledge with conservation in redress of the current biodiversity crisis (Wolverton and Lyman 2012). Beyond these applications, archaeologists might also pursue environmental justice agendas to enact systemic societal change by documenting conditions that have historically concentrated the harmful social, economic, and health consequences of environmental damage on marginalized groups. Because the choice to follow politically engaged research is a matter of academic freedom, the IACA code does not make specific recommendations here. Instead, research positionality is treated in the "IACA Best Practice Guide," where members are encouraged to reflect on the nature of their ethical engagement with contemporary environmental matters in relation to their responsibility to society, future generations, and Earth's systems.

Publication

Because archaeology faces many ethical issues that are not unique to the field, there is a wealth of available external resources that can provide guidance, particularly in terms of publishing and authorship. The International Committee of Medical Journal Editors (ICMJE 2019) and Committee on

Publication Ethics (COPE 2020) both offer comprehensive guidelines for public reference. Our code ultimately recommended that all IACA members read the COPE guidelines (Committee on Publication Ethics 2020).

However, we also pulled out and highlighted specific issues we felt were especially relevant for Caribbean archaeology. For instance, there is sometimes an impulse to "reward" those who contributed in fieldwork (e.g., local community members, undergraduate students) with authorship. Gifting authorship to supervisors, although they may not have contributed substantively to the research design, its development and execution, or the interpretation and publication of results, is also common. This practice can be problematic if such authors did not contribute significantly to the article and are now responsible for content they may know little about. Those who made minimal contributions may be offered the opportunity to contribute as an author where appropriate, but sometimes these contributions may best be rewarded as acknowledgments.

Harassment and Discrimination

IACA's original code of ethics did not mention harassment, discrimination, or any other interpersonal ethical violations by IACA members. Defined in the new "IACA Code of Ethics" as including but not limited to "unwanted photography or recording, intimidation, stalking, sustained disruption of conference presentations, inappropriate physical contact, physical violence, unwelcome sexual and intimate attention, and revenge pornography" (Cunningham et al. 2022b: 2), harassment was the issue (see Wade 2019) that originally stimulated development of this document. The working group was aware that harassment was a risk at archaeological conferences and workplaces, and during fieldwork (Wade 2019; Voss 2021), and wanted to ensure that there would be an ethical standard against which it would be possible to hold IACA members to account for their behavior. It was considered particularly important to protect women, youth, scholars of color, and members of the LGBTQ+ community from harassment by those in positions of power over them. This section of the document also covers any type of discrimination or bullying relating to protected identities such as race, gender, age, nationality, class, and religion. The working group wanted to ensure that the informal, close-knit IACA community can be a safe and welcoming space for everyone. We also wanted to ensure that perpetrators of harassment and discrimination would be held accountable, as other organizations have had trouble implementing their processes of intervention. We discussed potential situations in which the board would contact local authorities if a crime had been committed in relation to these issues.

In the development of this section, the working group consulted existing anti-harassment documentation from diverse organizations, including the Swedish Council for Higher Education (UHR 2020), the Canadian Standards Association (CSA) (Ferron and Kovacs 2019), and the Chartered Institute for Archaeologists (CIfA) in the UK (CIfA 2019). Some of these materials were more comprehensive than others, but ultimately the section on harassment and discrimination in the "IACA Code of Ethics" is short, providing a blanket statement that covers any type of harassment and discrimination, while the "IACA Best Practice Guide" provides references to organizations that can help those affected by these issues in the Caribbean. These organizations include, for example, None In Three (Barbados and Grenada) and Collectif de lutte contre le harcèlement sexuel dans l'enseignement supérieur (France). The guide also features training and awareness resources, for example Right To Be (2022) (formerly known as Hollaback!), and the workplace culture book *The No Asshole Rule* by Robert Sutton (2010). These resources and the links to them will have to be updated regularly as the links expire; regardless, it was important to give examples of support networks available.

Process of Intervention

In addition to having the above ethical standards, there must be a process for dealing with violations of any code. Depending on the nature of the infraction, some cases require immediate action, while others may allow (or require) more time for consideration. The previous (unratified) version of the IACA code included a process similar to what the working group ultimately recommended, but we also drew on various intervention models from other organizations. The newly implemented process at the SAA (Society for American Archaeology), inspired by the incident at its 2019 annual conference, is an example of one such model that we consulted (Society for American Archaeology [SAA] 2020). Whereas the SAA originally employed a single ombudsperson to handle complaints, our approach evolved into a panel of three to five members, which ensures greater accountability (the SAA also now employs several ombudspersons). The IACA panel investigates any reported violations and provides their findings to the board, which then determines and takes the appropriate action.

While the SAA model governs conduct at its annual meetings, the IACA intervention process was expanded to provide an adjudication mechanism that could address violations to the ethical codes beyond the confines of the congress. The process we developed was repeatedly "tested" and refined using hypothetical scenarios and input from the working group. Specific steps were added (e.g., investigation, board decision, appeals process) and a process flow graphic was developed to visualize and communicate the intervention procedure.

Critical Reflection

Within the diverse cultural and legal contexts of the Caribbean region, the matter of decolonization must be acknowledged. Recognizing the relationship of colonialism to the development of archaeological practices and methodologies is crucial to the application and dissemination of ethical procedures (Rizvi 2020), particularly within the Caribbean—a region itself deeply marked by prevalent imperialism and exploitation. The colonial past has significantly shaped the ways in which archaeological research has been conducted, often marginalizing local perspectives and knowledge. Therefore, it is imperative to critically examine and address these historical imbalances to foster a more inclusive and equitable approach to archaeology.

An essential pathway discussed by the IACA Ethics Working Group to address this issue was through conscious efforts toward hands-on engagement with local communities. Establishing relationships and partnerships through community-based participatory research (CBPR) is key. When CBPR is combined with academic efforts and guided by clearly delineated and reciprocal ethical standards, it leads to a better understanding and respect for the archaeological record and heritage in general. Additionally, such community-based research advances social justice (Wright 2022). This approach, encouraged by the new "IACA Code of Ethics," can promote a more holistic and respectful portrayal of Caribbean heritage, enabling more sustainable archaeological projects to flourish in the region. To underline this even more strongly, updates to the new "IACA Code of Ethics" should be developed in consultation with local communities.

The IACA codes were designed to be dynamic and adaptable by the entire IACA membership. In future versions, it will be important to include a section on the ethics of digital methods in archaeology. Digital archaeology is not only a subfield represented by, for example, the use of GIS, 3D scanning, and big data, but it in fact permeates the entire field of archaeology. Every archaeologist today uses a computer, a camera, and a GPS device, among other digital tools. Additionally, online replacements for air travel to other locations introduce their own ethical issues of accessibility. Thus, every archaeologist must reckon with the new ethical issues that this introduces (see Herrera Malatesta, this volume). The recent emergence of generative artificial intelligence (AI) and large language models (LLM) has yet to be fully determined implications for publication ethics and equity, training of the next generation of practitioners, and knowledge mobilization. We anticipate that as disciplinary norms around AI crystalize, these considerations will find their way into future revisions to the code of ethics.

An area in which the new "IACA Code of Ethics" was innovative was the inclusion of a section on environmental impact and sustainability, underscoring the necessity of considering the ecological footprint of archaeological work and acknowledging that while it is currently unavoidable, it must be thoughtfully managed. While some such documents briefly mentioned consideration for the environment (American Schools of Oriental Research 2019; Instituto Nacional de Antopología e Historia 2017: 11), at the time of approval by the membership in July 2022, the new "IACA Code of Ethics" and the "EAA Principles" were the only such documents in the discipline of archaeology that included whole sections on the topic (EAA 2022). This is a significant achievement for IACA, and we anticipate that it will become standard across the discipline in the future, particularly in the Caribbean where the effects of climate change are already being felt (Douglass and Cooper 2020).

Furthermore, the new code of ethics, while designed to be updated as necessary, does not include an automatic trigger for review and potential revision, relying instead on a reactive approach to updates and improvements. This structure requires the IACA membership to take an active role in the ongoing development of the codes, which can be a strength or a drawback depending on the buy-in of the association's individual members. On the one hand, it allows for sensitive and timely adjustments to be made. On the other hand, if there are no members taking responsibility for the document, then it may stagnate. We hope that the installation of the IACA Ethical Conduct Panel (consisting of four members plus one board representative) will prevent the document from passing into irrelevance. Additionally, future revisions could formalize a mechanism for regular reviews and updates, anchoring this process within the codes themselves. By allowing for this level of adaptability and member involvement, the IACA codes are poised to remain up to date in a rapidly changing professional landscape.

Finally, the "IACA Code of Ethics," while having no legislative power, can nevertheless encourage much-needed reciprocity between professionals, amateurs, and community members who have a vested interest in exploring and documenting Caribbean heritage. The current state of archaeology in the Caribbean is marked by both exciting opportunities and significant ethical challenges, and the development of the "IACA Code of Ethics" represents a critical step forward in promoting ethical standards, protecting cultural heritage, and fostering inclusive and respectful research practices.

Acknowledgments

Many thanks are due to Andreana Cunningham and Tibisay Sankatsing Nava for assistance in the development of the "IACA Code of Ethics" and "IACA Best Practice Guide," and to Marianny Aguasvivas and Gérard Richard for translating them into Spanish and French. Thanks also to the IACA board and membership for their support.

Notes

1 It is an *association loi 1901 à but non lucratif* (not-for-profit organization under the 1901 law).
2 "Association Internationale d'Archéologie de la Caraïbe" (AIAC) in French and "Asociación Internacional de Arqueología del Caribe" (AIAC) in Spanish.
3 As detailed in Ostapkowicz (2021), the Paredones scandal involved the creation of forged, precolumbian stone carvings in the Dominican Republic that were planted in archaeological sites and "discovered" during excavations by professional archaeologists, deceiving the archaeological community for more than 20 years until the hoax was publicly exposed in the late 1960s.
4 Although digital collaborations and online engagement may not be accessible to all, we note that these can be important tools for reducing greenhouse gas emissions arising from air travel for professional activities. For example, the IACA Ethics Working Group conducted its business with its internationally distributed members entirely through video conferencing.

References Cited

Agorsah, E. Kofi, Reg Murphy, and James Petersen. 2005. "Code of Ethics for the International Association for Caribbean Archaeology." Edited by Mary Hill Harris. International Association for Caribbean Archaeology (IACA).

American Schools of Oriental Research (ASOR). 2019. "Policy on Professional Conduct." Alexandria: American Schools of Oriental Research. https://www.asor.org/about-asor/policies/policy-on-professional-conduct/ (accessed June 13, 2024).

Atalay, Sonya. 2012. *Community-Based Archaeology: Research with, by, and for Indigenous and Local Communities.* Los Angeles: University of California Press.

Braje, Todd J. 2015. "Earth Systems, Human Agency, and the Anthropocene: Planet Earth in the Human Age." *Journal of Archaeological Research* 23: 369–396.

Chartered Institute for Archaeologists (CIfA). 2019. "Code of Conduct." Available at https://www.archaeologists.net/codes/cifa (accessed July 19, 2023).

Committee on Publication Ethics (COPE). 2020. "Promoting Integrity in Scholarly Research and Its Publication." Available at https://publicationethics.org/ (accessed April 18, 2023).

Council of Europe. 1992. "European Convention on the Protection of the Archaeological Heritage." Valetta: Council of Europe.

Cummins, Alissandra. 2006. "The Role of the Museum in Developing Heritage Policy." In *Art and Cultural Heritage: Law, Policy and Practice,* edited by Barbara T. Hoffman, 47–51. Cambridge: Cambridge University Press.

Cunningham, Andreana, Felicia J. Fricke, Christina Giovas, Jonathan A. Hanna, Tibisay Sankatsing Nava, John Shorter, and Amy A. Victorina. 2022a. "International Association for Caribbean Archaeology (IACA) Best Practice Guide." Translated by Marianny Aguasvivas and Gérard Richard. International Association for Caribbean Archaeology.

Cunningham, Andreana, Felicia J. Fricke, Christina Giovas, Jonathan A. Hanna, Tibisay Sankatsing Nava, John Shorter, and Amy A. Victorina. 2022b. "International Association for Caribbean Archaeology (IACA) Code of Ethics." Translated by Marianny Aguasvivas and Gérard Richard. International Association for Caribbean Archaeology.

Dalglish, Chris. 2012. "Archaeology and Landscape Ethics." *World Archaeology* 44(3): 325–341.

Dawson, Tom, Courtney Nimura, Elías López-Romero, and Marie-Yvane Daire. 2017. "Public Archaeology and Climate Change." In *Public Archaeology and Climate Change,* edited by Tom Dawson, Courtney Nimura, Elías López-Romero, and Marie-Yvane Daire, 1–9. Oxford: Oxbow Books.

Douglass, Kristina, and Jago Cooper. 2020. "Archaeology, Environmental Justice, and Climate Change on Islands of the Caribbean and Southwestern Indian Ocean." *PNAS* 117(15): 8254–8262.

Ecological Society of America (ESA). 2023. "What Is Ecology?" Available at https://www.esa.org/about/what-does-ecology-have-to-do-with-me/ (accessed April 15, 2023).

European Association of Archaeologists (EAA). 2022. "EAA Principles." Available at https://www.e-a-a.org/EAA/About/EAA_Codes/EAA/Navigation_About/EAA_Codes.aspx?hkey=714e8747-495c-4298-ad5d-4c60c2bcbda9 (accessed July 19, 2023).

Fricke, Felicia, and Rachel Hoerman. 2023. "Archaeology and Social Justice in Island Worlds." *World Archaeology* 54(3): 484–489.

Ferron, Era Mae, and Jill Kovacs. 2019. "Preventing Violence and Harassment in Canadian Workplaces: A Focus on Education, Healthcare, Government and Emergency Services, and Service Sectors." Toronto: Canadian Standards Association.

Geijskes, D. C. 1961. "Het eerste internationale congres voor de studie van de prae-Columbiaanse culturen in de Kleine Antillen." *New West Indian Guide* 41(1): 272–284.

Giovas, Christina, Claudia Kraan, and Amy A. Victorina. 2023. "The CCitRes Initiative: Using Citizen Science and Public Archaeology to Build Heritage Management Capacity in Curaçao." Paper presented at the Society for American Archaeology Conference, Portland, Oregon, March 29–April 2, 2023.

Gnecco, Cristóbal, and Dorothy Lippert, eds. 2015. *Ethics and Archaeological Praxis.* New York: Springer.

Goold, Imogen. 2014. "Why Does It Matter How We Regulate the Use of Human Body Parts?" *Journal of Medical Ethics* 40(1): 3–9.

Haber, Alejandro, and Nick Shepherd, eds. 2015. *After Ethics: Ancestral Voices and Post-Disciplinary Worlds in Archaeology.* New York: Springer.

Hanna, Jonathan A. 2021. "Spice Isle Sculptures: Antiquities and Iconography in Grenada, West Indies." In *Real, Recent, or Replica: Pre-Columbian Caribbean Heritage as Art, Commodity, and Inspiration,* edited by Joanna Ostapkowicz and Jonathan A. Hanna, 206–243. Tuscaloosa: University of Alabama Press.

Haviser, Jay, Rose Mary Allen, Luc Alofs, Richenel Ansano, Xiomara Balentina Ishmael Berkel, Alissandra Cummins, Matthieu Ecrabet, Kevin Farmer, Alexandra Jones, Teresa Leslie, Reg Murphy, Raimie Richardson, Paul Spanner, and Joshua Torres. 2022. "Report of the Statia Heritage Research Commission (SHRC) for the Government of St. Eustatius, Netherlands Caribbean." Oranjestad: Statia Heritage Research Commission (SHRC).

Hofman, Corinne L., and Jay B. Haviser, eds. 2015. *Managing Our Past Into the Future: Archaeological Heritage Management in the Dutch Caribbean.* Leiden: Sidestone Press.

Instituto Nacional de Antropología e Historia. 2017. Código de Conducta de los Servidores Publicos del Instituto Nacional de Antropología e Historia. Mexico: Secretaría de Cultura. https://www.inah.gob.mx/images/transparencia/20170529_codigodeconducta.pdf (accessed June 13, 2024).

International Association for Caribbean Archaeology (IACA). 2003. "Statutes of the International Association for Caribbean Archaeology." International Association for Caribbean Archaeology.

International Association for Caribbean Archaeology (IACA). n.d. "Welcome to the IACA Web Site." Available at https://blogs.uoregon.edu/iaca/ (accessed March 22, 2023).

International Committee of Medical Journal Editors (ICMJE). 2019. "Recommendations for the Conduct, Reporting, Editing, and Publication of Scholarly Work in Medical Journals." International Committee of Medical Journal Editors.

Janes, Robert R. 2021. "Humanizing Museum Repatriation." In *Museum Innovation: Building More Equitable, Relevant and Impactful Museums,* edited by Haitham Eid and Melissa Forstrom, 159–171. London: Routledge.

Kador, Thomas. 2014. "Public and Community Archaeology—an Irish Perspective." In *Public Participation in Archaeology,* edited by Suzie Thomas and Joanne Lea, 35–47. Woodbridge: The Boydell Press.

Mickleburgh, Hayley L. 2015. "Skeletons in the Closet: Future Avenues for the Curation of Archaeological Human Skeletal Remains in the Dutch Caribbean and the Rest of the Region." In *Managing Our Past into the Future: Archaeological Heritage Management in the Dutch Caribbean,* edited by Corinne L. Hofman and Jay B. Haviser, 113–130. Leiden: Sidestone Press.

National Trust for Historic Preservation and African American Cultural Heritage Action Fund. 2018. "Engaging Descendant Communities in the Interpretation of Slavery at Museums and Historic Sites: A Rubric of Best Practices Established by the National Summit on Teaching Slavery." Montpelier: James Madison's Montpelier.

Nicholson, Desmond, and Peter Harris. n.d. "I.A.C.A. History." The International Association for Caribbean Archaeology. Available at https://blogs.uoregon.edu/iaca/francais-historique/ (accessed March 22, 2023).

Ostapkowicz, Joanna. 2021. "Caribbean Indigenous Art Past, Present, Future: The View from the Greater Antilles." In *Real, Recent, or Replica: Pre-Columbian Caribbean Heritage as Art, Commodity, and Inspiration,* edited by Joanna Ostapkowicz and Jonathan A. Hanna, 1–35. Tuscaloosa: University of Alabama Press.

Ostapkowicz, Joanna, and Jonathan A. Hanna, eds. 2021. *Real, Recent, or Replica: Precolumbian Caribbean Heritage as Art, Commodity, and Inspiration.* Tuscaloosa: University of Alabama Press.

Peacock, James, Carolyn Fluehr-Lobban, Barbara Frankel, Kathleen Gibson, Janet Levy, and Murray Wax. 2003. "Code of Ethics of the American Association of Physical Anthropologists." American Association of Physical Anthropologists (AAPA).

Redfern, Rebecca, and June Jones. 2019. "BABAO Code of Ethics." British Association for Biological Anthropology and Osteoarchaeology (BABAO).

Riede, Felix, Per Andersen, and Neil Price. 2017. "Does Environmental Archaeology Need an Ethical Promise?" *World Archaeology* 48(4): 466–481.

Right To Be. 2022. "Who We Are." Available at https://righttobe.org/ (accessed April 18, 2024).

Rizvi, Uzma Z. 2020. "Community-Based and Participatory Praxis as Decolonizing Archaeological Methods and the Betrayal of New Research." In *Archaeologies of the Heart,* edited by Kisha Supernant, Jane Eva Baxter, Natasha Lyons, and Sonya Atalay, 83–96. New York: Springer.

Rockman, Marcy. 2011. "The Necessary Roles of Archaeology in Climate Change Mitigation and Adaptation." In *Archaeology in Society: Its Relevance in the Modern World,* edited by Marcy Rockman and Joe Flatman, 193–215. New York: Springer.

Shaw, Julia. 2017. "Archaeology, Climate Change and Environmental Ethics: Diachronic Perspectives on Human: Non-Human:Environment Worldviews, Activism and Care." *World Archaeology* 48(4): 449–465.

Siegel, Peter E., and Elizabeth Righter, eds. 2011. *Protecting Heritage in the Caribbean.* Tuscaloosa: University of Alabama Press.

Society for American Archaeology (SAA). 2020. "Meeting Safety Policy." Available at https://www.saa.org/annual-meeting/meeting-policies/Meeting-Safety-Policy (accessed April 28, 2023).

Society for American Archaeology (SAA). 1996. "Principles of Archaeological Ethics." Available at https://www.saa.org/career-practice/ethics-in-professional-archaeology (accessed July 19, 2023).

Stichting Infrastructuur Kwaliteitsborging Bodembeheer (SIKB). 2018. "Kwaliteitsnorm Nederlandse Archeologie, Version 4.1." Available at https://www.sikb.nl/archeologie/richtlijnen/brl-sikb-4000 (accessed July 19, 2023).

Sutton, Robert I. 2010. *The No Asshole Rule: Building a Civilized Workplace and Surviving One That Isn't.* New York: Business Plus.

Swedish Council for Higher Education (UHR). 2020. "Efforts to Prevent Sexual Harassment in Academia: An International Research Review." Solna: Swedish Council for Higher Education.

Victorina, Amy A., and Claudia Kraan. 2019. "Archaeological Protocol Bonaire." Curaçao: National Archaeological Anthropological Memory Management (NAAM).

Voss, Barbara L. 2021. "Disrupting Cultures of Harassment in Archaeology: Social-Environmental and Trauma-Informed Approaches to Disciplinary Transformation." *American Antiquity* 86(3): 447–464.

Wackernagel, Mathis, and William Rees. 1996. *Our Ecological Footprint: Reducing Human Impact on the Earth.* Gabriola Island: New Society Publishers.

Wade, Lizzie. 2019. "#MeToo Controversy Erupts at Archaeology Meeting." *Science* 364(6437): 219–220.

Wolverton, Steve, and R. Lee Lyman, eds. 2012. *Conservation Biology and Applied Zooarchaeology.* Tucson: University of Arizona Press.

Wright, Alice P. 2022. "From the Trowel's Edge to the Scholarly Sidelines: Community-Based Research in Academic Archaeology, 2012–2021." *Humans* 2022(2): 277–288.

2

Homegrown, Organic, Heritage Conservation on Saint Croix

Afro-Crucian Logics for Preserving the Historical Memory

WILLIAM A. WHITE III

Because they are a territory of the United States, the US Virgin Islands (USVI) are subject to the National Historic Preservation Act (NHPA) and territorial historic preservation regulations. The NHPA of 1966 (as amended) is at the heart of historic preservation, heritage conservation, and archaeological practice in the United States. This is because most of the archaeology in the United States is conducted by the cultural resource management industry (CRM), which is a conglomeration of government and commercial archaeologists working under the structures of historic preservation regulations like the NHPA. Academic archaeology participates in CRM to a lesser extent, primarily through training and certifying future archaeologists (Altschul and Klein 2022; King 2012). Regulatory contexts like the NHPA are designed to be as flexible as possible because they have the mission of providing for the identification and preservation of "historic properties" for the benefit of all American citizens, in perpetuity. When it comes to CRM, archaeologists are tasked with the identification and evaluation of historic properties so that their presence can be known by state historic preservation offices (SHPOs), as well as land administering and permit-granting government agencies, because these laws call upon agencies to mitigate any adverse effects their undertakings may have on historic properties that are eligible or recommended to be eligible for inclusion in the National Register of Historic Places (NRHP). Basically, CRM archaeologists are hired for their professional opinion as to the significance and integrity of archaeological sites. Their determinations strongly influence how these sites are subsequently treated.

Historic preservation is administered by the Virgin Islands Historic Preservation Commission. The commission is composed of six members of the Virgin Islands Planning Board, which is under the Office of the Governor. The Department of Planning and Natural Resources (DPNR) is also within the Planning Board. The Historic Preservation Office is a division of the DPNR. Additionally, the DPNR commissioner serves as the state historic preservation officer. While historic preservation in the Virgin Islands appears to mirror the systems in place in the States, the DPNR has also been tasked with protecting other aspects of cultural heritage like folklife and the arts (US Virgin Islands Code 2019a, tit. 3, § 402–404). For example, the DPNR also administers the Virgin Islands Cultural Heritage Institute, which exhorts, "It is appropriate and necessary to preserve, protect, and promote Virgin Islands culture in order to contribute to an understanding of the complex problems of our society, to encourage unity and economic viability of all of the Territory's people, to respect the tradition bearers and their lasting contributions, and to celebrate the Virgin Islands example throughout the Caribbean as a people of strong belief in freedom and self-development" (US Virgin Islands Code 2019b, tit. 3, § 408).

Regulations continue to declare protections for unique local practices like stories, handicrafts, foods, and linguistic elements. Virgin Island regulations have codified a unique regulatory context of historic preservation and heritage conservation provides pathways for Afro-Crucians to pursue truly unique forms of preservation. This can be seen in the ways they approach archaeology as an aspect of heritage conservation.

Regulations like the NHPA outline methods for evaluating archaeological sites as historic properties, but they fall short when it comes to identifying sites that are significant for many "traditionally associated people." The National Park Service (NPS), which administers the NRHP, defines traditionally associated people as groups that form a community that: (1) regards significant resources as essential to its distinct cultural identity; (2) has been associated with the park for at least two generations (40 years); and (3) had this association began prior to establishment of the park (Masur 2009: 85; National Park Service 2006: 159). In this chapter, the author has applied this definition to historic properties evaluated under the NHPA. One of the biggest shortfalls in structured historic preservation archaeology is its lack of efforts to include subaltern cultural understandings in significance determinations (e.g., culturally specific knowledge held by traditionally associated people who are underrepresented in the NHPA consultation process). While consultation is proscribed by law, collaboration with communities is not called for in current amendments to the NHPA, even though it could greatly expand our understanding of the past and lead to the discovery of whole new cultural landscapes.

While the NHPA, NPS, and CRM strongly influence how we think about archaeological sites as historic properties, non-archaeologists have different parameters through which they evaluate and engage with historical places. One example is how persons of African descent on the island of Saint Croix in the US Virgin Islands (USVI) conduct heritage conservation work. Existing outside the strictures of regulatory contexts like the NHPA, Afro-Crucian people have a broad system of teaching youth about the past as well as remembering those ancestors who came before them. In a 2020 Antiracism Workshop sponsored by Columbia University and the Society of Black Archaeologists (SBA), Saint Croix scholar and elder ChenziRa Davis-Kahina enlightened a breakout group of archaeologists about the activities she and others on Saint Croix had been doing to increase the number of Black youth involved in historic preservation and how to keep them in what is an industry that is largely dominated by professionals of European descent in the United States. Davis-Kahina said much of what is being done on Saint Croix takes place outside the CRM system, even though it involves historic properties that are in the NHPA and recognized archaeological sites. She spoke about a system that involves taking youth out into historical landscapes, teaching them about the events that took place there, and doing memory work that inculcates the youth into the world they will need to foster in the future. This system is what Davis-Kahina called "homegrown local heritage and identity conservation" (Davis-Kahina, personal communication, June 8, 2020).

Recent excavations by the Society of Black Archaeologists at Estate Little Princess on Saint Croix provide an example of Afro-Crucian homegrown heritage conservation strategies in practice. They show that American archaeologists do not have a monopoly on determining site significance. As currently practiced, structured historic preservation executed under historic preservation laws like the NHPA are missing the intangible aspects that African diasporic people like Afro-Crucians value in the places they consider significant historical sites.

I believe archaeologists working on African diasporic sites should incorporate Black vernacular histories in their interpretations. Not only would this increase our understanding of Black pasts, but it would also help Black communities connect with their archaeological heritage because, as stakeholders, they would have a vested interest in what happens to these sites and how they are described to the world. Inclusion could also increase the likelihood that Black sites are identified and recommended as eligible for historic preservation. Not only would this diversify our understanding of the past, but increasing Black collaboration and Black understandings of heritage conservation is also an ethical issue since Black historic properties are sorely underrepresented in the National Register of Historic Places (NHPA). Black sites are overlooked because few archaeologists have the cultural knowledge necessary to define the significance of Black historic properties and Black communities are not always consulted on sites important to their cultural identity. Including Black histories is an important step toward a more regenerative, inclusive, and ethical archaeology in the United States.

The State of Black Historic Properties in the United States

Engagement with Native Americans has shown the flexibility of the NHPA when it comes to addressing understated and unrecognized histories. Archaeologists working in the African diaspora can learn much from these studies. In the United States, African-descended people live with two different narratives of history: the "official" history as deduced from documents created by "colonizers," and histories circulated among traditionally associated people, which is oftentimes passed down by elders by way of memory and spoken word (Pagán-Jiménez 2006). This "untold," subaltern history is what many Black communities feel is a more truthful and accurate interpretation of past events since it is created by themselves for themselves. However, archaeologists rarely incorporate Black interpretations of the past when they evaluate African diasporic historic properties, most of the African diasporic archaeology conducted under a regulatory nexus is produced without incorporating Black American understandings of the past. African diasporic sites are considered significant at a lower rate than European American and Native American sites, which has resulted in less recognition of African-descended people in the archaeological record and less preservation of their sites (Babiarz 2011; Barile 2004; Franklin et al. 2022a, 2022b).

Other archaeologists have noted how African diasporic sites are frequently overlooked by projects conducted under the NHPA. Barile's work in east Texas (2004) highlights the difficulties associated with preserving African diasporic sites in the west through the NHPA. Regarding how CRM conducted under the NHPA tends to privilege historic properties with more substantial, elaborate architectural elements, Barile explains (2004, 98) that African diaspora-related historic properties have suffered because of the way the regulations have failed to "give proper recognition to site historic context where race and class figured largely." In this paradigm, simple African American-related properties are less likely to be preserved. Furthermore, the emphasis on "single-approach methodologies" (i.e., the identification of bounded properties) has resulted in a drastic reduction of post–Civil War NRHP-eligible sites, especially those associated with African-descended people in Texas (Barile 2004: 98). Babiarz calls this a silencing of Black heritage caused by white privilege, writing about how the NHPA has not served Black communities in Annapolis, Maryland, because those survey-ing for historic properties (e.g. scholars in the CRM industry) do not have enough command of Black history and culture to effectively evaluate Black properties even if they wanted to. Babiarz suggests preservationists reach out to communities and suggests they learn through cross-cultural learning from Black activist scholars (Babiarz 2011: 54). This work puts the onus on individual archaeologists, which is where we will need to start given the lack of protections under the NHPA.

A group of archaeologists from across the United States conducted a review of SHPOs' efforts to document African diasporic sites from 2020 until 2022 (Franklin et al. 2022a, 2022b). The Black Heritage Resources Task Force was an ad hoc group of archaeologists representing CRM, academia, and state historic preservation organizations. The task force's goal was to evaluate the most recent historic preservation plans for: (1) their efforts regarding the identification and management of African diasporic historic properties; (2) their implementation of diversity initiatives; and (3) their role in consulting with Black stakeholders (Franklin et al. 2022a: 2); as well as (4) to make rec-ommendations on best practices (as they currently exist) and potential ways SHPOs could increase their efforts to document Black heritage sites in their states (Franklin et al. 2022b). In accordance with Section 101 (b)(3)(C) of the NHPA, each SHPO must present a historic preservation plan to the National Park Service (NPS) to access the Historic Preservation Fund, federal funding designated to help SHPOs undertake their tasks. This plan must outline the state's preservation goals for the next five years that can be implemented by stakeholders, state agencies, preservationists, and other organizations. These plans also outline the state's efforts to reach out to the public and professionals in the state (Franklin et al. 2022a: 7).

In addition to reviewing the plans, the task force also conducted a survey of SHPOs to help illuminate their practices regarding the identification of cultural and ethnic affiliation for archaeological resources, diversity initia-tives, and representation among the Black community. Some SHPOs were responsive enough to contribute to a follow-up interview about their efforts to increase diversity and record African diasporic sites (Franklin et al. 2022a: 3). This process revealed several trends among state historic preservation plans:

1. *African Americans are mentioned but there is little effort to consult with Black stakeholders:* Of the 44 historic preservation plans that mention African Americans, only 18 of them discuss consultation with Black communities.
2. *Most states do not have plans to increase diversity within the SHPO:* Only 13 of the 53 plans mention efforts to increase diversity in their SHPO. Very few states mention increasing diversity in any of their planning. When it comes to historic preservation planning, nine states and one US territory do not mention diversity at all.
3. *Most states do not have African American historic contexts:* Only 10 of the 53 states and territories reviewed have Black historic contexts. Statewide historic contexts are important because they notify CRM professionals of the existence of certain site types that they may otherwise be unaware of (for example, Black sites) and help them contextualize these sites within historic preservation regulatory frameworks.
4. *Most states do not systematically document ethnic or racial affiliation of archaeological sites:* Archaeological site identification and documentation includes the process of placing sites within meaningful categories that can be used in future analyses. Without identifying African diasporic sites as significant for their connection to important data and events in Black pasts, it is difficult to measure how many Black sites exist in a state and how frequently they are recommended eligible for the National Register of Historic Places. This means African-descended peoples and state agencies do not know how much Black heritage is present and how those sites are regarded by the SHPO. It also makes it difficult for us to know how effective historic preservation regulations are at documenting Black sites.

The Black Resources Heritage Task Force discussed how these deficiencies could be partially remedied by consulting with African-descended people in their states. The task force recommended partnerships be created with Black stakeholders and that those stakeholders be asked for advice on historic preservation needs. It also recommended that Black heritage commissions be created, and that Black history museums, organizations, and community groups play a role in historic preservation decisions. Finally, the task force recommended that historic preservation plans include initiatives designed to recruit and train a generation of Black heritage conservation professionals (Franklin et al. 2022b: 8–9).

These aspirational suggestions will do much to help with the dearth of Black heritage conservationists in the United States. It is hoped that through significance determinations will include more Black historic properties if Black conservationists are involved in decision-making. Increased consultation may also help more Black Americans pursue careers in heritage conservation, which could help these suggestions live for generations to come. However, these suggestions overlook the existing, vernacular heritage conservation system Black people have already created over the years. These homegrown, organic heritage conservation systems are a response to the discrimination, disinvestment, and racism faced in the Western Hemisphere. The activities of Afro-Crucians in the United States Virgin Islands provide an example of Black responses to white histories designed to marginalize Black people.

History and the Island of Saint Croix

Persons of African descent have called the island of Saint Croix home since the sixteenth century. Christopher Columbus's second voyage to the Caribbean brought Saint Croix into European awareness, and when he landed on the north shore of the island in 1493 the island was occupied completely by Indigenous people. After the colonization of the Indigenous original inhabitants, the island was contested by ambitious French, English, and Dutch powers during the sixteenth century as European agricultural entrepreneurs sought to establish lucrative agricultural ventures. The first permanent European settlement was established on the island by English planters in 1631; however, the island remained claimed by Spain. These English squatters were attacked soon after their settlement was built, but this did not deter French planters who built a settlement on the island in 1634. The English made another attempt in 1636 and the Spanish reasserted their sovereignty by attacking the French and English. Nonetheless, large land patents were granted to English planters in the 1640s and a settlement was established on the west end of the island near present-day Frederiksted. In 1642, the Dutch West India Company landed on the island and built a settlement near the Salt River. The Dutch were joined by 120 French colonists in subsequent years as the French expanded their presence on the island. By the 1650s, Saint Croix was dominated by the French who established the French West India Company in 1665 to govern the island (Dookhan 1994; Hardy 2007).

Enslaved Africans comprised a significant portion of the island's population throughout the enslavement period. It is likely the French were responsible for introducing African enslavement to Saint Croix. This system was greatly enlarged once the Kingdom of Denmark-Norway entered the plantation economy in the Caribbean. In 1625, Christian VI issued the first Danish charters for a factory in what is now Ghana to obtain Africans to work on Caribbean islands administered by the Danish. This led to the establishment of the Danish West India Company in 1671 to secure agreements to establish plantations on Caribbean islands as well as a charter to establish a fort on the West African coast in 1672. Denmark claimed the islands of Saint Thomas (1672) and Saint John (1675) with the goal of producing cash crops using the plantation economy (Dookhan 1994). These ventures were incorporated through the West Indian and Guinean Company, WIGC (Vestindisk-Guineisk Kompagni) in 1674, which had a monopoly on the slave trade in the Danish West Indies. Denmark purchased the island of Saint Croix in 1733, expanding its colonialist enterprises in the Caribbean (Dookhan 1994).

While the French introduced African enslavement in the Danish West Indies (DWI), it was the Danish who greatly expanded it. Hardy (2007: 18) estimates that 600 Africans were part of the 1,300 residents on the island in the 1680s. While 631 Danish indentured servants and convicts were sent to the DWI between 1671 and 1755, their numbers paled in comparison to the approximately 53,000 human beings the Danish imported directly from West Africa between 1733 and 1802 (Green-Pedersen 1975; Hvid 2016). More recently, researchers have also realized that a significant proportion of additional enslaved Africans were obtained through purchases from other islands (Green-Pedersen 1975, 1980).

Danish colonization of Saint Croix lasted from 1733 until the islands were sold to the United States in 1917. During the eighteenth and early nineteenth centuries, sugar cultivation and processing became the primary Danish industry in the DWI, which was an industry greatly reliant upon enslaved labor (Dookhan 1994). Denmark encouraged and expanded African enslavement on the island during this period, with enslaved populations peaking at 32,213 in 1797 (Jensen and Simonsen 2016: 484–485). The importation of Africans from Danish forts on the coast of West Africa was banned by an edict issued by the Danish Crown in 1792, an edict that was supposed to go into full effect in 1803 (Flygare 2016; Green-Pedersen 1975; Røge 2014). However, there is evidence that Africans continued to be bought and sold as late as 1807 (Green-Pedersen 1975, 1980). Slavery in the DWI ended when enslaved Africans from across Saint Croix manumitted themselves in a mass action against the Danish fort in Frederiksted on July 3, 1848 (Hall 1992). After this, an insidious contract labor system replaced slavery in the DWI with the primary aim of keeping the sugar plantations in operation. The onerous terms of these contracts led to another mass uprising in 1878 called "Fireburn," an event that remains celebrated by Afro-Crucians today (Hall 1984).

During this period, Danish administrators, planters, and other residents of European descent crafted a racialized social and legal hierarchy that limited Black people, both enslaved and free. Free Black populations and economic power steadily increased during the eighteenth and nineteenth centuries. Legal documents illustrate how Black residents in the DWI were not supposed to testify in Danish colonial courts; however, they frequently found themselves recorded as witnesses and defendants in court records (Simonsen 2016). Analysis of these records by Simonsen (2016) and Hall (1992) reveals a complicated world where persons of African descent frequently circumvented proscriptions of their liberty to engage in a world designed to discriminate against them. Historical documents and cultural knowledge reflect attempts to increase agency throughout Black Crucian history. This ongoing campaign for freedom is acknowledged by today's Afro-Crucians along with a veneration of those ancestors who made the present world possible. Glimpses of this struggle were only sometimes captured in documents but cultural knowledge positions it in places, across landscapes, and on the land, and passes these understandings across generations in a way that is difficult to capture under historic preservation regulatory structures. This means that the places that make Afro-Crucian heritage slip through modern historic preservation frameworks.

Heritage Conservation Is More Than Historic Properties on Saint Croix

Present-day Afro-Crucians trace their lineages to enslaved and free Africans who arrived on the island at some point in the past; however, the specific African ethnicities of the enslaved Africans imported to Saint Croix is unclear. Spiritual traditions and values with roots in Africa persisted and diversified across the African diaspora. Both enslaved and free Africans drew upon these traditions to make sense of the world in which they lived. Scholars of African spirituality have long noticed how Christian and West African elements had blended into unique regional expressions by the twentieth century (Hurston 1938 [1990]). As early as the 1930s, scholars of the African diaspora recognized that Black spirituality transformed into several mixtures of traditional West African belief systems syncretized with Christianity. It has been noted that Yoruba concepts form the core corpus within these systems that developed in the wake of the slave trade (Karade 2020; Matory 2005; Murrell 2010). In the Caribbean, several syncretic African belief systems also developed and have become religions like Obeah, Vodou, and Santería (de la Torre 2004; Murrell 2010).

Historical documents record the presence of traditional religion practitioners as Christian colonial governments sought to eliminate Africanisms as part of their many-pronged strategy to acculturate Africans to enslavement. In the colonial Caribbean, historical documents frequently describe an African belief system practiced by Black residents called Obeah, which was a catchall term referring to a complex of shamanistic practices with origins in Africa. After Obeah was connected to Tacky's Rebellion on Jamaica (1760–1761), in which Obeah practitioners were linked to its planning, colonial administrators became even more concerned with monitoring spiritual behaviors (Browne 2008). Obeah was prosecuted by British authorities, which forced its practice into hiding, and spiritual specialists worked outside recognized Christian churches (Brown 2008). Colonial records note their efforts against traditional African spiritualists called "Obeah men" (Savage 2012). Practicing Obeah and other African syncretic religions were also prosecuted in British, Dutch, Spanish, and French colonial territories (Browne 2008; Crosson 2015). Restrictions on Obeah remained in some countries until 2000 (Crosson 2015: 151). It is important to note that attempts to suppress these activities did not stop their practice by Africans in the Western Hemisphere. Obeah is still practiced today.

While known to have been practiced widely, these African spiritual traditions only leave occasional traces in the archaeological record. Archaeologists recovered the buried remains of an African spiritual healer in Barbados in the 1970s who was interred with a range of material culture that has been connected to a suite of West African traditions. These items include metal finger rings, bracelets, teeth from a dog, an iron knife, a carnelian bead, and a clay pipe. A specific spiritual tradition was not identified for this individual; however, the artifacts harken to historical traditions in present-day Ghana (Handler 1997). Archaeological excavations of a Candomblé terreiro in Salvador, Brazil, demonstrates that urban Blacks modified houses into religious spaces where Candomblé ceremonies could be practiced (Gordenstein 2016). Matory (2005) asserts that Yoruba spiritualists and practitioners strongly influenced the development of Candomblé in Brazil where it was mixed with saints and other concepts in Catholicism. However, practicing the religion was suppressed by colonial and Brazilian law enforcement into the twentieth century. Since Candomblé was persecuted by law enforcement, the terreiros were in underground basements where practice could proceed undetected. Gordenstein (2016: 72) explains that Candomblé was brought to Bahía in the nineteenth century by Yoruba practitioners from Dahomey. The religion maintained a core in Yoruba spiritual practices, masked by a Christian veneer.

More recently, excavations at Estate Little Princess on Saint Croix in 2022 revealed a ferrous horseshoe buried beneath the threshold of a cabin once occupied by enslaved Africans (Flewellen et al. 2023). Horseshoes have also been found archaeologically within spiritual bundles elsewhere within the African diaspora (Leone 2020: S281). As was the case among other cultures, including European ones, placing a horseshoe near the doorway of a home could have been an effort to improve the well-being of those who enter this dwelling. The construction date of this building is unknown, but it was likely built after the Danish edict to improve conditions for the enslaved in the DWI, which included rebuilding enslaved cabins out of stone, coral, bricks, and bagasse (Jensen 2012). Jensen (2012: 147–148) notes that Obeah was a major aspect of healthcare among the enslaved in the Danish West Indies and was integrated with herbalism. Orser Jr. (2023: 153–176) chronicles archaeo-logical evidence of African spirituality across several sites in North America. These finds suggest charms and other items found in archaeological features provide glimpses of the connection between African spirituality tapped to help navigate the dangerous spiritual world, which is beyond time and place, and pervades all spaces, and the material world in which living people reside. While I have no personal experience with the beliefs expressed in each of these archaeological finds, they demonstrate that African-influenced spiritual beliefs were alive and well among enslaved Africans and free Blacks in the Caribbean. Some of these practices and beliefs have been maintained by Black people living on Saint Croix today and have seeped into their understanding and expression of heritage conservation.

When it comes to heritage conservation among Afro-Crucian people, I have come to understand that their ways of commemorating the past are rooted in their presence on the land and a desire to commemorate ances-tors who paved the way for people living in the present. Afro-Crucians also acknowledge elements like water and earth as important for the human experience in the past, present, and future. Strategies for conducting this memory work draw upon African spirituality and do not depend on owning the historic properties that contain the material remains left behind by their ancestors. One example is how Afro-Crucian elders explain the intertwined concepts of ancestor veneration, African spirituality, historic preservation, and the SBA's archaeological work at the Estate Little Princess.

In the ceremonies I have been privileged to witness, Afro-Crucian traditional spirituality is connected to the land and sea. Archaeological work at Estate Little Princess begins with a site-opening ceremony led by a Black elder who has resided on Saint Croix for decades. Through this ceremony, it is acknowledged that those of us working at the site today have been called to do this work. We are also told that the spirits of those who once lived here, both enslaved and slave-owner, continue to resonate in this space; therefore, the space in which we are remains the stage where ancestral spirits continue to exist in another plane. All of those working on the project are asked to say a few words about what they feel will come from this project. They are also told to be particularly mindful of feelings and dreams as these could be ancestors of this space or your own ancestral lineage attempting to send you a message. Other site-opening activities include pouring libations (e.g., clean water) in the area where archaeological excavations will take place and purifying project participants with smoke. Even after the site-opening ceremony, archaeologists remain in contact with Black elders, informing them about the things we are finding and any archaeological features that may have spiritual significance. Occasionally, elders are called to the site to bless features and finds.

While the exact sequence of steps in the site opening ceremony changes each year, the core elements, and the motivations behind them remain consistent. The elders officiating these ceremonies want excavators to understand that they are working in a place where human ancestors once lived, worked, and dreamed. These persons have passed out of the material world we currently occupy and now reside in a spiritual space where other human ancestors dwell. It is unclear whether these spirits act upon living human lives; some believe this is possible while others do not, and it is made clear that acknowledging the memory of these ancestral spirits, even anecdotally, is important for the success of the archaeological excavations because the earth contains the residues of their past activities. This is not strange for archaeologists to understand; however, elders presiding over these ceremonies make it clear that archaeology also involves revealing the stories and knowledge these residues contain. This is difficult to explain to archaeologists in a non-archaeological manner. Artifacts, ecofacts, and features exist and can be interpreted archaeologically but, in this case, these archaeological data sources are also imbued with echoes of the spirits of those who came before us. It is these echoes that whisper what the ancestors want us to know in the present. Therefore, one measure of the project's success is how well we listened to the ancestors' voices because the elders tell us that the message each of us receives will be different depending upon our own personal experiences that we bring with us to the project.

Regardless of whether we believe ancestral spirits are acting upon the lives of project participants, I have observed that the process of holding the site-opening ceremony helps participants enter a psychological state where they are more receptive to internalizing the impact of the project on local Afro-Crucians as well as in their own lives. At Estate Little Princess, practically the whole crew working on this project is of African descent, Afro-Crucian, or a member of the African diaspora. All of us know we are the descendants of slaves, the very same social group of people who lived, worked, and died on plantations across the Western Hemisphere. The site where we are working may not be connected to our own ancestry; however, everyone on the project shares the somber reminder that our people lived through this. We are the children of survivors. I believe this makes us more receptive to this sort of ceremony. It is difficult to explain to other archaeologists in words how this feels to each of us. We take it with us long after the field season is over.

Afro-Crucian elders approach heritage conservation from another perspective as well, one of veneration, connection, and spiritual survivance. While it is unclear whether the elders collaborating with archaeologists belong to a specific African spiritual orthodoxy, their approach contains elements found in Yoruba orişa traditions (e.g., those that recognize spiritual divinities called orişa), specifically when it comes to honoring ancestors (called egun in orişa traditions). In orişa worship, ancestral shrines (e.g., oju egun translated as "the face of the ancestors") represent monuments to those in each individual's lineage who lived in the past, preparing the earth in the past in anticipation of the present. Orişa traditions understand that the egun continue to live on another plane of existence after their time in the material world is over, but they can still interact with those living in the present in the material world (Correal 2003: 63–65). Holding communion with the egun takes place in different ways but leaving offerings, saying prayers, and asking for guidance are common activities. While ancestral shrines are typically made for individuals or families, I have seen offerings placed at trees, walls, buildings, and at archaeological sites on Saint Croix, especially in locations where enslaved Africans lived and worked. Some of these shrine-places at archaeological sites are actively maintained, demonstrating that engaging with places in this way is still part of Afro-Crucian life. The presence and maintenance of these shrine-places and the reminders from collaborating elders that our work engages with their ancestors demonstrates that Afro-Crucians recognize the land as a repository for ancestral human experiences. Activities on the land that venerate and maintain connection to these ancestors are important pathways for personal growth, as well as survivance and cultural reconciliation. When it comes to heritage conservation, these aspects are the most important elements to Afro-Crucian collaborators, but they are the most difficult to manage under historic preservation structures in the United States.

Conclusion

Heritage conservation in the form of regulated historic preservation has ethical difficulties integrating the intangible into its models. In the United States the primary mechanism for preservation emphasizes materiality and property. While this system is flexible, its practitioners' unfamiliarity with the unique, emotional, and spiritual ways descendant communities connect to preserved materials and places only amplifies shortcomings in regulations like the NHPA, even though these emotional and cultural ties are the ones that bind descendant communities to historical sites. This, I propose, is an ethical problem. Taking religious, spiritual, and other non-archaeological understandings into account does not mean we are no longer doing archaeology (Carman 2015: 159; Schadla-Hall 2004).

There are many possible ethical solutions, but they call upon archaeologists to change. When it comes to addressing archaeology conducted within communities, Carman (2015: 173–174) calls upon archaeologists to understand: (1) that communities pre-date the archaeologist's arrival; (2) that communities already have an "established sense of identity"; and (3) "that identity is grounded in what they perceive as their past as represented by certain kinds of material." Carman also states that these assumptions can be challenged based on the archaeologist's experiences, which implies that they are not static rules but observations made by archaeologists. Communities may have different values altogether when it comes to archaeological materials and the archaeological record.

Additionally, the presence or discovery of archaeological remains that contribute to that community's sense of identity can lead to a recursive process where the sites are accepted as part of the community's heritage, leading community members to acknowledge patrimony over more sites. It can also motivate archaeologists to discover ways to adjust archaeological narratives, so that they better contribute to that sense of identity (Carman 2015: 174–175). This "arborescent" model of heritage seeks to explain how the preexisting roots of a community's sense of identity can intermix with archaeology in such a way that they are cocreated through the processes of social interaction (Russell 2010). In the case of Afro-Crucian heritage conservation praxis, community-based participatory archaeology adds authority to local identity narratives while helping archaeologists better understand archaeological knowledge through a Caribbean, African diasporic cultural lens. The ethical way forward is a co-creation of knowledge; however, I believe archaeologists are learning more from local residents than they are from archaeologists because much of the archaeological data corroborates things local elders already knew about the past.

It may seem like archaeologists are gleaning more cultural knowledge under this model, but the situational identities of the Black American archaeologists working at Estate Little Princess have potential to reach audiences that would not otherwise partake in archaeological knowledge. Carman (2015: 177–178) warns that since white, middle- to upper-class people are the most likely to visit heritage sites, community archaeology may be talking "to those who already speak in our language and share our values." Optics contribute deeply to community connections. The fact that the work at the Estate Little Princess was conducted by an all-Black group of archaeologists who were invited to do this work by community elders who are also Black has made a deep impact on the local society. Black archaeologists who have similar family histories have allowed sincere knowledge sharing because both Afro-Crucians and African descended people from the mainland can relate to each other on many levels. The work proceeds at the speed of trust and I have found it easier to trust my Afro-Crucian colleagues as they have found it easier to trust us. We are working with people who speak our language and share our values, and those values and language are different than those of most archaeologists because of the cultural experiences that African diasporic people share.

Afro-Crucians can teach archaeologists about deeper connections to sites that extend to a spiritual level because they have not been as disenfranchised from the land or African spiritual practices to the extent of most African descended people on the mainland. The biggest difference is that, on the mainland, African diasporic people do not have as much control over the local government. Control over governance is important when it comes to historic properties since it is the local government and SHPO that approve

National Register forms, and apply a state-level recognition of the historicity of a property. But there are ways that mainland African diasporic communities and Afro-Crucians agree when it comes to historic properties. As members of the African diaspora, the true value of historic properties goes beyond the material property itself. A property's value to traditional communities is the way it carves places out of multivalent landscapes and sets them aside so that communities can continue their practices in the ways they see fit. Archaeology only adds texture to these persistent, integral practices. Adding this texture is not only good science but an ethical imperative given archaeology's checkered past with African diasporic communities.

Acknowledgments

There are too many people to whom I owe a deep, sincere debt of gratitude. First, to Dr. ChenziRa Davis-Kahina and Frandelle Gerard, elders who have helped me learn everything I know about how Afro-Crucian people relate to historic properties. To my colleagues at the Society of Black Archaeologists who kept the archaeological excavations at Estate Little Princess going before and after the pandemic: Ayana Flewellen, Alexandra Jones, Justin Dunnavant, and Alicia Odewale. To the Nature Conservancy, for letting us dig on their preserve for four years. To all the undergraduate, graduate, and local Crucian students who used shovels, trowels, machetes, and their beautiful minds to explore this small slice of the African diaspora. And, to all the people of Saint Croix who showed me what it looks like to live in a Black place created by Black ancestors operated by Black people for the benefit of Black children. Aṣẹ.

References Cited

Altschul, Jeffery H., and Klein, Terry H. 2022. "Forecast for the US CRM Industry and Job Market, 2022–2031." *Advances in Archaeological Practice* 10(4): 355–370.

Babiarz, Jennifer. 2011. "White Privilege and Silencing within the Heritage Landscape: Race and the Practice of Cultural Resources Management." In *The Materiality of Freedom: Archaeologies of Post-Emancipation Life,* edited by Jodi Barnes, 47–58. Columbia: University of South Carolina Press.

Barile, Kerri S. 2004. "Race, the National Register, and Cultural Resource Management: Creating an Historic Context for Postbellum Sites." *Historical Archaeology* 38(1): 90–100.

Brown, Vincent. 2008. *The Reaper's Garden: Death and Power in the World of Atlantic Slavery.* Cambridge: Harvard University Press.

Browne, Randy M. 2008. "The Reaper's Garden: Death and Power in the World of Atlantic Slavery." (Review.) *William and Mary Quarterly* 68(3): 451–480.

Carman, John. 2015. *Archaeological Resource Management: An International Perspective.* Cambridge: Cambridge University Press.

Correal, Tobe Melora. 2003. *Finding Soul on the Path of* Orişa: *A West African Spiritual Tradition.* Berkeley: Crossing Press.

Crosson, J. Brent. 2015. "What Obeah Does Do: Healing, Harm, and the Limits of Religion." *Journal of Africana Religions* 3(2): 151–176.

De la Torre, Miguel. 2004. *Santería: The Beliefs and Rituals of a Growing Religion in America.* Grand Rapids, Michigan: William B. Eerdmans Publishing Company.

Dookhan, Isaac. 1994. *A History of the Virgin Islands of the United States.* Kingston, Jamaica: Canoe Press.

Flewellen, Ayana, William A. White III, Justin Dunnavant, Alexandra Jones, Suzanne Pierre, and Benjamin David Siegel. 2023. "Estate Little Princess End of Fieldwork Report, Summer 2022." Prepared for the Nature Conservancy, Washington, DC. Society of Black Archaeologists Report 001–2023.

Flygare, Signe Haubroe. 2016. "The Free Negro Company of Christiansted: Struggles for Equality, 1773–1799." *Scandinavian Journal of History* 41(4–5): 586–607.

Franklin, Maria, Anna Agbe-Davies, Kimball Banks, Jodi A. Barnes, Thomas Cuthbertson, Sarah Herr, J. W. Joseph, Edward Morin, Burr Neely, Holly Norton, Tsim Schneider, and William White. 2022a. *Documenting U.S. State and Territorial Approaches to Black Heritage, Diversity, and Inclusion in Preservation Practices 2022.* Black Heritage Resources Task Force, United States. https://core.tdar.org/document/470407/documenting-us-state-and-territorialapproaches-to-black-heritage-diversity-and-inclusion-in-preservation-practices-2022 (accessed October 14, 2023).

Franklin, Maria, Anna Agbe-Davies, Kimball Banks, Jodi A. Barnes, Thomas Cuthbertson, Sarah Herr, J. W. Joseph, Edward Morin, Burr Neely, Holly Norton, Tsim Schneider, and William White. 2022b. *Recommendations for Raising the Visibility of Black Heritage Resources and Engaging with Black Stakeholders: Results from a Survey of State and Territorial Historic Preservation Offices and State Archaeologists.* Black Heritage Resources Task Force, United States. https://core.tdar.org/document/470405/recommendations-for-raising-the-visibility-of-black-heritage-resources-and-engaging-with-black-stakeholders-results-from-a-survey-of-state-and-territorial-historic-preservation-offices-and-state-archaeologists (accessed October 14, 2023).

Gordenstein, Samuel Lira. 2016. "Planting Axé in the City: Urban Terreiros and the Growth of Candomblé in Late Nineteenth-Century Salvador, Bahia, Brazil." *Journal of African Diaspora Archaeology and Heritage* 5(2): 71–101.

Green-Pedersen, Svend E. 1975. "The History of the Danish Negro Slave Trade, 1733–1807: An Interim Survey Relating in Particular to Its Volume, Structure, Profitability and Abolition." *Revue française d'histoire d'outremer* 62(1–2): 196–220.

Green-Pedersen, Svend E. 1980. "Colonial Trade under the Danish Flag: A Case Study of the Danish Slave Trade to Cuba, 1790–1807." *Scandinavian Journal of History* 5(1–4): 93–120.

Hall, Neville A. T. 1984. "The Victor Vanquished: Emancipation in St. Croix: Its Antecedents and Immediate Aftermath." *Nieuwe West-Indische Gids / New West Indian Guide,* 58(1/2): 3–36.

Hall, Neville A. T. 1992. *Slave Society in the Danish West Indies: St. Thomas, St. John, St. Croix.* Baltimore: Johns Hopkins University Press.

Hardy, Meredith D. 2007. *Archeological Investigations at Salt River Bay National Historical Park and Ecological Preserve.* SEAC Accession Number 1953. Tallahassee: Southeastern Archaeological Center.

Handler, Jerome. 1997. "An African-Type Healer/Diviner and His Grave Goods: A Burial from a Plantation Slave Cemetery in Barbados, West Indies." *International Journal of Historical Archaeology* 1(2): 91–130.

Hurston, Zora Neale. 1938 [1990]. *Tell my Horse: Voodoo and Live in Haiti and Jamaica.* New York: Harper & Row.

Hvid, Mirjam Louise. 2016. "Indentured Servitude and Convict Labour in the Danish-Norwegian West Indies, 1671–1755." *Scandinavian Journal of History* 41(4–5): 541–564.

Jensen, Niklas Thode. 2012. *For the Health of the Enslaved: Slaves, Medicine, and Power in the Danish West Indies, 1803–1848.* Copenhagen: Museum Tusculanum Press.

Jensen, Niklas Thode, and Gunvor Simonsen. 2016. "Introduction: The Historiography of Slavery in the Danish-Norwegian West Indies, c. 1950–2016." *Scandinavian Journal of History* 41(4–5): 475–494.

Karade, Baba Ifa. 2020. *The Handbook of Yoruba Religious Concepts.* Newburyport, MA: Weiser Books.

King, Thomas F. 2012. *Cultural Resource Law and Practice.* Fourth Edition. Lanham, Maryland: AltaMira Press.

Leone, Mark P. 2020. "The Problem: Religion within the World of Slaves." *Current Anthropology* 61(22): S26-S288.

Masur, Jenny. 2009. "Working with Traditionally Associated Groups: A Form of Civic Engagement." *The George Wright Forum* 26(3): 85–94.

Matory, J. Lorand. 2005. *Black Atlantic Religion: Tradition, Transnationalism, and Matriarchy in the Afro-Brazilian Candomblé.* Princeton, New Jersey: Princeton University Press.

Murrell, Nathaniel Samuel. 2010. *Afro-Caribbean Religions: An Introduction to their Historical, Cultural, and Sacred Traditions.* Philadelphia: Temple University Press.

National Park Service. 2006. *Management Policies 2006.* Washington, DC: US Department of Interior.

Orser, Charles E., Jr. 2023. *Living Ceramics, Storied Ground: A History of African American Archaeology.* Gainesville: University Press of Florida.

Pagán-Jiménez, Jaime R. 2006. "Is All Archaeology at Present a Postcolonial One?" *Journal of Social Archaeology* 4(2): 200–213.

Røge, Pernille. 2014. "Why the Danes Got There First—A Trans-Imperial Study of the Abolition of the Danish Slave Trade in 1792." *Slavery and Abolition* 35(4): 576–592.

Russell, Ian. 2010. "Heritages, Identities, and Roots: A Critique of Arborescent Models of Heritage and Identity." In *Heritage Values in Contemporary Society,* edited by George S. Smith, Phyllis M. Messenger and Hilary A. Soderland, 29–42. Walnut Creek, California: Left Coast Press.

Savage, John. 2012. "Slave Poison / Slave Medicine: The Persistence of Obeah in Nineteenth-Century Martinique." In *Obeah and Other Powers: The Politics of Caribbean Religion and Healing,* edited by Diana Paton and Maarit Forde, 149–171. Durham, North Carolina: Duke University Press.

Schadla-Hall, Tim. 2004. "The Comforts of Unreason: The Importance and Relevance of Alternative Archaeology." In *Public Archaeology,* edited by Nick Merriman, 255–271. London: Routledge.

Simonsen, Gunvor. 2016. *Slave Stories: Law, Representation, and Gender in the Danish West Indies.* Aarhus, Denmark: Aarhus University Press.

US Virgin Islands Code. 2019a. Title 3—Executive; Chapter 22—Department of Planning and Natural Resources. § 402–404: Division of Planning, Historic Preservation Commission and State Historic Preservation Officer. https://law.justia.com/codes/virgin-islands/2019/title-3/chapter-22/402/. Accessed June 25, 2024.

US Virgin Islands Code. 2019b. Title 3—Executive; Chapter 22—Department of Planning and Natural Resources. § 408: Virgin Islands Cultural Heritage Institute. https://law.justia.com/codes/virgin-islands/2019/title-3/chapter-22/408/. Accessed June 25, 2024.

3

Developing Collective Ethics on Sint Eustatius

The Case of the Golden Rock African Burial Ground

marjolijn kok

The excavation of 69 burials of enslaved people at the Golden Rock Plantation site on the island of Sint Eustatius in 2021, without the consultation of descendant communities, has led to local social upheaval and more widespread ethical concerns. In a time when codes of ethics have become an integral part of the archaeological professional field, the specific situation on Sint Eustatius can be seen as a lapse in such international ethical codes. These codes often appeal to individual morality in the sense that they assume individuals will try to do good. In this chapter, I explore how ethical behavior can be thought of as a community practice. The question is, how do we approach heritage if the associated ethics are not only part of professional codes, but also are created with the community? Here, I propose a collaborative approach where descendant communities and others such as heritage professionals work together to safeguard Caribbean heritage. I am a white, queer, Dutch independent researcher and was asked by the Alliance to help them with archaeological issues, such as reading archaeological reports and policies. I had no prior engagement with Caribbean archaeology as from my point of view it is a colonial context and I could only work there by invitation of local communities. In the European Netherlands I work especially on the postcolonial issue of the archaeological heritage of Moluccan camps. My activism pertains to all types of inequality as we are only free when everybody is free. This chapter therefore reflects my personal views and experiences as an activist/archaeological adviser of the St. Eustatius Afrikan Burial Ground Alliance (SE-ABG Alliance).

Ethical Codes

Since the early 2000s, ethics have become a part of the archaeological field, as is evident from scholarly publications (Gnecco and Lippert 2015; González-Ruibal and Moshenska 2015; Haber and Shepherd 2015; Meskell and Pels 2005; Scarre and Scarre 2006; Vitelli 1996) and many written ethical codes.[1] Most codes of ethics in archaeology are aligned to professional associations such as the Society for American Archaeology (SAA) (2024), the European Association of Archaeologists (EAA) (2022), the World Archaeology Congress (WAC) (2024), and the International Association for Caribbean Archaeology (IACA) (2022), to only name those most relevant to the Caribbean. These codes rely on the moral integrity of the person, because they are not legally binding. Members of these associations are expected to read and adhere to the codes, although this is usually not the reason people join these associations. This reliance on the assumed moral integrity of archaeologists has not been paired with sufficient oversight, which leads to a general pattern where the enforcement of the codes of ethics by these organizations is not common practice (Newson and Young 2022: 156; Pels 2005; Zimmerman 1998). Therefore, although the intentions behind the codes of ethics may be good, they can also be viewed as "window dressing," and in the worst cases they can be used as a mechanism with which to conceal unethical practices (Zorzin 2015), especially in (former) colonial territories or in areas where local heritage laws are minimal or absent. Newson and Young (2022) write about this problem of minimal presence or complete absence of heritage laws in post-conflict situations in countries such as Lebanon, Cambodia, and Rwanda, but this situation also prevails in (parts of) the Caribbean. Another problem related to the Caribbean is that codes of ethics, such as those of the SAA and WAC, aim to protect the rights of Indigenous communities, but seem to overlook Black people and other groups who have not had the same protection as white colonizers when it comes to their heritage.

Codes of ethics tend to focus on continuing the discipline of archaeology from a Western science perspective, where other ways of knowing are sometimes acknowledged but not accorded the same value as scientific knowledge (Curtoni 2015; Wylie 2005; also see Herrera Malatesta, this volume). Objective science and disciplinary best practices are often equated with ethical behavior. Especially in the context of colonized countries, the propagation of Western epistemologies within archaeological codes make these epistemologies a potential tool of the colonizer, and by extension, of neo-colonization by global neoliberal capitalism (González-Ruibal 2018).

The emphasis on a universal, objective science separates the archaeologist from political issues, thereby supporting the status quo and avoiding debates related to social justice (Gnecco 2015; Hamilakis 2007; Scarre and Scarre 2006; Wylie 2005). In this sense, archaeology can become a tool of the neoliberal colonizer just by claiming objectivity, and by failing to question the consequences that archaeological research may have for others. Therefore, several authors rightly question whether codes of ethics are made in order to protect the discipline or to engage with society (Ferris and Welch 2015; Gnecco 2015; Hamilakis 2007; Meskell and Pels 2005; Wylie 2005). This is complicated by the fact that much archaeological work in Europe, the United States, and the Caribbean is now carried out as part of contract archaeology, which takes place within neoliberal capitalist projects.

As mentioned above, the Western perspective on (codes of) ethics tends to focus on the behavior of individuals (Colwell-Chanthaphonh and Ferguson 2006; Pels 2005). It is assumed that archaeologists are persons with the right moral standards, and that they will automatically try to do the right thing. Even critiques of the codes of ethics do not seem to challenge the emphasis on the individual (Tarlow 2001). At the same time, many view ethics as a situated practice that only gains its meaning within a specific context with social and political implications (McDavid and Brock 2015; Meskell and Pels 2005; Newson and Young 2022). Situated practice is, in my view, never a solitary practice. We situate ourselves in relation to other people and perspectives. This is not an abstract methodology, but involves actions that affect people and communities. If we take this point of view, it would be strange not to include these people and communities in evaluating our ethics. Archaeologists may find their behavior ethical, but the public or descendant community might think differently, and therefore ethical practice should be discussed with the communities concerned (McDavid and Brock 2015; Tarlow 2006; Zimmerman 1994). I propose that we adopt a collective ethics situated in the local context (see also Hamilakis 2007; Meskell and Pels 2005; Tarlow 2006). This means discussions must take place prior to any project, with all the relevant groups, to come to a mutually agreed upon set of ethical values, and as Meskell and Pels (2005) suggest, responsibilities that guide further practices. These discussions can be difficult, as they concern people's cultural and professional norms about what a just practice is. Different viewpoints and cultural backgrounds may challenge people's foundational beliefs, whether related to their profession or community. Furthermore, collective ethics means giving up some authority and power, and sometimes limiting academic freedom. Some find this troubling, as they assume that science is for the good of all. But this assumption can no longer be seen as self-evident (Bauer 2010; Ferris and Welch 2014; González-Tennant 2014; Lane 2005; Meskell and Pels 2005; Reardon and TallBear 2012; Wylie 2000; Zimmerman 1998). A possible limit to research should not only be discussed in negative terms, as the engagement with descendant communities can lead to other insights and new research questions (Wylie 2008; Zimmerman 1998).

The discussions and engagement that need to take place are long-term processes, as a meaningful outcome cannot emerge in just a few meetings. People need time to process each other's values and to adapt to a collective situation in which conflict and emotional confrontations cannot and should not be avoided. Collective ethical codes are always in motion, and therefore there is no finalizing moment but rather continuous interaction and adaptation (Wylie 2000).

The Golden Rock Plantation African Burial Site of Sint Eustatius

As ethical codes are considered situated practice, I will now turn to the Dutch Caribbean island of Sint Eustatius. This will provide the context in which ethical concerns did arise, which is discussed in the next section. The 2021 excavation of the eighteenth-century African burial ground at Sint Eustatius airport, also known as Golden Rock Plantation, has stirred the local community.[2] The way in which the archaeological process was executed, including the lack of community engagement, has exposed flaws in the management of cultural heritage on the island that are informative for the archaeological field in the wider Caribbean and beyond. Here, I will give a brief history of the events related to the excavation of the African burial ground and indicate the moments where ethical concerns were raised. It will become clear that it is not just personal actions but also systemic circumstances that have led to these concerns. Finally, I will propose an alternative way of looking at ethical concerns that may prevent these issues from happening again in the future.

On July 2, 2020, a board member of the St. Eustatius Center for Archaeological Research (SECAR) saw excavators employed by the local government digging for sand to be used for construction in a protected area within the airport premises.[3] The next day a letter about the archaeological potential was sent from SECAR to the government. In the following days, information was exchanged and the local government asked SECAR to provide a desk-based assessment (DBA) and field investigation (van Keulen et al. 2020: 1). The DBA showed the area to have high archaeological potential and high integrity with some minimal cable disturbances. The local government should already have been aware of these facts, as the 2013 Archaeological Predictive Map indicates that the airport area has high archaeological potential (Dutch Caribbean Nature Alliance 2024). To gain more accurate information, a test excavation started on September 16, 2020, carried out by SECAR. In the relevant report, there is no reference to a program of requirements. Test trenches yielded 15 visible burial outlines, and a total of 60–70 burials were expected within the project area (van Keulen et al. 2020: 26). The burials were thought to be those of enslaved people from the eighteenth century, as historic maps show a nearby settlement for enslaved people. The importance of the archaeological remains was immediately grasped; this could be one of the largest excavated African burial grounds in the Caribbean (van Keulen et al. 2020). According to SECAR, they sent several proposed press releases to the local government, which the latter allegedly decided not to release. SECAR itself, and especially the principal investigator of the excavation, were also reluctant to share information with the local community, expecting that there might be opposition to the excavation of their ancestors (Haviser 2022). A community consultation and engagement plan was commissioned by SECAR and presented to the government, but no community consultation or engagement took place in advance of the full excavation. Community engagement at the site was ultimately limited to visits by school children and the invitation of local volunteers.

The open-area excavation started on April 21, 2021, with the participation of a full team of international experts, including an osteologist. Since as of September 2025 there is still no publicly available report of the excavations, the details of the excavation findings are not accessible. In June 2021, people on the island realized that an ancestral burial ground was being excavated. The descendant community started protesting, and they demanded the excavation be stopped and the reburial of their ancestors. Representatives of the Ubuntu Connected Front, Brighter Path Foundation St. Eustatius, grassroots movement St. Eustatius Awareness and Development Movement (SEAD), and public health research institute EcoRAY wrote a letter stating their demands to the local government on June 20, 2021 (Ubuntu Connected Front 2021b). At that moment, the excavation was already in its final stage, and it ended the next day. The evening of the last day of excavations, a town meeting was held, where public concerns were cut short by the moderator from the government information department (Statia Government 2021). The public protests continued, and on July 3 an online petition was launched aimed at stopping the excavation of the ancestral remains and requesting the inclusion of the descendant community in the archaeological research. At this point, I became aware of the issues and got involved with the group St. Eustatius Afrikan Burial Ground Alliance as an unpaid independent archaeological adviser. For me it was logical as an advocate for inclusive ethical archaeology to participate in a grassroots movement when directly asked, even though I had always avoided doing archaeology in colonial territories.

In response to the complaints, on July 9, 2021, the Sint Eustatius government prohibited any destructive analyses on the ancestral remains, but at the same time gave no definite answer on where to store these remains properly. On September 23, the government issued an article about establishing the Statia Heritage Research Commission (SHRC), with the goal of reviewing the process and making recommendations for future heritage management on the island. The alliance during this time wrote articles published in local newspapers, thus keeping pressure on the government. They also started talks with UNESCO NL, the Cultural Heritage Agency of the Netherlands, and the Dutch Ministry of the Interior and Kingdom Relations. The SHRC report was published in January 2022 (Haviser 2022). Its most important conclusions were: (1) there had been a government policy of turning a blind eye to heritage; (2) the public was deliberately not informed about the burial site; and (3) legislation relating to heritage management was inadequate. The local government formed the Statia Cultural Heritage Implementation Committee (SCHIC) at the end of 2022 with the intent to put the report's recommendations into practice. At the time of writing this contribution in September 2025, the SCHIC is still working on implementation of the SHRC recommendations. One of the members of the alliance is part of this committee. However, the committee has come across some difficulties. The SCHIC is in the midst of community engagement, but their work is hindered by a lack of accurate information from the government.[4] Recent developments, such as the curation of archaeological materials and ancestral remains by the government at a location known as a "heritage house" have not been handled in a transparent or community-focused manner and have excluded the SCHIC (Statia Government 2023). The proper storage of ancestral remains could have provided an opportunity to engage with the community and involve them in a ceremony or other event that acknowledged the humanity of these ancestors. All in all, decisions seem to have been made in a hurry to repair damage instead of thinking through how to engage with the community in a more meaningful way.

Ethical Concerns

The outline of the events surrounding the Golden Rock Plantation African burial site raises several ethical concerns, ranging from the overall system to personal actions. I will highlight three of my main concerns here, although there are many more smaller ethical issues surrounding the project.

Firstly, there was a lack of protection of heritage sites at a governmental level. The area was already known to have high archaeological potential, but this had not led to protective measures (de Waal et al. 2019: 161). Here, the unethical behavior of developing an area with high archaeological potential is not so much a personal responsibility as it is embedded in a system that does not value Dutch Caribbean heritage in the same manner as Dutch European heritage. In the European Netherlands, planning policies automatically involve an assessment of the potential cultural and natural impact of all terrain developments. In the Dutch Caribbean, there are to date no comparable policies or legislation (although the SCHIC is working on developing such legislation for Sint Eustatius). The Dutch government did not deem it necessary to update the heritage policies when the islands Bonaire, Sint Eustatius, and Saba (BES) became fully integrated into the Netherlands in 2010. The outdated BES monuments law, a mere three and a half pages long, has remained in use on the islands (Rijksoverheid Nederland 2024). However, the main problem was a lack of enforcement. Local governments can protect archaeological heritage if they choose, but they are not obliged to do so if they do not deem it necessary. New initiatives to improve the legal and policy situation, such as those of the SCHIC, are being developed but are not yet complete. In Dutch archaeology there has been little discussion on this point, except for some sessions at the Reuvensdagen (the national archaeology conference in the Netherlands). These discussions do not yet, however, flow over into general debates about heritage management. Archaeologists not directly involved in the Caribbean do not seem to feel the same responsibility for the protection of Caribbean heritage as they would for European Dutch heritage. Although an archaeological company (Archol) working in the Dutch Caribbean does conform to Dutch standards, there is a feeling among stakeholders I spoke to that local institutions (SECAR) and international universities such as Texas State University seem to take advantage of the lack of legislation by not making their methods and results publicly available. There is also the assumption by most Dutch people that, because nearly every public aspect of life is regulated in the European part of the Netherlands, things will be regulated in the Caribbean too. The Dutch government calls the islands "special municipalities" (bijzondere gemeenten), which suggests they are governed by Dutch legislation. But in reality the islands are public bodies (openbare lichamen), which have a different juridical status (Rijksoverheid Nederland 2024). Not all Dutch laws apply to the islands; for example, the islands are exempt from minimum wage law and the compulsory use of social security numbers. Moreover, because they do not belong to a Dutch province, there is a lack of provincial heritage support and facilities such as archaeological depots and erfgoedhuizen (in the European Netherlands, "heritage houses" play a role in policy development and general support). This may be because the Caribbean islands are seen as complicated and difficult by policymakers, with the added reluctance of Dutch civil servants to enforce policies that might be considered colonial. This was communicated to the alliance during several meetings with officials from the Ministry of the Interior and Kingdom Relations and the Cultural Heritage Agency of the Netherlands. In my view, this brings to the fore the fact that unethical behavior can be constituted merely by inattention or inaction.

Another ethical concern is SECAR's lack of engagement with the Sint Eustatius community relating to the excavation of ancestral remains. Since the 1990s it is no longer deemed ethical to excavate human remains without involving the descendant community (Franklin 1997; Nicholas and Hollowell 2009; World Archaeological Congress 1989; Zimmerman 1998). What makes the situation here of extra concern is that, according to the SHRC report, the lack of communication was not just a general oversight but communication was purposefully avoided by the principal investigator as he anticipated problems (Haviser 2022). This constitutes the misleading of a descendant community for personal (academic) gain. Furthermore, the situation was complicated by the fact that members of the excavation team who protested against this approach had little power to affect the situation, due to—for example—contractual obligations with SECAR (Fricke 2022).

The failure to involve the descendant community shows a lack of respect for the culture under research, and harms not only the community but also the field of archaeology. There was enough time between the test trenches project and the actual excavation to allow for community engagement, or even to find alternatives for the soil extraction and to preserve the site in situ. Furthermore, some members of the excavation team had extensive experience with community engagement but were allegedly prevented from utilizing this experience. In discussions with the alliance on Sint Eustatius in December 2020, SECAR pointed to the fact that the community's governmental representatives had given them permission to excavate. In cases like this, and especially on Sint Eustatius where there is not a full democracy,[5] permission from the local government cannot be equated with that of the local (descendant) community.

A final point of concern is the lack of publicly available information. According to the BES monuments law, the local government can ask for all kinds of archaeological information—reports and data—to become part of the public domain, but the local government is not legally obliged to do so (Rijksoverheid Nederland 2024). In fact, the local government was monitoring neither the excavations nor their outcomes (Haviser 2022). A 2015 mandate from the island governor gave SECAR the far-reaching power to decide who would have access to the archaeological heritage of the island.[6] In essence, this meant that there was no compulsory public access to archaeological reports, artifacts, or other documentation. In the European Netherlands the system might not be perfect, but something like this is not likely to happen, as archaeologists are obliged to deposit their artifacts, documentation, and reports in public depots within two years, and all archaeological research in the field has to be reported and geolocated.

On Sint Eustatius the community therefore has no way to gain accurate information about what is researched, or where the archaeological artifacts and ancestral remains are stored. In December 2022 I was on the island with several members of the alliance and we could neither visit the ancestral remains to pay our respects, nor obtain information on where exactly the ancestral remains were kept. In November 2024 the alliance was able to visit the ancestral remains, as they are now at the Heritage House. It was also very difficult to get access to archaeological reports, and even when reports were provided, not all of the requested material was included. If it is nearly impossible for me as a professional archaeologist to get accurate information, what would this mean for the descendant community? Access to one's own past is a human right (United Nations General Assembly 1948), and that is violated here.

Access to one's own heritage is also hindered by the fact that archaeological materials are sometimes sent abroad and that the research done by foreign students and researchers does not reach a wider audience, including the local community. As an example from Sint Eustatius, Texas State University has conducted student projects with archaeological materials from the Godet African Burial Ground of Sint Eustatius (Bowden 2019), but no reports or information about these materials are publicly available. In essence, it seems to me that the cultural heritage of Sint Eustatius is still exploited in a colonial manner, in which the benefits do not return to the local community but are extracted by companies abroad or reaped by archaeologists who stay on the island temporarily. SECAR is not an exception in this regard, as the extractive model is a widely recognized problem in contract archaeology (Ferris and Welch 2015; Haber and Shepherd 2015). SECAR's official monopoly on archaeological heritage only served to further aggravate the situation.

Toward Collective Ethics

While on the island, I invited several local people, including representatives of SECAR and the local government, to collaborate on this article by writing a short piece on how ethical heritage practice should develop on the island. In person, everybody confirmed their willingness to participate, but in the end no one stepped forward. There was interest from the descendant community, and four members of the community gave their opinion in interviews. Their willingness to participate and their responses strengthened my idea that if we want to move in a more ethical direction, this has to be done collectively, with representatives of all parties.

Because I want to gain insight into people's experience in their own words, the interviews were semi-structured in nature. Each interviewee was asked three questions,[7] on which they could elaborate as much as they wanted. At the outset, I explained that the responses would be used in this chapter and I made it clear that I am an archaeologist and a member of the alliance. Participants were also informed that they could withdraw their cooperation at any time, and contact information was exchanged for this purpose. A draft of this article was sent to interviewees for approval. No information on their background was recorded, but they were all adults from the descendant community living on Sint Eustatius.

A striking fact about the interviews is that, generally, there was a similar experience of archaeological heritage, and it was seen in a wider context concerning other aspects of living on the island. Of course, this is not a representative sample, and I met the participants during community engagement activities, which biases the responses, but if I triangulate them against informal conversations that I had with people on the street, the same feelings were expressed.

First, all of the interviewees expressed the idea that they initially thought archaeology was not for them. In their view, archaeology was not related to their own heritage as it was carried out by people from outside the island. Over the years, many archaeologists have come to the island to excavate; they might have told the public an archaeological narrative that had no relevance to the audience, and then they left, often taking artifacts with them. Archaeologists, just like so many other people, were seen to come to the island to do a job and leave without really affecting local circumstances. With the excavation of their ancestors, the respondents started to think about the ethical problems associated with archaeology and wider implications this could have. This is not surprising, as many ethical discussions in archaeology around the world have started when people questioned or protested against the excavation of their ancestors (Colwell 2016; Haber and Shepherd 2015; LaRoche and Blakey 1997; Zimmerman 1998).

Secondly, the interviewees felt local history education was lacking. Although recently the local high school has tried to teach more local history, the main curriculum is based on European Dutch history, which makes people feel it is not for them as it does not relate to their circumstances. One of the interviewees expressed the sentiment like this: Why should I or my children go to the local museum if they show nothing that is of interest to us?

Thirdly, as the respondents learned about archaeology, it interested them, but they also related it to their present-day situation. For example, when we came to the subject of DNA analysis, one interviewee wondered if it would help answer why, in the interviewee's perception, so many Black people on Sint Eustatius die of cancer. They were certainly interested in having a greater say in what happened during excavations and subsequent research.

And last but certainly not least, interviewees' responses indicated it was generally seen as unethical to excavate ancestral remains. Even when done in a way that archaeologists might find ethical or respectful, in principle it was seen as disrespectful to excavate people, especially as these individuals had already been deprived of so many things in life. This said, despite the unethical behavior of the archaeologists, the respondents were generously still willing to talk to archaeologists and to look toward a joint future, working together.

How does this all work toward a more collective way of dealing with ethics and responsibilities? Working toward a more ethical and responsible archaeology is a long process. The issues that arise ought to be discussed widely, and should not be superficially "fixed" in order to gloss over deeper problems. The Golden Rock Plantation African burial site can be seen as a turning point in dealing with heritage on Sint Eustatius, and it should serve as a learning opportunity for all involved. Although the present focus is on this specific site due to the public attention, the ethical concerns discussed above relate to the entire archaeological heritage on the island and also beyond. If we take the situatedness of ethics seriously, local circumstances and local communities become central. Archaeological heritage should not be seen as just in the past, where the value of objects lies in the scientific information they may convey. For descendant communities this heritage can be part of their present-day living culture (Meskell 2002; Tarlow 2006; Wylie 2005). The collective ethical approach therefore extends into broader discussions on the value of local heritage and how to take care of it within a community context. The lessons learned can be extended to the national level, as the archaeological field is currently exploring the consequences of the implementation of the Faro Convention (Rijksdienst voor Cultureel Erfgoed 2022).

Sint Eustatius's situation—as a small island with limited resources dependent on a country on the other side of the Atlantic Ocean—is complex but could also be seen as an opportunity, because the Dutch legislative restrictions on direct public participation in archaeological heritage are absent. The handling of the island's heritage can be vastly improved, but the degree in which this succeeds will depend upon how this opportunity is utilized. New legislation could integrate the Valletta Treaty and the Faro Convention[8] into one, balancing the interests of the field of archaeology with that of the local community. Although the SHRC report does not refer directly to the Faro Convention, its recommendations can be read as having similar goals. In the European Netherlands, the Valletta Treaty has led to a disengagement of the public, due to the overregulation of direct access to archaeology (van der Horst, van Soomeren, and Hopstaken 2021, 15–16; Reith 2022, 36). With the new adherence to the Faro Convention, in which people's access and control over their own heritage is anchored, the tension between archaeological legislation and the public comes into view. However, legislation for Sint Eustatius should be tailored to the local situation; it cannot simply be a copy of the Dutch Valletta legislation. For one thing, certain aspects such as the Kwaliteitsnorm Archeologie (KNA, translated as "archaeology quality norm") would not suit Caribbean archaeology and heritage because, for example, experience working in the European Dutch territory is required to obtain certification. Instead, the legislation should be developed in a careful process supported by various groups including heritage professionals and community members. The complexity of combining both the protection of archaeological heritage and public accessibility could lead to a new idea of heritage and its management. In that way, Sint Eustatius could emerge from a lagging position to serve as an example for others to follow.

Today, SECAR no longer has an official monopoly on the island regarding contract archaeology and no longer receives any governmental support. Any future project can learn from the mistakes of the past. Public lectures, for example, are often seen as public engagement, but they only reach a certain portion of the people on the island and only give information. Other forms of communication may be more effective in becoming community engagement instead of outreach only. We can only truly communicate when we employ language that everybody understands, because presenting facts accurately is only ethical if the listener understands the wording used (Allen 2015). I would add that the engagement can only be truly ethical if the setting in which discussions take place is welcoming to the community. Moreover, the engagement should not be one-directional. What is needed is a conversation about the past (McDavid 2002). Everybody has their own knowledge and ways to engage with heritage. We can use the concept of "braided knowledge" (Atalay 2020) here, where different types of knowledge are used to tell the narrative of the local heritage. It is a mistake to think that scientific practice is compromised in a collaborative or collective process. Archaeologists bring their scientific know-how to the table. Collective practice means that we realize that others contribute their own know-how as well. By combining these different approaches, new insights can be gained. Differences and disagreements will most likely arise, but common ground can be found as well. If you share responsibility about specific issues, it is in everybody's interest to reach solutions that work within the community.

Community-wide engagement is essential, but has to be embedded in a durable structure. My emphasis on good legislation can be seen as a top-down approach, but I see this legislation as a starting point for further developments. This point is also made by the SHRC in its report (Haviser 2022: 31). Ideally, this legislation should enhance the accessibility of archaeological heritage, which makes it possible for more people to engage meaningfully with their heritage and have a say in what happens to that heritage. It should not be the case that a commercial company decides on the heritage of a whole community. If you share responsibility, it becomes more difficult to hide behind others, since you are all working toward the same goal. It is therefore important to agree on the goals of any heritage project taking place within the community. In the conversations around ethics and heritage, questions such as "Who decides over whose heritage?" and "Who benefits from the archaeological project?" have to be central, grounding the archaeological heritage in its local context and community.

Difficult or emotional heritage does not need a quick fix—it needs thoughtful engagement and time to heal. Only then can we come to an ethical approach to heritage and its communities.

Conclusion

To conclude, the main ethical concerns relating to archaeological research into Sint Eustatius's past have concerned a lack of legislation and legislation enforcement, a lack of descendant community involvement, and a lack of access to accurate information and archaeological heritage. Both the government and the archaeological community bear responsibility for these matters, but the question is how these concerns can be resolved, especially regarding future archaeological research. An individual, top-down approach is not the way to go; we need a process that includes healing the wounds of the unethical practices that have taken place on the island. So, how can we approach heritage practices in an ethical manner, involving the community?

The excavation of the Golden Rock African burial ground has become a pivotal event as it has sparked wider discussion about how to deal with heritage on Sint Eustatius. If all involved take responsibility, a collective way of engaging with archaeology can come to fruition. Legislation and policies should be put into place ensuring that community engagement becomes a priority. These rules should not be an endpoint, but should be the continued adaptive practice of collective collaboration on heritage projects. Ethical standpoints should be discussed continuously as a shared responsibility beyond reactions to immediate conflicts. As became clear in the interviews, there is a willingness to collaborate with the archaeological field. The interviewees certainly had ideas for research directions and ethical approaches. The road will not be easy but it can lead to Sint Eustatius becoming an example for the Caribbean and the wider area of heritage practice that benefits the local community as much as the field of archaeology.

Acknowledgments

I would like to thank the people on Sint Eustatius for their warm welcome and our conversations, especially Althea Merkman, Charles Woodley, Rosabell Blake, Geoffrey Blake, Carlos Lopes, Derrick Simmons, Kenneth Cuvalay, Petra Ploeg, and Jamal Berkel.

Notes

1 Although not complete, for example, the Archaeological Ethics Database has links to 97 codes of ethics (Register of Professional Archaeologists & the Chartered Institute for Archaeologists 2024).

2 For example, the combined press release of several groups (Ubuntu Connected Front 2021a).

3 I received a list of events concerning the excavations from a board member of SECAR.

4 Information provided by the SCHIC committee member representing the alliance.

5 For a short description of the political situation, see kok 2022.

6 On February 10, 2015, the island governor issued a mandate which stated that SECAR "is appointed as the sole entity for the execution of the identification, investigation and preservation of the diverse marine and terrestrial archaeological heritage of St Eustatius, or oversight of other parties involved in these activities." The author has a scan of the mandate dated February 15, 2015.

7 These questions were: (1) When and how did you become aware of the excavation of the African burial site at the Golden Rock Plantation? (2) What are your feelings and thoughts about the excavation of the African burial site? (3) What would you like to be done differently in the future?

8 The Valletta Treaty is mainly concerned with the protection of archaeological heritage and regulation of the field of archaeology. The goal of the Faro Convention is that everybody has not only access to but also a say in what happens to their cultural heritage.

References Cited

Allen, Mitchell. 2015. "Ethics in the Publishing of Archaeology." In *Ethics and Archaeological Praxis,* edited by Cristóbal Gnecco and Dorothy Lippert, 185–199. Ethical Archaeologies: The Politics of Social Justice 1. New York: Springer.

Atalay, Sonya. 2020. "Indigenous Science for a World in Crisis." *Public Archaeology* 19(1–4): 37–52.

Bauer, Alexander A. 2010. "Cultural Property: Internationalism, Ethics, and Law." In *Handbook of Postcolonial Archaeology,* edited by Jane Lydon and Uzma Rizvi, 285–294. Walnut Creek, California: Left Coast Press.

Bowden, Taylor. 2019. "Exploring Enslaved African Lifeways: An Isotopic Study of an 18th Century Cemetery (SE600) on St. Eustatius, Caribbean Netherlands." MA thesis, Texas State University.

Colwell, Chip. 2016. "Collaborative Archaeologies and Descendant Communities." *Annual Review of Anthropology* 45: 113–127.

Colwell-Chanthaphonph, Chip, and T. J. Ferguson. 2006. "Trust and Archaeological Practice: Towards a Framework of Virtue Ethics." In *The Ethics of Archaeology: Philosophical Perspectives on Archaeological Practice,* edited by Chris Scarre and Geoffrey Scarre, 115–13. Cambridge: Cambridge University Press.

Curtoni, Rafael Pedro. 2015. "Against Global Archaeological Ethics: Critical Views from South America." In *Ethics and Archaeological Praxis,* edited by Cristóbal Gnecco and Dorothy Lippert, 41–47. Ethical Archaeologies: The Politics of Social Justice 1. New York: Springer.

Dutch Caribbean Nature Alliance. 2024. "Sint Eustatius, Caribbean Netherlands: Archaeological Predictive Map." https://www.dcbd.nl/sites/default/files/documents/ARGEOgraph%282013%29_archeologicalPredictiveMapStatia.pdf (accessed June 25, 2024).

European Association of Archaeologists. 2022. EAA Codes and Principles. https://www.e-a-a.org/EAA/About/EAA_Codes/EAA/Navigation_About/EAA_Codes.aspx?hkey=714e8747-495c-4298-ad5d-4c60c2bcbda9 (accessed June 25, 2024).

Ferris, Neal, and John R. Welch. 2014. "Beyond Archaeological Agendas: In the service of a Sustainable Archaeology." In *Transforming Archaeology: Activist Practices and Prospects,* edited by Sonya Atalay, Lee Rains Clauss, Randal H. McGuire, and John R. Welch, 215–237. London: Routledge.

Ferris, Neal, and John R. Welch. 2015. "New Worlds: Ethics in Contemporary North American Archaeological Practice." In *Ethics and Archaeological Praxis,* edited by Cristóbal Gnecco and Dorothy Lippert, 69–92. Ethical Archaeologies: The Politics of Social Justice 1. New York: Springer.

Franklin, Maria. 1997. "'Power to the People': Sociopolitics and the Archaeology of Black Americans." *Historical Archaeology* 31(3): 36–50.

Fricke, Felicia. 2022. "Comments on the SHRC Report on the Golden Rock Excavation, St Eustatius." https://www.feliciajfricke.com/post/comments-on-the-shrc-report-on-the-golden-rock-excavation-st-eustatius (accessed July 19, 2023).

Gnecco, Cristóbal. 2015. "An Entanglement of Sorts: Archaeology, Ethics, Praxis, Multiculturalism." In *Ethics and Archaeological Praxis,* edited by Cristóbal Gnecco and Dorothy Lippert, 1–17. Ethical Archaeologies: The Politics of Social Justice 1. New York: Springer.

Gnecco, Cristóbal, and Dorothy Lippert, eds. 2015. *Ethics and Archaeological Praxis.* Ethical Archaeologies: The Politics of Social Justice 1. New York: Springer.

González-Ruibal, Alfredo. 2018. "Ethics of Archaeology." *Annual Review of Anthropology* 47: 345–360.

González-Ruibal, Alfredo, and Gabriel Moshenska, eds. 2015. *Ethics and the Archaeology of Violence.* Ethical Archaeologies: The Politics of Social Justice 2. New York: Springer.

González-Tennant, Edward, 2014. "The 'Color' of Heritage: Decolonizing Collaborative Archaeology in the Caribbean." *Journal of African Diaspora Archaeology & Heritage* 3(1): 26–50.

Haber, Alejandro, and Nick Shepherd, eds. 2015. *After Ethics: Ancestral Voices and Post-Disciplinary Worlds in Archaeology.* Ethical Archaeologies: The Politics of Social Justice 3. New York: Springer.

Hamilakis, Yannis. 2007. "From Ethics to Politics." In *Archaeology and Capitalism: From Ethics to Politics,* edited by Yannis Hamilakis and Philip Duke, 15–40. Walnut Creek, California: Left Coast Press.

Haviser, Jay, ed. 2022. Report of the Statia Heritage Research Commission (SHRC) for the Government of St. Eustatius, Netherlands Caribbean. St. Eustatius: Statia Heritage Research Commission (SHRC).

Horst, Annelies van der, Soomeren, Paul van der, and Hopstaken, Lotte. 2021. *Cultureel erfgoed voor en met iedereen. Overwegingen bij het ratificeren Verdrag van FARO.* Amsterdam: DSP-group BV.

International Association for Caribbean Archaeology. 2022. Code of Ethics. https://blogs.uoregon.edu/iaca/announcements/ (accessed June 25, 2024).

Keulen, Fred van, Stelten, Ruud, and Hinton, Alex. 2020. An Archaeological Desk-Based Assessment and Field Investigations for the F.D. Roosevelt Airport on St. Eustatius, Caribbean Netherlands. SECAR Report. St. Eustatius: St. Eustatius Centre for Archaeological Research.

kok, marjolijn. 2022. *A Future That Does Not Forget: Collaborative Archaeology in the Colonial Context of Sint Eustatius (Dutch Caribbean).* Rotterdam: Bureau Archeologie en Toekomst, BAT-report 1.

Lane, Paul 2005. "The Material Culture of Memory." In *The Qualities of Time: Anthropological Approaches,* edited by Wendy James and David Mills, 19–34. London: Routledge.

LaRoche, Cheryl J. and Blakey, Michael L. 1997. "Seizing Intellectual Power: The Dialogue at the New York African Burial Ground." *Historical Archaeology* 31(3): 84–106.

McDavid, Carol. 2002. "Archaeologies That Hurt; Descendants That Matter: A Pragmatic Approach to Collaboration in the Public Interpretation of African-American Archaeology." *World Archaeology* 34(2): 303–314.

McDavid, Carol, and Brock, Terry P. 2015. "The Differing Forms of Public Archaeology: Where We Have Been, Where We Are Now, and Thoughts for the Future." In *Ethics and Archaeological Praxis. Ethical Archaeologies: The Politics of Social Justice 1,* edited by Cristóbal Gnecco and Dorothy Lippert, 159–183. New York: Springer.

Meskell, Lynn. 2002. "Negative Heritage and Past Mastering in Archaeology." *Anthropological Quarterly* 75(3): 557–574.

Meskell, Lynn, and Pels, Peter, eds. 2005. *Embedding Ethics.* Oxford: Berg.

Newson, Paul, and Young, Ruth. 2022. "Post-Conflict Ethics, Archeology and Archaeological Heritage: A Call for Discussion." *Archaeological Dialogues* 29: 155–171.

Nicholas, George, and Hollowell, Julie. 2009. "Decoding Implications of the Genographic Project for Archaeology and Cultural Heritage." *International Journal of Cultural Property* 16: 141–181.

Pels, Peter. 2005. "'Where There Aren't No Ten Commandments': Redefining Ethics during the darkness in El Deroda Scandal." In *Embedding Ethics,* edited by Lynn Meskell and Peter Pels, 69–99. Oxford: Berg.

Reardon, Jenny, and TallBear, Kim. 2012. "Your DNA Is Our History" Genomics, Anthropology, and the Construction of Whiteness as Property. *Current Anthropology* 53(5): 233–245.

Register of Professional Archaeologists & the Chartered Institute for Archaeologists. 2024. Archaeological Ethics Database. https://archaeologicalethics.org/code-of-ethics/ (accessed June 25, 2024).

Reith, Maarten, ed. 2022. *Onderweg naar Faro, Uitvoeringsagenda Faro Deel I.* Amersfoort: Rijksdienst voor Cultureel Erfgoed.

Rijksdienst voor Cultureel Erfgoed. 2022. Welcome. https://faro.cultureelerfgoed.nl/welcome (accessed June 25, 2024).

Rijksoverheid Nederland. 2024. Monumentenwet BES. https://wetten.overheid.nl/BWBR0028429/2010-10-10, consulted 27–7-2023 (accessed June 25, 2024).

Scarre, Chris, and Scarre, Geoffrey, eds. 2006. *The Ethics of Archaeology: Philosophical Perspectives on Archaeological Practice.* Cambridge: Cambridge University Press.

Society for American Archaeology. 2024. Ethics in Archaeology. https://www.saa.org/career-practice/ethics-in-archaeology (accessed June 25, 2024).

Statia Government. 2021. Town Hall Meeting, June 22, 2021. https://www.facebook.com/watch/live/?extid=NS-UNK-UNK-UNK-IOS_GK0T-GK1C&ref=watch_permalink&v=979937822753610 (accessed June 25, 2024).

Statia Government. 2023. Ancestral Remains Being Relocated. https://www.facebook.com/100066531756444/posts/pfbid02kGdjaqfx1P3anqP1D63nRebiiW5hxK4cFH-P53AgKtZcM6Y3URLbPG2Lo7Mbm2mD3l/?sfnsn=mo&mibextid=6aamW6 (accessed June 25, 2024).

Tarlow, Sarah. 2001. "Decoding Ethics." *Public Archaeology* 1(4): 245–259.

Tarlow, Sarah. 2006. "Archaeological Ethics and the People of the Past." In *The Ethics of Archaeology: Philosophical Perspectives on Archaeological Practice,* edited by Chris Scarre and Geoffrey Scarre, 199–216. Cambridge: Cambridge University Press.

Ubuntu Connected Front. 2021a. Press Release. https://ubuntuconnectedfront.com/wp-content/uploads/2021/07/PRESS-RELEASE-UCF_Stop_Excavations_African_Burial_Ground_St_Eustatius_2021_July12.pdf, consulted 5–6-2024 (accessed July 12, 2021).

Ubuntu Connected Front. 2021b. Letter to St. Eustatius Government and Island Council. https://afrikanhistoryandconsciousness.blogspot.com/2021/06/ (accessed June 25, 2024).

United Nations General Assembly 1948. Universal Declaration of Human Rights. Paris, 10 December 1948. https://www.un.org/en/about-us/universal-declaration-of-human-rights (accessed May 8, 2024).

Vitelli, Karen. 1996. *Archaeological Ethics.* Walnut Creek, California: AltaMira Press.

Waal, Maaike S. de, Jochem Lesparre, Ryan Espersen, and Ruud Stelten. 2019. "The Effectiveness of Archaeological Predictive Maps: Management and Protection of Sites on St Eustatius and Saba, Caribbean Netherlands." *Journal of Cultural Heritage Management and Sustainable Development* 9(2): 149–164.

World Archaeology Congress. 2024. "Code of Ethics." https://worldarchaeologicalcongress.com/code-of-ethics/ (accessed June 25, 2024).

World Archaeological Congress 1989. "The Vermillion Accord on Human Remains." https://worldarchaeologicalcongress.com/code-of-ethics/ (accessed June 25, 2024).

Wylie, Alison. 2000. "Some Reflections on the Work of the SAA Committee for Ethics in Archaeology." *Canadian Journal of Archaeology* 24(2): 150–156.

Wylie, Alison. 2005. "The Promise and Perils of an Ethics of Stewardship." In *Embedding Ethics,* edited by Lynn Meskell and Peter Pels, 47–68. Oxford: Berg.

Wylie, Alison. 2008. "Legacies of Collaboration: Transformative Criticism in Archaeology." Patty Jo Watson Distinguished Lecture, Archaeology Division, American Anthropological Association, San Francisco, November 21, 2008.

Zimmerman, Larry. 1994. "Sharing Control of the Past." *Archaeology* 47(6): 65–68.

Zimmerman, Larry. 1998. "When Data Become People: Archaeological Ethics, Reburial, and the Past as Public Heritage." *International Journal of Cultural Property* 7(1): 69–86.

Zorzin, Nicolas. 2015. "Archaeology and Capitalism: Successful Relationship or Economic and Ethical Alienation?" In: *Ethics and Archaeological Praxis,* edited by Cristóbal Gnecco and Dorothy Lippert, 115–139. Ethical Archaeologies: The Politics of Social Justice 1. New York: Springer.

4

Starting at the Start

Approaches to Ethical Research
with Indigenous Peoples and Heritage
in the Southeastern Caribbean

OLIVER ANTCZAK,
LAURIANE AMMERLAAN, ASHLEIGH JOHN MORRIS,
AND FIDEL RODRÍGUEZ VELÁSQUEZ

September 9, October 14,[1] and January 1 are important dates on the islands of Margarita, Trinidad, and Bonaire. The Dia de los Guaiquerí, the Santa Rosa First Peoples Festival, and the Maskarada Festival respectively are celebrated on these dates, and each, in their way, commemorates the Indigenous heritage of their islands. These events are only the most visible faces of communities whose historical legacies and present-day identities question the narratives that herald an "extinction" of Caribbean Indigenous populations as a result of European colonialism. The Dia de los Guaiquerí and the Santa Rosa First Peoples Festival are celebrations associated with Catholicism. On Margarita, a large procession heads out of El Poblado toward the church where the image of the Virgen del Valle is located, while on Trinidad, the inhabitants of Arima organize their festivity together with the church of Santa Rosa where they honor the patron saint of the old mission around which their community was united for centuries. The case of Bonaire is substantially different. The Maskarada celebration consists of the use of costumes and masks accompanied by music and theater. This celebration is also claimed to be associated with the Indigenous legacy of the island, although in the context of deep Indigenous erasure here, the legacy persists more diffusely than in Margarita and Trinidad (Antczak 2018).

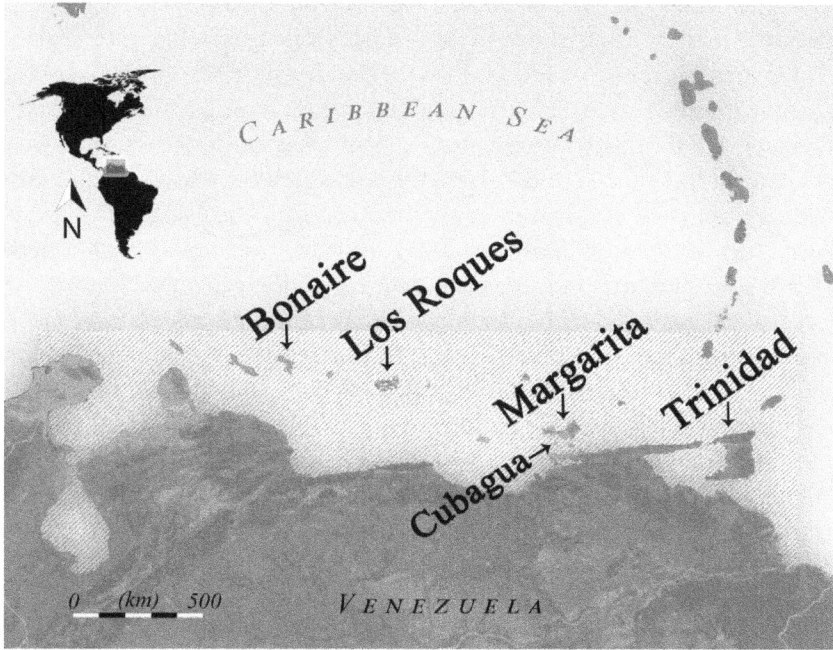

Figure 4.1. Map of the Southeastern Caribbean region (denoted as striped area) with each island highlighted. Map by Oliver Antczak using data from ISAS/JAXA, 2018.

These examples serve to introduce some of the complexities of the Caribbean region and its multifarious expressions of Indigenous history, identity, and recognition. In thinking about the ethics of archaeological practices with Indigenous peoples, heritage, and archaeology in the Caribbean, we argue that comprehensively discussing the right and wrongs, or the dos and don'ts, is an impossible and irresponsible task. The Caribbean is a rainbow patchwork that displays nearly every color imaginable. Entanglements of archaeology and Indigenous peoples are dependent on a vast diversity of local contexts that rely on histories, cultures, economies, geographies, politics, and more axes of difference. Recognizing this, within this chapter we aim to bypass generalizing discussions of ethics, focusing rather on particular examples from the Southeastern Caribbean, a subregion of the Caribbean ranging from Aruba in the west to Trinidad in the east, and from Grenada in the north to the coasts of Venezuela in the south (see area marked in Figure

4.1). This area is like a fractal of the Caribbean. It appears to display many of the same characteristics as, and to face similar challenges to, the wider region.

We further argue that focusing on the Southeastern Caribbean is useful for four specific reasons. Firstly, it highlights the area as having a close relationship with the nearby Venezuelan mainland. Secondly, it sets it somewhat apart from the Greater and Lesser Antilles, which have been much more widely researched as representative case studies for the Caribbean (Grunberg 2015; Rodríguez Velásquez 2023). Thirdly, it reflects a commitment to this subregion that in some ways defies common generalizations of the larger Caribbean and allows us to concretely tackle ethical issues as made explicit in discrete examples of practice on these islands. Consequently, we think of this frame as a helpful window to look through, to rethink some of the classic (or hegemonic) narratives that have been constructed about the Caribbean in other, more intensively researched, areas. Finally, this category emphasizes the interrelations between a set of islands and communities that, while overtly distinguished by linguistic, socioeconomic, political, and cultural borders, continue sharing tacit similarities and relationships that have spanned millennia.

In this chapter, we engage with the Southeastern Caribbean as four experts bridging these borders to come together in discussion. The discussion is contextualized within a rising tide of critical and decolonial conversations and research taking place across academic and nonacademic spaces, particularly surrounding research ethics and design—especially when working with Indigenous peoples (Atalay 2006; Jácome 2020; Machado 2013; Ramos 2023; Wylie 1996). As early-career researchers and practitioners in archaeology, heritage, and history, we have applied a lens that looks ahead toward possible future ethical practices in the Caribbean. We aim to discuss past practices, present-day implications, and future aspirations for ethical engagements with Indigenous peoples in this region. In this chapter, we all share our long-term relationships with the islands as a result of having been born, been raised, and lived in the region. In parallel, we have maintained our own relationships with Indigenous identities and the people who hold them. We hope that with contributions like this chapter, we can continue nuancing the many ways in which Indigeneity expresses itself in the Southeastern Caribbean, and consequently, the complex identity constructions that some of our authors ascribe to, given colonial erasures, our political positions, and pervasive uncertainties, that will be described below. With experiences on Trinidad, the islands of the Venezuelan Caribbean with emphasis on Margarita, Cubagua and Los Roques, and Bonaire, we hope to outline case studies that are unique but also shared in the Southeastern Caribbean and that perhaps offer a window for the greater circum-Caribbean.

In the following sections, we discuss the case studies of Bonaire, Los Roques, Margarita, and Trinidad to further three main points that need to be addressed for future ethical engagements with Indigenous peoples in the region. The first is countering pervasive narratives of Indigenous extinctions. The second is being aware of and engaging with local narratives *about* archaeologists, which are formed alongside disciplinary narratives *by* archaeologists. The third is the development of projects with awareness of Indigenous multi-vocality in the region. We suggest that, beyond these case studies, future ethical approaches need to "start at the start," a conceptual recasting of archaeological practice that questions what the discipline prioritizes and values from the earliest stages of research and allows archaeologists to shed the "armor of expertise" (Smith 2004).

Framing Archaeological Practice in the Southeastern Caribbean

Before the establishment of clear rules of conduct, archaeologists acted according to their individual senses of ethics (Beaudry 2009: 17). The earliest archaeologists of the Southeastern Caribbean, such as H. R. van Heekeren and Theodoor de Booy, were collectors of curiosities, educated travelers, priests, and explorers, fascinated by "exotic" vestiges of the past, often taking these back to collections in Europe or North America (Curet and Galban 2019). Already in these earliest manifestations, archaeologists furnished themselves in an "armor of expertise," a concept we use to refer to archaeologists' claim of special access to, and exclusive stewardship over, the resources of the past (based on Smith 2004: 194). Rather than connect the pieces that were found to the people living around them, early archaeologists harkened back to a deep and exotic past, privileging themselves as the only ones able to appropriately access it. As archaeological practice became standardized in the early twentieth century, academics from Europe and North America accelerated the development of archaeology in the region. The cult of expertise was a constant feature of the period; contemporary inhabitants of the subregion continued to be distanced from the peoples and objects being dug up at the time, and archaeology heavily favored academic expertise and colonial documents over local oral histories.

Since the 1970s, archaeologists and anthropologies in the Caribbean have seen increasing concern about the ethics of their practice, for example the 1971 Declaration of Barbados, which marked key steps for nation-states, religious missions, and anthropologists to support Indigenous "liberation" in Latin America and the Caribbean (Anonymous 1973). Communities played a key role in voicing their concerns, demanding more significant consideration in archaeological work, and more equitable and decolonizing research practices (see Gómez 1991). We must remember that this also occurred during a time of Caribbean independence movements and a profound critique of imperialism and colonialism. Foreign scholars and their theoretical apparatuses for interpreting the past were usually seen and criticized as part of these colonial practices and as evidence of a continued dependence of Latin American and Caribbean nations on colonial metropolises (Navarrete Sánchez 2012). As archaeologists and heritage experts beginning our careers, we position ourselves within this ongoing process and propose future directions. The following are our reflections based on our experiences on the islands of the Southeastern Caribbean.

Bonaire and the Kingdom of the Netherlands: Narratives of Extinction

Bonaire, a small Dutch public body (see kok, this volume) close to Curaçao, has faced intense erasure of its Indigenous historical and present peoples as a result of colonial efforts. Many inhabitants of the island contend that the original inhabitants, known popularly as the Caquetío, were all removed from the island by Spanish slavers or indieros in the early sixteenth century, never to return (Antczak 2018). Despite this narrative that persists in school books, Indigenous identity does maintain itself on Bonaire, and close historical readings, conscious archaeological work, and heritage research make this clear (Antczak 2018; Haviser 1991). Thus far, it has been an immense bottom-up effort for Bonaireans to reconnect with their Indigenous heritage and overturn centuries of erasure. Indigenous Bonaireans express their identity in a diversity of ways that have ensured the persistence of their identity through violent colonialism, erasure, and transculturation. These efforts have largely gone unrecognized by academics who perceive them as inaccurate, and claim that the "true" Indigenous people disappeared generations ago (Bullbrook 1939; Van Heekeren 1960: 103; see also Newton 2022).

Within this context, the Bonaire Archaeological Institute (BONAI) was founded in 2003 by Jay Haviser, Jackie Bernabela, and Hubert Vis, who were all active in heritage management on the island. The institute was created through an initiative of the Netherlands Antilles government, which was looking for innovations in the public educational system of the Dutch islands. Haviser was stationed on Bonaire for three years to set up this pilot youth program, not only to stimulate more local youth to get involved in science-based careers, but also to counterbalance the dominance of foreign specialists in archaeological research (Haviser 2003). The program was also geared to prepare youth to become leaders in ecotourism and heritage/nature conservation (Haviser 2014). Ethics in archaeology and heritage management formed the base for this youth program that has been running for more than 20 years and within which one of the coauthors was raised.

The experience of growing up in this program helped participants overcome many of the shortcomings of the current educational curriculum on Bonaire. Since October 10, 2010, Bonaire, Saba, and Sint Eustatius are formally a part of the Netherlands and their school textbooks are designed in the Netherlands. From personal experience, these history books continue telling a story of the Caribbean region from a European point of view. Indeed, such phenomena have been reported across the Caribbean (Con Aguilar 2020). This educational slant is felt clearly by Bonaireans who have lived their whole life on the island and to whom the books do not speak adequately. In the books, information about precolonial times and the Indigenous slave trade is scant and the myth of Indigenous extinction continues to be promoted.

Following adjacent conversations within sociology, psychology and education, we argue that if youth do not learn about their heritage, culture, and history in a familiar voice, they become dissociated from it (see, for example, Barton and Levstik 2004). Youth develop their perspective toward the past based on what they begin to value at an early age, and this is where ineffective and inaccurate education from a colonial metropole can cause children to be alienated from their heritage, culture, and history. We argue that adequate ethical practices in managing the past cannot develop in the present circumstances, as the current curriculum creates unsound premises. Through this process, Bonaireans continue being misled about the disappearance of Indigenous peoples from the island.

Over its years of existence, BONAI has headed various projects of conservation, excavation, and restoration at sites around Bonaire, including Washington Slagbaai National Park (see Figure 4.2) and the Tanki Maraka Heritage Park, what is left of a World War II US military base (Nicolaas et al. 2005). Through these efforts, the youth of Bonaire were introduced to the tools of archaeology: fieldwork, scientific methods, documentation, registration, conservation, academic writing, press communication, and policy work. The youth program has now trained students who have turned out to be government officials, lawyers, heritage managers, and much more across

Figure 4.2. Bonaire Archaeological Institute (BONAI) group picture after activities at Tanki Maraka Heritage Park (US military base Bonaire) in 2023. Photo courtesy of BONAI, 2023.

Bonaire's job landscape, setting the stage for more ethical engagements with the past. With the support of various organizations, Haviser argues that BONAI has become a regional model for Caribbean youth and archaeology programs (Haviser 2015: 138).

Where schoolbooks and traditional educational techniques have thus far failed in connecting Bonaireans with their past, particularly with the Indigenous past, BONAI has succeeded in creating a new generation of stakeholders who are knowledgeable about their heritage and capable of protecting it. Recognizing the dissociation from heritage, culture, and history that is experienced in Bonaire, it becomes apparent that archaeologists and heritage professionals need to carry a toolkit that can facilitate overcoming these narratives of extinction, leading stakeholders and broader audiences to value their archaeology and heritage in a way that they may not have been officially educated to do.

We argue that tailored outreach programs such as BONAI can be one of the tools that archaeologists use to patch the fissures caused by narratives of Indigenous extinction that still pervade the Southeastern Caribbean. Such programs could also focus on professionals in various sectors and on elders, the latter often feeling that they are not knowledgeable enough about their own past (Antczak 2018). We suggest that in cases such as Bonaire, the need for such a program also extends to professionals who are brought to the island to work in powerful positions, but who have never lived there before.

The case of Indigenous identity is not unique to Bonaire. Subtle and unexpected (to outsiders) expressions of Indigenous identity are a feature across the Caribbean and are a result of adaptations in heritage and identity methods to resist active and violent colonial erasure. We argue that archaeologists need to openly engage with and recognize these expressions, facilitate the connections of present-day Indigenous peoples with their past, and actively design their research with policy and educational components that cater to the specificities of the region and to the challenges it has historically faced and overcome.

The Venezuelan Caribbean: Parallel Stories

Shifting focus to the east, we reach the islands of the Venezuelan Caribbean. We argue that any attempt to think about the ethical implications of doing archaeology on these islands, particularly Margarita, Cubagua, and Los Roques archipelago, which have seen the most research, must always begin with a historical reconstruction of the communities' experiences with archaeology. That is, archaeologists must recognize that just as archaeology has constructed a history of the region from the material culture recovered in fieldwork, local inhabitants and communities have simultaneously constructed a history of archaeology and of their own experiences with archaeological projects. In some cases, these community histories represent the only source, other than the archaeologists themselves, for reflecting on the history of archaeology.

The history of archaeology across the islands of Cubagua, Margarita, and the archipelago of Los Roques can be summarized in six periods. The first is marked by the founding works of Adolfo Ernst in the archipelago of Los Roques (1871) and of Theodoor de Booy in Margarita Island (1915). The second period launched with discussions between researchers of the Universidad Central de Venezuela and the Instituto Pedagógico de Caracas in 1948 on the "discovery" of the remains of the city of Nueva Cadiz on Cubagua (see Rodríguez Velasquez and Antczak 2023). A third moment was initiated with the works of José María Cruxent on Cubagua in 1954 and Pedro Jam in 1956 in the archipelago of Los Roques. The declaration of the "Ruins of Nueva Cadiz" as national patrimony of Venezuela in 1974 denotes the following period. Next, a fifth period began in 1982 with the foundation of the project "Archaeology of the Venezuelan islands" by Andrzej Antczak and Maria Magdalena Antczak (Antczak and Antczak 2006). Finally, the sixth moment began in the 2000s and was marked by wider and more diverse participation and larger international projects. This period featured community archaeology initiatives in the archipelago of Los Roques led by the Unidad de Estudios Arqueológicos of the Universidad Simón Bolívar (UEA-USB) (Antczak et al. 2013); the declaration of the island of Cubagua as a "property of cultural interest"; and successive projects led by the Instituto de Patrimonio Cultural (IPC). These projects included new excavations at the Nueva Cadiz site and the rest of Cubagua Island; the project to create an archaeological, geological, and paleontological park; the museum exhibition on Nueva Cadiz; and the candidacy of Cubagua Island as a World Heritage Site before UNESCO (see Rodríguez Velasquez 2020).

The community correlate of these experiences persists in the memory of many locals and Indigenous peoples, particularly fishermen, with whom the authors have worked in recent years. Some of them recall that part of their childhood was spent in the midst of the archaeological excavations initiated by José María Cruxent in 1954 in Cubagua. Others remember their childhood during the beginnings of the project in Los Roques in 1982 by Andrzej Antczak and Maria Magdalena Antczak (see Figure 4.3). These community members worked as assistants, as key informants, and as patrons, guaranteeing vital resources for the fieldwork, such as maritime transportation between the islands and lodging, as well as water and food for the archaeologists. Consequently, archaeological stories have become deeply woven into the heritage and identity of the region decades after the archaeologists themselves have left. The experiences on the islands of Cubagua and Margarita, as well as those of the Los Roques Archipelago, show two possible types of relationship that archaeologists can forge with communities.

In the case of Cubagua and Margarita, when listening to the stories of archaeology told by the community, the first great contrast that arises is related to the academic valuation of the results of these works and their dissemination among the community actors who were involved in the development of these investigations. That is, what appears in the disciplinary narrative as a coherent history of successive scientific projects with results that have deepened the knowledge of the pre-Hispanic and colonial history of these islands, is instead presented by the community as a series of successive cycles of a history that repeats itself. Namely, long periods of absence and total abandonment of the island, punctuated by short periods in which new archaeologists arrive with new excavation projects. Rarely do any of

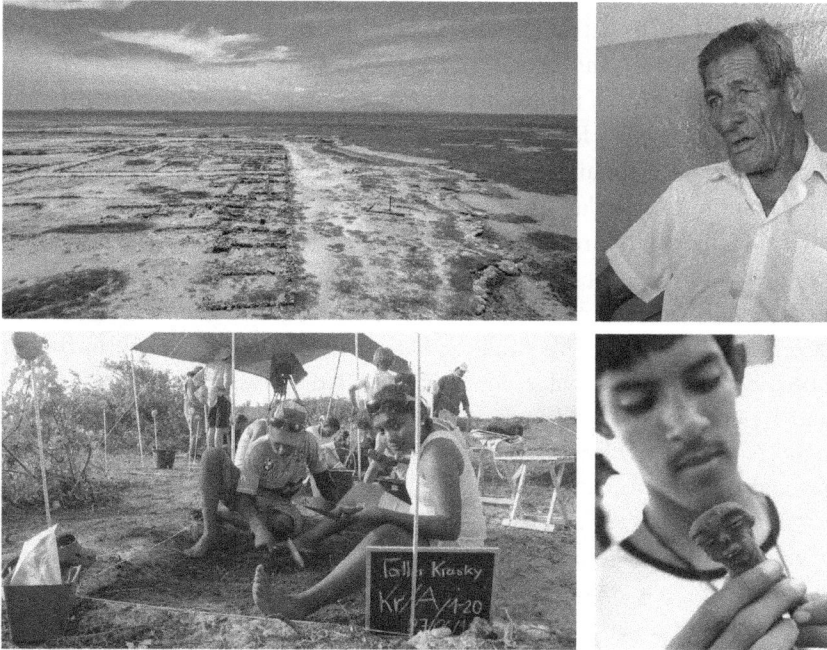

Figure 4.3. *Top:* At left, aerial view of the ruins of Nueva Cadiz in Cubagua (photo courtesy Giancarlo Orco, 2022), and at right, Cristóbal Rojas, a fisherman and worker at the first archaeological excavations on Cubagua in the 1950s (photo courtesy of Cesar Escalona, 2014). *Bottom:* Community archaeology work done in Los Roques, on the left excavations done in Krasky in 2015 (photo courtesy of M. M. Antczak, 2015), and on the right in Boca de Sebastopol in 2007 (photo courtesy of M. M. Antczak, 2007).

those archaeologists return to present results or reengage with the site or its communities. This archaeology is characterized in community narratives as pioneering efforts that are isolated and without any kind of continuity over time. As demonstrated in interviews with fishermen from Cubagua and Margarita Island by a team coordinated by Fidel Rodríguez Velásquez as part of a local history project in 2014,[2] the consequences of these perceptions are important. This history of repetitive cycles has generated distrust and resistance in stakeholder communities, which perceive each new project as another tired episode in the repetitive cycles of great absences and brief presences.

In addition, it should not be overlooked that, amid the great absences, the community has created its own mechanisms to discuss, analyze, and co-write its history. This brings into focus the second contrast, which has to do with the history of the results of archaeological research on the islands. There have been very few publications directed at local actors, and most of the texts produced by archaeologists remain partially (if not totally) unknown to the community today. This vacuum has meant that most of the archaeological studies in the region have not been translated into knowledge that can be used by teachers in schools, and for many teachers, it is very difficult to distinguish legitimate archaeological work from circulating versions that lack a scientific basis. This situation has greatly hindered the appropriation of archaeological knowledge, which has resulted in the proliferation of myths and stereotypes that end up being an obstacle to the dissemination of the region's history. Ultimately this lack of access to knowledge alienates the present inhabitants from their past.

The archipelago of Los Roques brings the two contrasts into clear view, particularly when looking at a series of community archaeology efforts carried out between 2006 and 2015 (Antczak et al. 2013). The communities inhabiting the research area here are not descendants of the peoples being "uncovered" archaeologically. Archaeological evidence suggests that the islands were visited seasonally by the inhabitants of the central Venezuelan coast between AD 1000 and ca. 1500 (Antczak and Antczak 2006). Meanwhile, the present-day Roqueños mostly settled from Margarita Island to the east, with a majority of permanent settlers coming during the twentieth century. Other influences and migrations have come from the mainland coast, for example from Caracas and La Guaira; from the Dutch Caribbean, specifically Bonaire and Curaçao; and more recently around the growing European tourist industry, especially from Italy, Spain, and Portugal. While in most of the Caribbean, the absent ancestor is largely a myth, in Los Roques it is a reality, not because the Indigenous inhabitants were "eradicated," as is insisted in pan-Caribbean myths, but rather because visitors only occupied the island for brief periods until they ceased to do so altogether. Los Roques becomes a counterpoint for the apparent "disconnection" elaborated upon in the case study of Margarita and Cubagua above, as the islands were inhabited seasonally, visited sporadically, and eventually settled permanently by different groups, and yet archaeology here has fostered a "connection."

Actively fostering relationships with a heritage they did not consider their own was one of the aims of the community archaeology work carried out with Gran Roque schoolchildren who were mostly of Margariteño descent.

Six community archaeology projects were undertaken with final-year school-children from the high school in Gran Roque, a community of some 3,000. Workshops involved the children in the archaeological work, excavating, documenting, cleaning, and interpreting the finds, while also receiving lectures from the archaeologists. The workshops took place on various islands of the archipelago and concluded in the Unidad de Estudios Arqueológicos laboratory at Universidad Simón Bolívar. The results of the project have been palpable with awareness of the history being visible in tangible artisanal products on Gran Roque, in informed tourist tours of the islands and particularly in the sensitivity and protectiveness of local inhabitants toward the past (Antczak et al. 2013). In more than one case, the network of parents contacted archaeologists when they found out about archaeological objects being discovered, and finds were reported to specialists.

The juxtaposition of the Los Roques example with that of Margarita and Cubagua leads us to reflect on how effective archaeologies can connect supposedly disconnected people with a heritage that is effectively theirs, and on how ineffective archaeologies can fail to do so even when the Indigenous inhabitants are active participants in the research project. Consistent with the arguments made by Antczak et al. (2013: 204), archaeological principles and expectations should be expanded to include "broader civic responsibility [so that] we can improve communities through archaeology and improve archaeology through communities." To improve local people's relationships with archaeological work in cases such as Cubagua and Margarita, archaeologists must always include considerations of community involvement and heritage management, and this should not be left to heritage experts alone. On the contrary, archaeological projects and commitments should include, from their inception, provisions and considerations for community involvement and heritage impacts that actively engage with local perspectives on, and commitments to, previous archaeological work.

Trinidad: Multivocality

For the final case study, we move farther east to Trinidad, one-half of a nation-state that also includes Tobago. Much like the rest of the Southeastern Caribbean, the trajectory of archaeological scholarship in this twin-island nation began during the mid-nineteenth century. Early archaeological ventures in Trinidad set the stage for an era of archaeological research in the twentieth century that has deeply impacted the present-day understanding of the island's Indigenous peoples and the nation's cultural heritage (Boomert

2000; Guppy 1984). Through the later part of the twentieth century and the early twenty-first century, there was a significant shift in research approaches and priorities as researchers focused on reconstructing Indigenous life-ways, conducting ethnohistorical research, and addressing cultural resource management (Boomert 2000; Boomert et al. 2013). This shift represented a broader recognition of the value and importance of cultural heritage in understanding Trinidad and Tobago's past.

Recently, the Red House archaeological project has emerged as a watershed moment in ethical archaeological research in the region. In 2013, during a restoration project at the Red House, the seat of Parliament in Port of Spain, an archaeological excavation unearthed the remains of 60 individuals and as-sociated artefacts (Reid 2018). Factions of Trinidad and Tobago's First People community were consulted on matters specifically related to the treatment of the discovered human remains, and permission was granted to conduct multidisciplinary investigations, including radiocarbon dating, DNA analy-sis, and stable isotopic analyses. However, approval was contingent upon the timely reinternment of all remains (not destroyed in sampling) at the site. The reinternment ceremony, held in 2019, was a regional affair attended by representatives from South American and Caribbean Indigenous groups who employed rites derived from their traditions (Figure 4.4).

In its disciplinary context, the reinterment ceremony at the Red House stands as a poignant example of ethical archaeological practices in the Carib-bean. It resonates with scholarly assertions that it is entirely feasible to honor the cultural and spiritual tenets of Indigenous communities whilst concur-rently safeguarding the multitudinous layers of archaeological, historical, and heritage significance (Agbe-Davies 2010; Colwell-Chanthaphonh and Ferguson 2008; Hofmann and Hoogland 2016). However, it also presents challenges that as of yet remain unaddressed: namely a disconnect in disci-plinary narratives and modern identities. Today, Trinidad is host to many Indigenous groups that identify variously as Nepuyo, Carib, Black Indian, Warao, Kalinago, and Santa Rosa First People, to name a few. It may seem obvious to say, but it is important to highlight here that each group, and individual who forms part of it, has their priorities that sometimes intersect with and even contradict the goals of others.

The overlapping narratives surrounding this site epitomize some of the challenges, and simultaneously the possibilities, of ethical archaeological heritage management in the Caribbean. Beyond its role as the active seat of government and its architectural significance, the Red House has today evolved into a multifaceted heritage site. It is simultaneously an archaeologi-

Figure 4.4. Reinterment ceremony at the Red House in 2019. Photo by Ashleigh Morris, 2019.

cal site, a national architectural landmark, an important government building, and a site of memory for the First Peoples' descendants. The Red House archaeological project illuminates the potential inherent in a collaborative framework of heritage management and underscores the many times previous archaeological work failed to implement such designs. However, while descendant First Peoples, archaeologists, and governmental bodies synergistically converged to deliberate upon the appropriate treatment of ancestral remains and the overarching management of the site, such a collaborative situation is not devoid of challenges. On the one hand, it undeniably presents a more encompassing and ethically robust model for heritage management than a total lack of multilateral engagement or open deliberation at all. But on the other, it raises new questions, such as how to effectively balance the interests and concerns of all stakeholders, how to ensure that the narratives presented do not marginalize or distort any particular group's perspective, and how to address potential conflicts that arise from differing interpretations of the site's significance.

This challenge was made evident for example when during the 2020 wave of protests and statue topplings, the Columbus statue in Tamarind Square, Port of Spain, was defaced and a public debate on it was initiated. Chief Ricardo Bharath Hernandez of the Santa Rosa First Peoples Community publicly opposed the movement to remove the statue as he preferred changes his people would feel more directly, stating, "If it is just removing Columbus' statue for the sake of removing it, I see no benefit and no merit. The removal must be replaced with something significant to advance our cause today" (in Forte 2020). Meanwhile, Donna Bermudez-Bovell, the Warao Queen, and several other Indigenous spokespeople, countered Chief Bharath Hernandez's claims, calling for the removal of the statue for its controversial message (see, for example, Anonymous 2020; De Souza 2018; Gioannetti 2020).

What this example and the example of the Red House reinterment show is that consultation and inclusion in archaeological and heritage work needs to always be a carefully designed process that consciously assesses stakeholders and their opinions, to the breadth of their expressions. Additionally, the complexities of establishing a hierarchy of importance among the various narratives, and determining which aspects to prioritize in heritage presentations to the public, become paramount. As in the case of the Red House, while a collaborative approach brings more voices to the table, it also demands a nuanced understanding and navigation of the cultural, political, and historical intricacies inherent in such a diverse group of stakeholders.

Determining the right stakeholder communities is particularly challenging in Trinidad. Archaeologically, Trinidad has been viewed as a sort of stepping stone in the population of the Lesser and Greater Antilles (Rouse 1947). Periods of successive migrations and population growth suggest that Trinidad was a patchwork of Indigenous communities of various identities in non-conflictual cohabitation and constant negotiation and adaptation (Kerrigan 2012). And yet, as critiqued by Kerrigan (2012: 27), "the work of well-intentioned archaeologists of the 20th century can be classed as neo-colonial in the sense of producing clear racial and ethnic divisions where a situation of prolonged and constant differential acculturation and interaction was more likely."

The diversity of identities and its translation into the early colonial situation, up to the present day, has been a challenge for both academics and the Indigenous peoples of Trinidad and Tobago. The historical, archaeological, and modern categories all speak over each other in the present identity landscape of Trinidad. Archaeological labels like "Arauquinoid," "Saladoid," "Barrancoid," and others have not been picked up as modern identities, and archaeologists have noted the difficulty in linking them to modern-day identities (Boomert 2016). "Carib" and "Arawak," long favored, are no longer used, as evidenced in the change in name of the Santa Rosa First Peoples Community.[3] Linguistic and/or ethnic labels such as "Kalinago," "Nepuyo," "Yao," and "Warao" have had more success and are more used—though they also are not always directly linked to precolonial groups, with the exception of the Warao. The result is that in the present day, there is still a broad range of diverse Indigenous identities and expressions in Trinidad, but heritage management and many archaeological endeavors tend to operate predominantly within the paradigms of government recognition.

In the case of the Red House reinterment, the Santa Rosa First Peoples Community played a protagonist role in the negotiations and consultations around the reinterment. As the only officially recognized Indigenous community on Trinidad, this was the clear path for government decision makers—but in a deeper-time and whole-island perspective, this stifled the involvement of a possible broader range of Indigenous groups. To be clear, we do not aim to undermine the self-organization and internally determined leaderships within Indigenous groups. Instead, we raise concerns about the currently limited scope of communications between academics and Indigenous peoples in an area that has historically always been marked by its diversity of Indigenous identities. We suggest that future engagements of this type must be supported by a comprehensive recognition of Indigenous expressions across the entire nation, and a responsible and sensitive appreciation of the wide diversity of identities that cover the twin islands.

Starting at the Start

In the sections above, we have raised three main points that we consider essential for ethical research with Indigenous peoples in the Southeastern Caribbean. Firstly, Indigenous peoples, like all peoples, change and transform without necessarily "losing" their identity and their Indigeneity. This must be made clear in publications and community engagements. In other words, archaeologists must actively counter narratives of Indigenous extinction in the Caribbean. Secondly, we highlight that local stories of archaeologists are created in tandem with academic stories made by archaeologists. We must be sensitive to these stories and create projects that improve and build on previous engagements. As made evident in the example of Margarita and Cubagua, archaeological publications and presentations are not enough. Thirdly, we highlight that work must also be cognizant of Indigenous communities beyond the officially recognized communities because identities can be widespread and diverse, and often relationships mediated through institutions and/or governments (as heritage work often is) privilege certain voices over others.

These points do not exist in isolation, and in each case, they rely on changes occurring at the first stages of research: research design. A key takeaway from the experiences described in this chapter is the need for locally sensitive research projects built on previous engagement with relevant stakeholder communities. We contend that doing so requires that archaeologists, at least to start, do away with the "armor of expertise" that they wear when interacting with stakeholder communities. As Lynne Meskell (2002: 293) points out, we need to move past a disciplinary "illusion that the subjects of our research are dead and buried, literally, and that our 'scientific' research goals are paramount." This also means that simple consultation with Indigenous and other stakeholder groups can no longer be seen as good enough (Smith 2004: 198). A changed and future-oriented ethical practice must "start at the start"—we must actively listen to people.

"Starting at the start" refers to a deep self-reflection upon and an active defiance against valued traditional academic practices that affect research from its inception. One notable example is the academic desirability placed on single-authorship, which continues being sought for position, grant, and studentship applications. Such academic pressures disincentivize archaeologists from sharing authorship with stakeholders and instead incentivize a certain blurring and generalization of knowledge sources that appropriates, redefines, and isolates knowledge in academia. In drastic contrast, some departments demand authorship to be attributed to laboratory heads or supervisors who are little involved in the research, but do not encourage or ensure sharing coauthorship with participants and teachers "in the field." Actively countering this would mean more liberally recognizing coauthorship of nonacademic stakeholders who contributed knowledge to research; removing the "armor of expertise" involves democratizing the ascription of coauthorship beyond just academics.[4] Another example is departmental and institutional guidelines, which are often inflexible and impose a certain standardization that leads to ineffective and problematic research that is not designed according to the specificities and needs of its context (Meskell and Pels 2005). We would encourage, instead or in tandem, that flexible and responsive ethical committees be developed that enforce training, parse ethics applications, follow up with oral questioning, and finally debrief upon the completion of fieldwork. Such a system would allow applicants to present and justify their approach to ethics, guided by community and stakeholder interactions, permitting ethical engagements to take a variety of forms not necessarily strictly in line with formal guidelines.

The aim of conceptualizing "starting at the start" is to pivot the direction of research and impact all stages, from the very start to the very end (if there is such a moment) of research. Such a change could redirect the amateur and professional impetus to discover the sensational and exotic (sometimes literal, but often metaphorical) "treasure."[5] The Caribbean is still exoticized for its headline stories about pirates, cannibals, treasure ships, and lost cities, but academically pursuing these topics can easily lead researchers to reissue a history of exploitation and looting of Caribbean riches at the cost of the local inhabitants, their heritage, economy, and environment. Sensitive research design and execution must be guided by awareness and an active countering of such sensationalism and exoticizing.

We suggest that to "start at the start," archaeologists must arrive at and interact with the area of research and its stakeholders in meaningful discussions that will guide the research design before any research officially begins. To shed the "armor of expertise" archaeologists must recognize "Indigenous and other non-positivist knowledge claims within archaeological theory" (Smith 2004: 202). And, as evidenced in the case of Trinidad, it must be done without falling into the trap of essentializing the community. To do this, archaeologists must cede the labels of archaeological material and archaeological heritage—in this way giving room for non-archaeological claims about the significance and meaning of these elements of the past (Smith 2004: 137). One major component of this is bringing oral histories to an equal standing with other sources of knowledge about the past, such as archaeology and written history.

Ultimately, starting at the start would lead to improved identification and publication of materials. Objects identified to static cultural groups and applying the cultural-historical model of one-to-one representation have failed repeatedly in the Caribbean both to tell a nuanced history of the region and in connecting modern-day descendants with their precolonial ancestors. For this to improve, archaeologists need to revise the theoretical underpinnings of much of Caribbean archaeology and shift their interpretations and categorizations into more fluid and less essential categories of identification that facilitate both richer understandings of the past and more diverse identification with that past. Doing so can start with understanding the historical changes, the present-day fluidity, and richness of Indigenous identity across the region, and letting go of notions of authenticity, a well-challenged notion within heritage studies (see Silverman 2015) that often determines archaeological responses to present-day Indigenous expression.

A final element of "starting at the start" is that it does not have a clear conclusion. Archaeologists today still often close field sites and research projects, never to return. We argue that in an archaeological engagement, relationships and entanglements never end—they continue long after the archaeologists remove themselves from the area. In this view, it is irresponsible for the archaeologist to "close" the research and artificially and one-sidedly end these relationships. We argue that if an archaeologist disturbs the soil, they cannot then leave it, expecting it to bring itself back to a normality. We urge future work to consider engagement with local communities as an open-ended engagement with no finality. This means leaving open channels of communication, maintaining open spaces for learning and sharing of knowledge, and continuing work with the heritage and didactic aspects of archaeology.

Many archaeologists would today likely agree that archaeology should not remain in the laboratory, and that it cannot be divorced from politics. As Meskell (2002: 293) develops, the "'terrain of ethics' lies in the 'nexus of politics and identity.'" A future archaeology that we hope to contribute to with this chapter would include shifting perspectives around looting and falsifying of objects (see Ostapkowicz and Hanna 2021: 56), and redefining notions of authenticity and ownership of heritage. Reburial, reconnection, restitution, and reparations would all be concerns of such an archaeology. In this way, we argue for an integration of the remits of heritage managers/researchers and archaeologists, so that both share the responsibility of how archaeological work is used and made relevant in the present (see Santikarn et al. 2022).

Notes

1 The date varies; sometimes August 20 is used.
2 Funded by the Facultad de Ciencias Económicas y Sociales (FaCES), Universidad Central de Venezuela.
3 The group originally went by the name Santa Rosa Carib Community.
4 Though it is important to note that anonymity should always be a possibility and choice for participants in research.
5 Legends exist in Venezuela surrounding *morocotas* (gold coins) and *entierros* (burial sites); the stories promise that whoever might find these while digging will be immensely rich but may also be cursed. Archaeologists are often accused by local inhabitants of looking for these treasures, and it is an interesting conceptual metaphor for reflecting on extractivism and the sensationalism of archaeology.

References Cited

Agbe-Davies, Anna S. 2010. "Concepts of Community in the Pursuit of an Inclusive Archaeology." *International Journal of Heritage Studies* 16(6): 373–389. https://doi.org/10.1080/13527258.2010.510923.

Anonymous. 2020. "'Traitorous' Bharath-Hernandez? CRFP Claim 'Disingenuous Chief Only Concerned with Tangible Benefits.'" *Wired868*. Blog. June 22, 2020. https://wired868.com/2020/06/22/traitorous-bharath-hernandez-crfp-claim-disingenuous-chief-only-concerned-with-tangible-benefits/ (accessed July 2, 2024).

Anonymous. 1973. "The Declaration of Barbados: For the Liberation of the Indians." *Current Anthropology* 14(3): 267–270.

Antczak, María Magdalena, and Andrzej T. Antczak. 2006. *Los ídolos de las islas prometidas: Arqueología prehispánica del archipiélago de los Roques.* Caracas: Equinoccio Editorial.

Antczak, Andrzej, Maria Magdalena Antczak, Gustavo Gonzalez Hurtado, and Konrad A. Antczak. 2013. "Community Archaeology in Los Roques Archipelago National Park, Venezuela." *Politeja* 24: 201–232.

Antczak, Oliver. 2018. "Unpicking a Feeling: Interrogating the Role of Heritage in Indigenous Collective Identity Formation on the Caribbean Island of Bonaire." MA dissertation, University of Cambridge.

Atalay, Sonya. 2006. "Indigenous Archaeology as Decolonizing Practice." *American Indian Quarterly* 30(3): 280–310.

Barton, Keith C., and Linda S. Levstik. 2004. *Teaching History for the Common Good.* London: Routledge.

Beaudry, Mary. 2009. "Ethical Issues in Historical Archaeology." In *International Handbook of Historical Archaeology,* edited by David Gaimster and Teresita Majewski, 17–29. New York: Springer. https://doi.org/10.1007/978-0-387-72071-5_2.

Boomert, Arie. 2000. *Trinidad, Tobago, and the Lower Orinoco Interaction Sphere: An Archaeological/Ethnohistorical Study.* Leiden: Universiteit Leiden.

Boomert, Arie, Birgit Faber-Morse, Irving Rouse, A.J.D. Isendoorn, Annette Silver, Yale University Department of Anthropology, and Yale Peabody Museum of Natural History. 2013. *The 1946 and 1953 Yale University Excavations in Trinidad.* New Haven, Connecticut: Yale University Department of Anthropology. Yale Peabody Museum of Natural History.

Boomert, Arie. 2016. *The Indigenous Peoples of Trinidad and Tobago from the First Settlers until Today.* Leiden: Sidestone Press. https://www.sidestone.com/books/the-indigenous-peoples-of-trinidad-and-tobago.

Bullbrook, J. A. 1939. "The Ierian Race." Lecture at the Historical Society of Trinidad and Tobago, Victoria Institute, Port of Spain, March 3.

Colwell-Chanthaphonh, Chip, and Thomas J. Ferguson. 2008. "Introduction: The Collaborative Continuum." In *Collaboration in Archaeological Practice: Engaging Descendant Communities,* edited by Chip Colwell-Chanthaphonh and Thomas J. Ferguson, 1–32. Lanham, Maryland: AltaMira Press.

Con Aguilar, Eldris. 2020. *Heritage Education. Memories of the Past in the Present Caribbean Social Studies Curriculum: A View from Teacher Practice.* Leiden: Sidestone Press. https://www.sidestone.com/books/heritage-education.

Curet, L. Antonio, and Maria Galban. 2019. "Theodoor de Booy: Caribbean Expeditions and Collections at the National Museum of the American Indian." *Journal of Caribbean Archaeology* 19: 1–50.

De Booy, Theodoor Hendrik Nikolaas. 1916. "Island of Margarita, Venezuela." *Bulletin Pan American Union* 42(5): 531–546.

De Souza, Janelle. 2018. "Uneasy Truce." *Trinidad and Tobago Newsday.* October 14, 2018. https://newsday.co.tt/2018/10/14/uneasy-truce (accessed July 2, 2024).

Ernst, Adolfo. 1871. "Notes on Some Indian Remains found in Venezuela." *Journal of Anthropology* 1(3): 7–9.

Forte, Maximilian C. 2020. "Trinidad: Chief Asks How Does Removing Columbus Statue Improve First Peoples?" *Review of the Indigenous Caribbean.* Reproduced from *Stabroek News,* June 15, 2020. Blog. June 16, 2020. http://indigenousreview.blogspot.com/2020/06/trinidad-chief-asks-how-does-removing.html (accessed July 2, 2024).

Gioannetti, Andrew. 2020. "Kambon 'Corrects' Chief of Santa Rosa First Peoples." *Trinidad and Tobago Newsday.* June 24, 2020. https://newsday.co.tt/2020/06/24/kambon-corrects-chief-of-santa-rosa-first-peoples/ (accessed July 2, 2024).

Gómez, Iván E. 1991. *Cubagua: Un llamado a la conciencia Nacional.* Caracas: Abre Brecha.

Grunberg, Bernard, ed. 2015. *À La Recherche Du Caraïbe Perdu: Les populations amérindiennes des Petites Antilles de l'époque précolombienne à la période coloniale.* Paris: L'Harmattan.

Guppy, R. J. Lechmere. 1984. "Notes on the Molluska Used as Food in Trinidad." *Proceedings of the Victoria Institute of Trinidad* 1: 27–31.

Haviser, Jay B. 1991. "The First Bonaireans." *Reports of the Archaeological-Anthropological Institute of the Netherlands Antilles* 10.

Haviser, Jay B. 2003. "A Grassroots Archaeology Project on Bonaire: Stimulating Antilleans to Take Their Own Initiatives." In *Proceedings of the 20th International Congress for Caribbean Archaeology,* 59–64. Santo Domingo, Dominican Republic.

Haviser, Jay B. 2014. "Bonaire Archaeological Institute (BONAI)." In *Encyclopedia of Caribbean Archaeology,* edited by Basil A. Reid and R. Grant Gilmore, 75–75. Gainesville: University Press of Florida.

Haviser, Jay B. 2015. "Community Archaeology as an Essential Element for Successful Archaeological Heritage Management." In *Managing Our Past into the Future: Archaeological Heritage Management in the Dutch Caribbean,* edited by Corinne L. Hofman and Jay B. Haviser, 133–51. Leiden: Sidestone Press.

Hofman, Corinne L., and Menno L. P. Hoogland. 2016. "Connecting Stakeholders: Collaborative Preventive Archaeology Projects at Sites Affected by Natural and/or Human Impacts." *Caribbean Connections* 5(1): 1–31.

Jácome, Camila Pereira. 2020. "Aprender e ensinar, algumas reflexões sobre arqueologias indígenas." *Revista do Museu de Arqueologia e Etnologia* 35(December): 14–35.

Kerrigan, Dylan. 2012. "Culture Contact: Trinidad 'Pre-History,' Historical Representation and Multiculturalism." *Journal of the Department of Behavioural Sciences* 1(1): 15–33.

Machado, Juliana Salles. 2013. "História(s) indígena(s) E a prática arqueológica Colaborativa." *Revista de Arqueologia* 26(1): 72–85.

Meskell, Lynn. 2002. "The Intersections of Identity and Politics in Archaeology." *Annual Review of Anthropology* 31: 279–301.

Meskell, Lynn, and Peter Pels, eds. 2005. *Embedding Ethics*. London: Routledge. https://doi.org/10.4324/9781003085249.

Navarrete Sánchez, Rodrigo. 2012. "¿El fin de la arqueología social latinoamericana? Reflexiones sobre la trascendencia historica del pensamiento marxista sobre el pasado." In *La Arqueologia Social Latinoamericana: de la Teoria a la Praxis,* edited by Henry Tantalean and Miguel Aguilar, 45–66. Bogotá: Ediciones UniAndes.

Newton, Melanie J. 2022. "Counterpoints of Conquest: The Royal Proclamation of 1763, the Lesser Antilles, and the Ethnocartography of Genocide." *William and Mary Quarterly* 79(2): 241–282.

Nicolaas, Mireille, Fleur Veldkamp, Douglas Abraham, and Cristopher Maldonado. 2005. "The BONAI Project on Bonaire after Two Years: Potentials for Youth Programs in the Caribbean." In *Proceedings of the 21st International Congress for Caribbean Archaeology,* 202–210. St. Augustine, Trinidad, University of the West Indies.

Ostapkowicz, Joanna, and Jonathan A. Hanna, eds. 2021. *Real, Recent, or Replica: Precolumbian Caribbean Heritage as Art, Commodity, and Inspiration.* Tuscaloosa: University of Alabama Press.

Ramos, Alcida Rita. 2023. "Indigenous Intellectuals Embrace Anthropology. Will It Remain the Same?" *Anuário Antropológico* 48(1).

Reid, Basil A. 2018. *An Archaeological Study of the Red House, Port of Spain, Trinidad and Tobago.* Port of Spain: University of the West Indies Press.

Rodríguez Velásquez, Fidel. 2020. "Excavando el pasado del Caribe insular venezolano: historia e historiografía de los primeros 100 años de arqueología en las islas de Cubagua y Margarita 1915-2019." *Caribbean Studies* 48(1): 93–133.

Rodríguez Velásquez, Fidel. 2023. "Enredados por las perlas: historias conectadas de los trabajadores indígenas, europeos y africanos en el Atlántico de las perlas (1498–1650)." PhD dissertation, Pontificia Universidade Católica do Rio de Janeiro.

Rodríguez Velásquez, Fidel, and Oliver Antczak. 2023. "Nueva Cádiz de Cubagua and the Pearl Fisheries of the Caribbean." In *The Oxford Research Encyclopedia of Latin American History,* edited by Stephen Webre. New York: Oxford University.

Rouse, Irving. 1947. "Prehistory of Trinidad in Relation to Adjacent Areas." *Man* 47: 93–98.

Santikarn, Alisa, Elifgül Doğan, Oliver Antczak, Kim Eileen Ruf, and Mariana P. L. Pereira. 2022. "Rethinking the Archaeology-Heritage." *Archaeological Review from Cambridge* 37(1): 1–11.

Silverman, Helaine. 2015. "Heritage and Authenticity." In *The Palgrave Handbook of Contemporary Heritage Research,* edited by Emma Waterton and Steve Watson, 69–88. London: Palgrave Macmillan UK.

Smith, Laurajane. 2004. *Archaeological Theory and the Politics of Cultural Heritage*. New York: Routledge.

Van Heekeren, Hendrik Robbert. 1960. "Studies on the Archaeology of the Netherlands Antilles: ii: A Survey of the Non-Ceramic Artifacts of Aruba, Curaçao and Bonaire." *New West Indian Guide* 40: 103–120.

Wylie, Alison. 1996. "Ethical Dilemmas in Archaeological Practice: Looting, Repatriation, Stewardship, and the (Trans)Formation of Disciplinary Identity." *Perspectives on Science* 4(2): 154–194. https://doi.org/10.1162/posc_a_00502.

5

From Theory to Practice

Evaluating a Decade of Progress on Ethical Approaches in Human Bioarchaeological Research in the Caribbean Region

Eleni Seferidou, Oriana Chiappa,
Daniel Antonio Brito-Pacheco,
and Nelda Issa Marengo Camacho

In the past decade, the discussion on ethical research on human skeletal remains has become a significant one in anthropological and archaeological sciences. Due to rapid technological and methodological advancements, especially in molecular and microscopic archaeology (i.e., aDNA, isotopic analysis, radiocarbon dating, proteomics), researchers have a variety of tools at their disposal to reveal a great amount of information about the human past, including evidence of mobility, health, and dietary patterns, as well as information about the genetic ancestry of archaeological populations (Squires et al. 2019: 265). However, most of these advances involve exporting samples for analysis and require destructive methods, which has led to discussions surrounding the ethical implications of studying ancient humans and the impact that this can have on both the descendant communities and on future research (Ávila-Arcos et al. 2022; DeWitte 2015; Squires et al. 2019; Squires et al. 2022).

These discussions have motivated multiple associations, institutions, and researchers around the world to publish codes of conduct and guidelines to carry out ethical research within the biological anthropology/bioarchaeology fields (i.e., AAPA 2003; BABAO 2019a, 2019b; Mays et al. 2013; NVFA 2023; SAA 2021; Schutkowski et al. 2017). This discussion has recently appeared in the Caribbean as well, where a code of ethics was composed and voted on by the International Association for Caribbean Archaeology in

2022 (Cunningham et al. 2022; also see Fricke, Giovas, Hanna, Shorter, and Victorina, this volume). However, these codes/guidelines have no legal implications, and therefore violations or noncompliance hold no legal repercussions (Tsosie et al. 2020). At the same time, legislation regarding the protection of cultural heritage varies in the Caribbean, depending largely on the state of self-governance of the island. In addition, heritage laws do not necessarily protect the interests of all stakeholders interested in and/or affected by an archaeological project, and therefore, do not guarantee the conduct of ethical work. As a result, in most parts of the world, including the broader Caribbean region, ethical (scientific) research into past peoples depends on the choices of the researchers and the means available to them.

The Caribbean region was one of the first to be colonized in the Americas by Europeans, and up until today, there are island states that have varied forms of independence from countries of the Global North[1] (Lewis 2013), marking more than 500 years of colonial presence. This has naturally affected the way research is performed, including archaeological and anthropological studies, which are still shaped by institutionalized neo-colonialism (Jean et al. 2024). The complexity of the broader Caribbean region, as one encompassing language differences, and past and present geopolitical and sociocultural intricacies, has made it difficult to promote a more collaborative, community archaeology. Community archaeology seeks to establish partnerships between (non-)local researchers and local communities, those who are impacted by and/or are interested in the research (see chapters by White, kok, and Antczak et al., this volume). This partnership entails the equal involvement of all parties in every step of the project, from formulating the objectives and the broader scope to cover the interests/needs of all stakeholders, and continues with equal terms throughout the duration of the project, as well as after its conclusion, when decisions about long-term curation are to be made (McDavid 2014; Londoño 2021; see Martin and Jean, this volume).

In recent years, discussions on community archaeology and ethics in bioarchaeology have also gained ground in scientific journals (i.e., Alpaslan-Roodenberg et al. 2021; Argüelles et al. 2022; Overholtzer and Argueta 2017). However, a question that emerges—and that is the main purpose of this chapter—is whether and how these discussions have moved beyond theoretical frameworks and have been implemented into anthropological and archaeological practice. To answer this question, the present study utilizes a data search in journal databases and evaluates scientific papers with a clear focus on scientific analyses on human skeletal remains from the broader Caribbean region published in the past decade. The main objective is to determine how discussions on ethics have been incorporated into practice and how this is communicated to the public.

More specifically, we are mapping trends in scientific interest in the Caribbean region in the past 10 years (2012–2022), using numbers of published research papers on Caribbean bioarchaeology. We look into which regions and countries within the Caribbean are most commonly studied as well as what percentage of the studies have been conducted by local and what percentage by foreign institutions. Lastly, we examine whether the collected studies performed destructive analyses on samples from human remains and whether they report engagement with the local communities of the area they were working in. Papers are divided into four categories according to how the role of the community is portrayed in the reported research activities, from not mentioned, to some form of acknowledgment of local communities or institutions, to some form of outreach activity to or with local communities, and lastly to some form of local involvement in research activities. Afterward, focusing on the studies that applied a collaborative focus in their project, we are interested in what ethical research, as mentioned in the articles, actually entails, and in what ways and at which stage the incorporation of collaborative aspects begins—whether it is a continuous collaboration (from project formulation until and after publication) or is limited to a certain part of the project (e.g., acquisition of permits). The research questions we will answer are:

1. How many studies have been published on Caribbean bioarchaeology, where analyses are performed on human remains, over the past 10 years (2012–2022)?
2. Which regions and countries within the Caribbean were most commonly studied?
3. What percentage of the studies have been conducted by local institutions and what percentage by foreign institutions?
4. How prevalent is destructive analysis in bioarchaeological research and how are the samples curated and/or returned to the institution that provided them?
5. How did researchers engage with the local community where research is performed?
6. Specifically, in what ways were locals involved in the research activities?

This study will provide a clearer picture of how much the efforts and discussions on ethical research during the past years have improved practice and collaboration between researchers and communities, how these are discussed or reported in journal articles, and which areas need to be improved.

Methodology

As mentioned previously, the aim of this chapter is to explore how discussions on ethics have been translated into practice. Given the scope and goal of this research, a mapping approach was chosen to answer questions about how researchers engage with the local community in the place where they conduct research. This approach entails collecting examples of studies where bioarchaeological research was conducted on human remains and performing quantitative analyses to understand the characteristics of community involvement. The methodology was organized similarly to a systematic mapping procedure as laid out in Petersen et al. (2008). The methods described by the authors were taken as broad guidelines and were adapted to fit the purposes of this study. The steps conducted here were as follows:

The above research questions were formulated, which are sought to be quantitatively answered. Online databases of research articles were scoured to find publications in which research on human skeletal remains in the Caribbean region was performed.

Publications were categorized with the goal of answering the research questions, and quantitative data were extracted from the information in the articles.

Search Process

A list of online databases was decided upon to search for publications to be analyzed, which included Elsevier ScienceDirect, PLOS One, Proceedings of the National Academy of Sciences (PNAS), Cambridge Core, Science, Taylor & Francis Online, and others. These were chosen as being likely to contain the main bulk of research in the field of interest. After trying several key words that correspond to our research focus, we decided on three that maximized the results ("Skeletal" AND "Caribbean" AND "archaeology"); we used these key words for the majority of the databases (with the exception of three databases, for which we had to slightly modify the search terms). An extensive description of the methodology followed for the search process is available from the authors upon request. The search was repeated with the same keywords in other official Caribbean languages (Spanish, French,

Dutch), which returned no results from these specific databases. All papers were analyzed after review to ensure that the following criteria were met:

1. Primary research papers focusing on bioarchaeological studies in the circum-Caribbean region, involving human skeletal remains
2. Papers published in the years 2012–2022 (inclusive)
3. Papers published in English, Spanish, French and Dutch

Conference proceedings, reviews, book chapters, dissertations/theses, and gray literature were excluded.[2]

The papers were split into four categories according to how the role of the community is portrayed in the reported research activities. The types of engagement are described as follows:

Type 1—Some form of acknowledgment of local communities, local government, or local academic institutions. The article may refer to some form of contribution to the research from any of these subjects without explicitly mentioning that they were involved in the research activities.

Type 2—Some form of outreach activity involving the local communities. The article reports that the research findings were shared with the local community members either during or after results had been obtained.

Type 3—Some form of involvement in research activities. The article reported that the local government, an academic institution, or some members of the local communities were involved in the archaeological activities carried out in order to perform the research. Any publication mentioning collaboration between a local and a foreign academic institution was also included in this type.

Not mentioned—The publication did not acknowledge or report any of the above activities pertaining to community engagement. This does not necessarily mean that a strategy was not followed, simply that it is not mentioned in the paper.

Results

The total number of publications found in the databases mentioned above in the past 10 years (2012–2022) focusing on bioarchaeology in the Caribbean region was 61. All results presented in this section are about these 61 publications. The articles were categorized in order to answer the initial research questions. It is important to note that in some categorizations, the

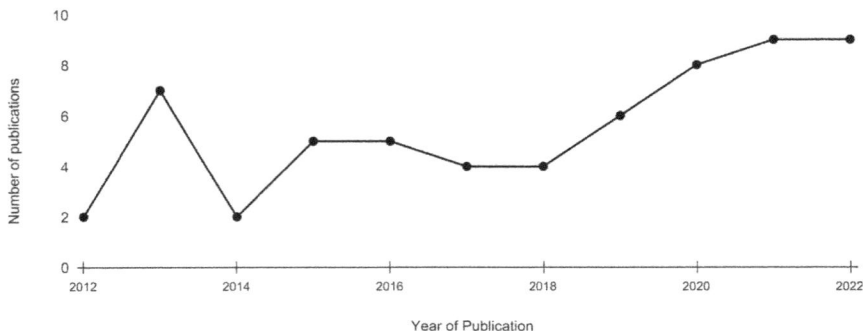

Figure 5.1. Number of publications focusing on Caribbean bioarchaeology per year of publication. Graph by Daniel Antonio Brito-Pacheco.

sum of the number of papers in the different categories may not be 61, since a paper may fall into several different categories. For example, when focusing on the countries the authors' affiliated institutions are located in, a given publication can fall into many categories, as coauthors from different regions contributed to the article. All percentages presented in this section have been rounded to the nearest whole number. No publications were found written in languages other than English in the databases searched; this is potentially because the majority of the publishing databases require their manuscript to be submitted in English (i.e., PLOS One, PNAS) or some (i.e., Springer Link) mention that they have only a few titles in other languages (Springer 2020). The categorization of the papers has been done with the information provided in the main publication and not in supplementary material.

Publications per Year

Figure 5.1 shows the number of papers that focus on bioarchaeology in the Caribbean region found each year between 2012 and 2022, inclusively. A slight upward trend is captured by the data, showing an increased interest in the topic in the past few years.

Geographical Distribution of Research

For each publication, we identified the region in the broader Caribbean in which the research was conducted. In cases where studies were conducted abroad, we identified the regions from which the samples originated. Results of this section are summarized in the first two columns of Table 5.1. It is im-

Table 5.1. Number of Publications of Each Engagement Type per Country/Region of Research

Region / Country of Research	Total Publications	Publications of Engagement Type 1	Publications of Engagement Type 2	Publications of Engagement Type 3	Publications of No Engagement
Cuba	12	3	0	0	9
Yucatan Peninsula (Mexico)	9	3	1	2	6
Puerto Rico*	8	2	0	1	5
Bahamas	8	4	0	1	4
Panama	8	4	0	1	4
Dominican Republic	6	3	0	1	3
Guadeloupe*	5	2	0	0	3
Venezuela	5	1	0	1	4
St. Lucia	4	3	1	2	1
St. Vincent and the Grenadines	4	2	0	0	2
Jamaica	4	1	1	0	2
Trinidad and Tobago	4	3	0	1	1
Haiti	4	2	0	1	2
Saba*	3	1	0	0	2
Barbados	3	1	0	0	2
US Virgin Islands*	2	1	0	0	1
Saint Martin*	2	0	0	0	2
Curaçao*	2	2	0	1	0
Belize	2	1	0	1	1
Guatemala	2	1	0	0	1
Honduras	2	1	0	0	1
Colombia	2	0	0	0	2
Guyana	1	0	0	0	1
Nicaragua	1	0	0	0	1
Aruba*	1	1	0	0	0
Florida (US)	1	0	0	0	0

Notes: The table shows which Caribbean islands/regions are attracting archaeological interest (quantified in the column "Total Publications"). Caribbean regions and territories that have different forms of independency from other countries are presented with an asterisk.

portant to note that each publication might cover more than one area, so the numbers in the table do not reflect the total number of publications found. (Engagement type, also displayed in the table, is explained in following text.)

According to our findings, the most researched areas in the Caribbean are located in Cuba, the Yucatan Peninsula, Puerto Rico, Bahamas, Panamá, and the Dominican Republic. In contrast, there were notably fewer studies found on regions such as Florida, Aruba, Nicaragua, Guyana, Colombia, Honduras, Guatemala, Belize, Curaçao, Saint Martin, and the US Virgin Islands, with only one to two publications found for each.

Involvement of Local Researchers

Publications were also classified according to the location of the authors' institutions of affiliation. When performing the classification, overseas territories inside the Caribbean were counted as a separate region, that is, an institution in Guadeloupe is officially part of France, but the institution was classified as being in Guadeloupe. This was done similarly for Puerto Rico, Turks and Caicos, Curaçao, and Saint Martin.

A country was only counted once per publication, meaning that if two or more authors' institutions are located in the same country/region, this country will only be counted once. A few authors' affiliations were found to be with the Smithsonian Tropical Research Institute, which is located in Panama but is headquartered in the United States; therefore, a special category was created called USA-Adj (USA-Adjacent) for publications written by authors in this institution. One publication was found to be partially authored by an independent researcher; therefore, a category was created to reflect this ("Independent Researcher"). Table 5.2 presents the results of this section, together with the community engagement type mentioned by country.

According to both these sections, 21 publications (34%) had some contribution from authors from local institutions, while 40 (66%) were authored exclusively by researchers based in foreign countries. We found no publications where all authors are affiliated with a local institution. Figure 5.2 shows the percentage of publications that include an author from a local institution by the year of publication. There seems to be no clear upward or downward trend.

Treatment of Samples

For the next part, we looked into how prevalent destructive analysis was in bioarchaeological research. Out of all the 61 publications found, 45 of them (74%) were identified to have performed destructive analysis, while the other

Table 5.2. Number of Publications of Each Engagement Type per Country/Region of Author's Affiliation

Country / Region of Author Affiliation	Total Publications	Publications of Engagement Type 1	Publications of Engagement Type 2	Publications of Engagement Type 3	Publications of No Engagement
US	38	13	0	4	24
Netherlands	20	8	2	3	11
Canada	14	5	1	3	9
UK	11	6	1	4	5
Cuba	9	3	0	1	6
Mexico	10	5	1	3	5
USA-Adj	7	3	0	0	4
Denmark	7	1	0	0	6
Germany	7	3	1	3	4
Spain	6	2	0	2	4
Bahamas	4	4	0	1	0
Puerto Rico	4	1	0	0	3
St. Martin	3	1	0	0	2
Austria	2	2	0	2	0
Belgium	2	2	0	1	0
Colombia	2	1	0	1	1
Curacao	2	2	0	1	0
Dominican Republic	2	1	0	1	1
Italy	2	1	0	1	1
Jamaica	2	0	1	0	1
New Zealand	2	0	0	0	2
Panama	2	2	0	0	0
Portugal	2	1	0	1	1
Venezuela	2	1	0	1	1
Turks and Caicos	2	1	0	1	1
Australia	1	1	0	1	0
Belize	1	1	0	1	0
Guatemala	1	0	0	0	1
Guyana	1	0	0	0	1
Independent Researcher	1	0	0	0	1
Ireland	1	0	0	0	1
Japan	1	1	0	0	0

(*continued*)

Table 5.2—*Continued*

Country / Region of Author Affiliation	Total Publications	Publications of Engagement Type 1	Publications of Engagement Type 2	Publications of Engagement Type 3	Publications of No Engagement
Trinidad and Tobago	2	2	0	1	0
St. Vincent and Grenadines	1	1	0	0	0
Switzerland	1	0	0	0	1
France	1	0	0	0	1
Guadeloupe	1	0	0	0	1
Saba	1	0	0	0	1

Notes: The table shows the country of affiliation of all the authors in the analyzed papers (quantified in the column "Total Publications"). The excavations on which the independent researcher project was based were carried out as a collaboration between a Caribbean archaeological institution and a European university.

16 (26%) carried out nondestructive techniques or used data from previously published research.

When the examination of the samples was performed abroad, in 10 (16%) publications, it was explicitly mentioned that remaining samples or intact fragments that were not utilized during the analysis process were returned. However, in 40 (66%) of the publications that required sampling abroad there was no information on whether the remaining samples were returned. In 3 publications (5%), the research was conducted by local or foreign scientists in local institutions or research centers, where the human remains were already housed. Table 5.3 shows the cross-count of papers in which destructive analysis was performed versus those mentioning the returning of samples.

Community Engagement

A total of 24 articles (39%) showed *Type 1* engagement of the community (some form of acknowledgment of local communities and/or institutions), 3 (5%) showed *Type 2* engagement (some form of outreach activity involving the local communities), 8 (13%) mentioned *Type 3* engagement (some form of involvement in research activities). Finally, 35 papers (57%) did not acknowledge any type of engagement, thus were classified as *Not Mentioned*. Table 5.1 and Table 5.2 present the number of papers where each engagement type was recognized. In Table 5.1, this is analyzed in regard to the region/country that the study focused on, and in Table 5.2, in regard to the region/country of affiliation of the authors.

Table 5.3. Cross-Count of Publications in Which Destructive Analysis Was Performed versus Publications that Mention That Samples Were Returned

	Unknown if Samples Were Returned	Samples Returned	Local Research
Destructive Analysis	35 (78%)	9 (20%)	1 (2%)
Nondestructive Analysis	5 (63%)	1 (13%)	2 (25%)

Note: Percentages are based on the totals in the row.

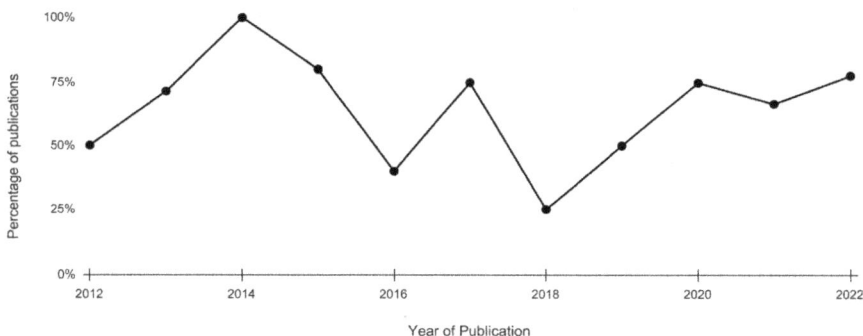

Figure 5.2. Percentage of publications that include at least one author from a local institution per year of publication. Graph by Daniel Antonio Brito-Pacheco.

Discussion

Publications per Year

One of the aims of this study was to evaluate how bioarchaeological research in the Caribbean region has evolved in the past decade (2012–2022), in relation to ethical considerations. The first goal was to identify the number of studies involving human skeletal remains that have been conducted across this time range, and whether this number has changed or remained stable. An observed—after 2018—increase in the number of published papers indicates an increase in scientific interest for the Caribbean people and their past (Figure 5.1).

The broader Caribbean region, together with others with a colonial past (and present) have historically, and for a variety of reasons, attracted the least archaeological Western interest. Since the beginning of the field, the majority of research has taken a Eurocentric focus. This is obvious from our search into English-based journal databases, where Eurasia is a focal point of interest, with the rest of the world following. Intensively investigating regions like East Asia, the Caribbean, or the Pacific islands has been a relatively recent phenomenon (Van Stipriaan, Alofs, and Guadeloupe 2023). Regardless, and even though archaeological contexts showed a rich precolonial history, with a variety of material indicating extensive culture variation, interest in these areas is still rather limited, at least in the English-speaking world (we only found 61 papers to match our criteria across 9 databases).

Moreover, until recently, archaeological expeditions in the Caribbean mostly focused on settlement patterns and material culture traditions, which were the basis for interpreting human behavior (i.e., Hofman and Hoogland 2011; Hoogland, Hofman, and Panhuysen 2010; Knippenberg 2006). A significant contributing factor to this was the poor preservation of human remains, due to climatological and geological conditions but also due to cultural mortuary practices (Crespo-Torres, Mickleburgh, and Valcárcel Rojas 2013; Hoogland and Hofman 2013). With technological advancements and the arrival of the field of molecular anthropology, scientists were given the opportunity to research past humans in depth, without the need for a good preservation of the entire skeleton. In addition, another great push forward has been the epistemological shift toward smaller geographical scales, where small groups and individuals are at the center. The potential to acquire a great amount of information on individual life stories looking directly at the human skeleton attracted more public interest (e.g., Fricke, Laffoon, and Espersen 2021). Lastly, another aspect that would have contributed to the increase in the bioarchaeological studies in the past decade and that is worth mentioning is the contribution of local researchers. More locals from the region choose the path of anthropological and archaeological research, especially in countries where an undergraduate degree on the topic is offered (Cuba, Puerto Rico), driving the interest in their own countries/islands and their ancestors (e.g., Daggers et al. 2018).

Geographical Distribution and Involvement of Local Authors

1. Which are the most common places in the Caribbean where research is conducted?

As seen in Table 5.1, Cuba appears as the most researched region in the Caribbean, accounting for the highest number of publications (12). This means that a great number of the published articles center on skeletal remains coming from archaeological sites found in present-day Cuba. This is followed by the Yucatan Peninsula, located in Mexico, with nine publications. The disparity of publications centered around skeletal remains from some countries or regions compared to others might be due to several factors. First, sample size and preservation might be playing an important role, as Cuba's geological conditions (such as caves, wetlands, or sand dunes) have allowed for good preservation of human remains. In fact, at some sites, such as El Chorro de Maíta, more than 100 individuals have been excavated (Crespo-Torres, Mickleburgh, and Valcárcel Rojas 2013).

In the case of the Yucatán Peninsula in Mexico, the large number of publications centered on this region is connected to the long-established field of research on Mayan archaeology in the area by local and foreign institutions (Márquez-Grant and Fibiger 2011; Morfín and Licón 2011). However, the value is still high when compared to the number of publications on skeletal remains from other countries with comparable sites of interest for Mayan archaeologists, such as Belize, Honduras, and Guatemala. This disparity could be related not only to the number of skeletal collections available (during the past decade), but also to the amount of resources and regulations dedicated to study, store, and preserve these collections, which could be the result of the focus of particular research institutes (Márquez-Grant and Fibiger 2011; Morfín and Licón 2011; Penados 2011).

In addition to sample size and preservation, political factors and legislation have an important role in deciding where research is conducted. Over the past decade, countries and territories of particular interest for bioarchaeologists have included the Bahamas archipelago, Panama, Puerto Rico, the Dominican Republic, Guadeloupe,[3] and Venezuela. These places (as well as many others listed in Table 5.1) do not have strict legislation regarding archaeological heritage, and specifically archaeological human remains (Hofman and Hoogland 2016; Siegel and Righter 2011; UNESCO 2023). In most of these regions, archaeological heritage management rules are restricted to monuments, materials, and objects, without much consideration for skeletal remains (see Marquez-Grant and Fibiger 2011; Siegel and Righter 2011; Van Stipriaan, Alofs, and Guadeloupe 2023). However, in regions where archaeological heritage is regulated in relation to Indigenous people's rights, less research has been conducted. For instance, in Table 5.1, we observe that human remains from archaeological sites in Florida and Guyana have been some of the least studied areas in the past 10 years (1 publication each). For the case of Florida (US), this region falls under NAGPRA legislation, leaving the analysis of human skeletal remains to the decision of Indigenous communities (National Park Service, n.d.). Similarly, Guyana is one of the Caribbean regions with more extensive legislation regarding Indigenous peoples' rights, as it follows the Amerindian Act that empowers Indigenous communities to make decisions regarding their heritage (Strecker 2017).

Sometimes, even when there are laws supporting stakeholders' rights, a lack of personal identification with archaeological heritage (due to cultural and social structures embedded in racism and colonialism) has prevented descendant communities from taking the initiative to exercise their rights and make decisions regarding skeletal remains found in excavations (Cucina 2013; Nieves-Colón et al. 2021; Ortega Muñoz 2011). However, it is becoming more common for Indigenous peoples and descendant communities to decide upon their heritage. For instance, in Guatemala, Mayan Indigenous communities have started requesting the restitution of objects and human remains found in excavation, which has resulted in the reburial of many individuals previously stored in museums (Castillo 2022; Penados 2011). This is not the case in the Mexican Yucatán Peninsula, where to date there are still no restitution claims on skeletal remains by the Indigenous communities.

2. Who Is Conducting This Research?

When looking into the regions being explored, it is important to consider the institutions or individuals responsible for conducting archaeological research at these sites. In Table 5.2, we can observe that 67% of the authors who have published data about Caribbean skeletal remains in the past decade are affiliated to an institution located in the Global North, while only 29% of researchers belong to institutions based in the Global South.[4] In addition, it was found that 21 publications (34%) had some contribution from authors from local institutions, while 40 (66%) were authored exclusively by researchers based in foreign countries.

This does not come as a surprise, as institutions from the Global North have more economic resources available to fund scientific research. In addition, many Caribbean regions and territories hold strong historic ties to foreign countries from the Global North, and some of them continue to have different forms of independence from said countries[5] (Boatcă 2021). These relationships have facilitated foreign institutions and researchers to finance and conduct multiple projects in various regions of the Caribbean, specifically those with fewer restrictions regarding sampling and export of human remains. Although these projects can lead to long-lasting collaborations with local researchers and communities, the lack of regulations can result in what has been referred to as "helicopter or parachute science." This is a type of research in which scientists from privileged settings collect, export, and process data from less privileged regions or areas without involving local communities and collaborators (Haelewaters, Hofmann, and Romero-Olivares 2021; Yáñez et al. 2022). With recent decolonization trends in our discipline, we expected an increase in the collaboration between local and foreign institutions, however, there was no upward trend, which forces us to reflect on the way we are producing research.

Another factor to consider for the disparity of publications authored by foreign versus local scientists is the lack of specialists in some regions. Many countries in the Caribbean do not provide academic programs in bioarchaeology, which creates an inherent disadvantage in the number of local specialists (Argüelles, Fuentes, and Yáñez 2022; Ávila-Arcos et al. 2022). In cases where such programs exist, such as Mexico and Cuba, not only do we see a higher number of researchers affiliated with local institutions compared to other Caribbean regions, but also a significantly higher number of published papers, which speaks to the importance of local researchers when producing knowledge. It is important to note that in this research we could not identify those local scientists who, for numerous reasons, live abroad, and therefore are affiliated to a foreign institution but conduct research activities in their home country. In these cases, collaborative projects occur often, as the diaspora scientists are already familiar with local communities and researchers.

Finally, behind the apparently smaller contribution of local researchers might be an economic and language factor, since to publish in "high impact" journals such as those analyzed for this research, finances play an important role, which can be an issue for institutions in the Caribbean, as well as for early career researchers (Ávila-Arcos et al. 2022; Collyer 2018; Demeter 2020; Yáñez et al. 2022). Likewise, these papers are published in English, which in most Caribbean regions is not a first language. This is potentially also the reason why we did not find any publications in languages other than English. Due to these factors, local academics often opt for publishing in local scientific journals, edited volumes, and other resources that were excluded from the search as many of these are often not indexed or digitized and may be more difficult to locate, again because of the unequal geopolitical power dynamics.

Treatment of Samples

Further, this study examined the percentage of bioarchaeological research papers that included destructive analysis and the curation strategies followed after a project's completion. The majority of examined publications appear to have performed destructive analysis (45), with only 10 of these mentioning the return of the samples to the institutions currently housing them. Most do not refer to samples' return or any other curation strategies followed. As stated previously, the fact that there is no information provided about the return and/or curation of samples does not necessarily mean that this was not part of the research project.

A significant aspect of conducting respectful and ethical research, especially when concerning human skeletal remains, is providing information regarding the handling process of the samples that have been used for the project's analyses. This refers to a clear explanation on how the samples have been stored after the end of the analyses, and whether or not they have been returned either to the institution that provided them or to another, or if they have not been returned, whose curation care they are under. The last point is one that can contribute to future research and the avoidance of further and unnecessary destructive resampling. The need for the documentation of the samples' handling process is present in multiple codes of conduct published by various anthropological and archaeological associations. The codes indicate the need for transparency for all parts of a project to all interested parties but lack any legal framework to enforce it (i.e., BABAO 2019a, 2019b; Cunningham et al. 2022; NVFA 2023).

An important point to be mentioned here is that curation of the remains is not the only option. In several cases, the decision was made to repatriate and rebury human remains. This decision should always be made after serious consideration of stakeholders' wishes and consultation with descendant communities. In the Caribbean region specifically, even after the destructive sampling of skeletal remains, cases of repatriation and reburial have been reported that benefited both researchers and the local community (i.e., the case of the Red House excavation in Trinidad, see de Souza 2019, and Antczak, Ammerlaan, Morris, and Rodríguez Velásquez, this volume).

Lastly, with the advancement of molecular analyses in archaeology, the need for curation is extended to the data derived from the analyzed skeletal material (i.e., isotope compositions, disease and lifestyle information, genetic data). In publications, it is important to mention where and in what ways these data are stored, who is given permission for their potential publication, and whether they are available for reuse in future research.

Community Engagement

One of the main objectives of this study was to research the ways in which scientists engage with local communities and how this is communicated in the associated publications. With decolonial discourses and community archaeology gaining significant traction in our discipline during the past decade, we expected publications to address this topic.

In fact, we found that most of the analyzed publications do not mention any type of local engagement at all (57%), and when they do, the most common way to address it is to recognize local communities and/or institutions in the acknowledgments section of the publication, without specifying the role of said participants in the research project. Only in eight publications (13%), was the contribution of local communities, individuals, and/or institutions directly specified, and these contributions were mostly based on local individuals aiding in manual labor (for example as excavators or divers), local governments providing permissions for research practices, local academic institutions providing samples to be analyzed, and collaborations with local researchers. Again, most of these contributions were only stated in the acknowledgments section of the article, and in very few exceptions was there an ethics segment addressing this topic. Here, it should be mentioned that we focused on the main paper and not on the supplementary material. However, in the main paper, there was no text referring the reader to the supplementary material for more information on community engagement strategies.

Multiple authors have highlighted the need to create long-lasting and equitable relationships with local communities in order to generate a two-way sustainable collaboration, and to avoid new ways of colonialism based on scientific extractivism (Ávila-Arcos et al. 2022; Wagner et al. 2020; Yañez et al. 2022). For this, it is essential to communicate results to stakeholders, which can be done by organizing outreach activities as well as through open-access publications. In this study we found that only three publications explicitly mention some sort of outreach activity in which the results of the research were shared with the local community. Projects should also communicate project objectives and limitations in advance with the public, to ensure transparency and broad collaboration (Londoño 2021). Nevertheless, in the publications reviewed for this article we did not find an explicit explanation of how (or whether) this was conducted, with most of them only mentioning the acquisition of legal permits for the analyses.

Although we are aware that some projects attempted and managed to create ties between local and foreign institutions as well as between researchers and local communities, community engagement constitutes an essential part of a project, and therefore we propose that the methodology followed to establish said collaboration should be clearly addressed in the publication (potentially in the "Materials and Methods" section). Moreover, as stated by Squires et al. (2022), more transparency in scientific publications can help promote community engagement as a higher priority, enhance the clear communication of information, and thus encourage relationships of trust with the general public.

A big reason for this lack of proper communication is that scientific journals can be rather limiting in the space they provide for discussions on community engagement. We anticipate that in the coming years scientific journals and funding agencies will begin to give more priority to these issues (see Springer Nature Limited 2024), and it is expected that more space will be provided for discussions on community engagement strategies. In the meantime, as researchers, we ought to prioritize this engagement from the project formulation (when setting the research direction) and throughout the project's duration, to ensure results reach the community, and we should address these strategies in our publications.

Conclusion

The aim of this study was to evaluate the ways in which the discussion on ethical bioarchaeological research in the Caribbean has been incorporated into archaeological practice.

In order to investigate this, we performed a data search across nine international bibliometric databases, to collect a list of scientific papers with a clear focus on scientific analyses on human skeletal remains from the broader Caribbean region, published in the past decade (2012–2022). Our goals were to examine whether or not studies performed destructive analyses, whether they engaged with the local community of the area they were working on, and how this was communicated. Furthermore, we investigated whether these studies have been performed by researchers from foreign or local institutions. We compiled a list of 61 publications, the majority of which reported research conducted by an institution of the

Global North and presented some kind of destructive analysis of the human remains. In addition, we recognized a limited number of studies published in these international journals led by researchers in local institutions, due to geopolitical disadvantages, such as economic, resource, and language limitations.

Given the increasing discussions on ethics in bioarchaeology that have emerged during recent years, we expected to see an upward trend in the number of collaborative projects in the past decade. Out of the 61 papers we examined, 35 did not mention any type of collaboration or engagement with the local community. Focusing on the studies that opted for a more collaborative project, description of the strategy followed to achieve this engagement was rather limited, mostly mentioning the involvement of local institutions. In the papers where some form of collaboration was mentioned, it was difficult to ascertain how this was achieved and what steps were followed, as most papers did not present details of their strategy for engagement and collaboration with local entities. One point that is made clear in this study is the need to include community engagement strategies as an integral part of publications' research methodology. This is a simple step toward communicating collaborative projects in detail and providing the "know-how" to an increasing number of researchers.

In conclusion, although ethical and collaborative research has gained significant popularity in our discipline, according to our results the impact of this is not yet visible on a practical level in Caribbean bioarchaeology publications. Specifically, regarding scientific analysis of human remains, we saw an increase in scientific interest in the region, but this was still dominated by institutions in the Global North. These results demonstrate that, as researchers, we still have much room for improvement in applying ethical practices in the study of human skeletal remains, and community engagement is one of them. A step forward would be to clearly address this issue in all our publications, report how and by whom samples are curated, and elaborate on community engagement strategies in a transparent way. In addition, we must continue to establish collaborations between international and local researchers, as well as demanding from academic and financial institutions the necessary resources to carry out long-lasting sustainable projects that prioritize collaboration with local communities from project formulation to publication.

Notes

1 Countries that have historically profited from colonialism and are still benefiting from this economic advantage. They are primarily located in the Northern Hemisphere except New Zealand and Australia (Haelewaters, Hofmann, and Romero-Olivares 2021).

2 These were omitted to limit our results to research studies, the involved sample analysis, and data production and to keep the number of publications low enough to efficiently analyze in the framework of this volume. In addition, the publication types are less accessible than the majority so would limit our ability to answer our research questions.

3 In the specific case of Guadeloupe, a law regarding this issue was approved as of December 2023 (République Française 2023).

4 Countries, regions, or territories located in the Southern Hemisphere that have been adversely affected by colonialism, often referred to as "developing countries" (Haelewaters, Hofmann, and Romero-Olivares 2021).

5 Territories marked with asterisk in Table 5.2.

References Cited

Alpaslan-Roodenberg, Songül, Anthony David, Babiker Hiba, Eszter Bánffy, Thomas Booth, Patricia Capone, and Arati Deshpande-Mikherjee, et al. 2021. "Ethics of DNA Research on Human Remains: Five Globally Applicable Guidelines." *Nature* 599: 41–46.

American Association for Physical Anthropology (AAPA). 2003. "Code of Ethics." https://physanth.org/documents/3/ethics.pdf (accessed June 27, 2024).

Argüelles, Juan M., Agustín Fuentes, and Bernardo Yáñez. 2022. "Analyzing Asymmetries and Praxis in aDNA Research: A Bioanthropological Critique." *American Anthropologist* 124(1): 130–140.

Ávila-Arcos, Maria C., Costanza de la Fuente Castro, Maria A. Nieves-Colón, and Maanasa Raghavan. 2022. "Recommendations for Sustainable Ancient DNA Research in the Global South: Voices from a New Generation of Paleogenomicists." *Frontiers in Genetics* 13: 880170.

Boatcă, Manuela. 2021. "Thinking Europe Otherwise: Lessons from the Caribbean." *Current Sociology* 69(3): 389–414.

British Association for Biological Anthropology and Osteoarchaeology (BABAO). 2019a. "Code of Ethics." https://babao.org.uk/resources/guidelines-codes/ (accessed June 27, 2024).

British Association for Biological Anthropology and Osteoarchaeology (BABAO). 2019b. "Code of Practice." https://babao.org.uk/resources/guidelines-codes/ (accessed June 27, 2024).

Castillo, Victor. 2022. "Zaculeu, Guatemala: Reflexiones y propuestas para un retorno local." *Revista De Arqueología Americana* 40: 163–182.

Collyer, Fran M. 2018. "Global Patterns in the Publishing of Academic Knowledge: Global North, Global South." *Current Sociology* 66(1): 56–73.

Crespo-Torres, Edwin, Hayley L. Mickleburgh, and Roberto Valcárcel Rojas. 2013. "The Study of Pre-Columbian Human Remains in the Caribbean Archipelago." In *The Oxford Handbook of Caribbean Archaeology,* edited by William F. Keegan, Corinne L. Hofman, and Reniel Rodríguez Ramos, 436–451. Oxford: Oxford University Press.

Cucina, Andrea. 2013. "Ética En Bioarqueología." *Temas Antropológicos: Revista Científica de Investigaciones Regionales* 35(2): 149–70.

Cunningham, Andreana, Felicia J. Fricke, Christina Giovas, Jonathan A. Hanna, Tibisay Sankatsing Nava, John Shorter, and Amy Victorina. 2022. "Code of Ethics." International Association for Caribbean Archaeology (IACA). https://blogs.uoregon.edu/iaca/announcements/ (accessed June 27, 2024).

Daggers, Louisa, Mark G. Plew, Alex Edwards, Samantha Evans, and Robin B. Trayler. 2018. "Assessing the Early Holocene Environment of Northwestern Guyana: An Isotopic Analysis of Human and Faunal Remains." *Latin American Antiquity* 29(2): 279–292.

Demeter, Marton. 2020. "The Dynamics behind the Problem of Inequality: The World-System of Global Inequality in Knowledge Production." In *Academic Knowledge Production and the Global South: Questioning Inequality and Under-Representation,* edited by Marton Demeter, 63–84. New York: Springer International Publishing.

De Souza, Janelle. 2019. "60 First Peoples Remains Laid to Rest at Red House." *Trinidad and Tobago Newsday.* October 20, 2019. https://newsday.co.tt/2019/10/20/60-first-peoples-remains-laid-to-rest-at-red-house/ (accessed June 27, 2024).

DeWitte, Sharon N. 2015. "Bioarchaeology and the Ethics of Research Using Human Skeletal Remains." *History Compass* 13(1): 10–19.

Fricke, Felicia, Jason E. Laffoon, and Ryan Espersen. 2021. "Unforgotten: The Osteobiography of an Enslaved Woman and Child from 18th Century Saba." *Journal of Archaeological Science Reports* 36(4): 102838.

Haelewaters, Danny, Tina A. Hofmann, and Adriana L. Romero-Olivares. 2021. "Ten Simple Rules for Global North Researchers to Stop Perpetuating Helicopter Research in the Global South." *PLoS Computational Biology* 17(8): e1009277.

Hofman, Corinne, L., and Menno L. P. Hoogland. 2011. "Unravelling the Multi-Scale Networks of Mobility and Exchange in the Pre-Colonial Circum-Caribbean." In *Communities in Contact. Essays in Archaeology, Ethnohistory & Ethnography of the Amerindian Circum-Caribbean,* edited by Corinne L. Hofman and Anne van Duijvenbode, 15–44. Leiden: Sidestone Press.

Hofman, Corinne. L., and Menno L. P. Hoogland. 2016. "Connecting Stakeholders: Collaborative Preventive Archaeology Projects at Sites Affected by Natural and/or Human Impacts." *Caribbean Connections* 5(1): 1–31.

Hoogland, Menno L. P., Corinne L. Hofman, and Raphael G. A. M. Panhuysen. 2010. "Interisland Dynamics: Evidence for Human Mobility at the Site of Anse à La Gourde, Guadeloupe." In *Island Shores, Distant Pasts: Archaeological and Biological*

Approaches to the Pre-Columbian Settlement of the Caribbean, edited by Scott M. Fitzpatrick and Ann H. Ross, 148–62. Gainesville: University Press of Florida.

Hoogland, Menno L. P., and Corinne L. Hofman. 2013. "From Corpse Taphonomy to Mortuary Behavior in the Caribbean: A Case Study from the Lesser Antilles." In *The Oxford Handbook of Caribbean Archaeology,* edited by Corinne L. Hofman, William F. Keegan, and Renial Rodríguez Ramos, 452–469. Oxford: Oxford University Press.

Jean, Joseph Sony, Eduardo Herrera Malatesta, and Katarina Jacobson. 2024. "Local Voices, the Uses of Archaeological Heritage in the Caribbean." In *Local Voices, Global Debates: The Uses of Archaeological Heritage in the Caribbean,* edited by Joseph Sony Jean and Eduardo Herrera Malatesta, 1–17. Leiden: Brill.

Knippenberg, Sebastiaan. 2006. "Stone Artefact Production and Exchange among the Lesser Antilles. Leiden University." PhD dissertation, Leiden University.

Lewis, Linden. 2013. *Caribbean Sovereignty, Development and Democracy in an Age of Globalization.* London: Routledge.

Londoño, Wilhelm. 2021. "Indigenous Archaeology, Community Archaeology, and Decolonial Archaeology: What Are We Talking About? A Look at the Current Archaeological Theory in South America with Examples." *Archaeologies* 17(3): 386–406.

Márquez-Grant, Nicholas, and Linda Fibiger, eds. 2011. *The Routledge Handbook of Archaeological Human Remains and Legislation: An International Guide to Laws and Practice in the Excavation and Treatment of Archaeological Human Remains.* London: Routledge.

Mays, Simon, Joseph Elders, Louise Humphrey, William White, and Peter Marshall. 2013. "Science and the Dead: A Guideline for the Destructive Sampling of Archaeological Human Remains for Scientific Analysis." Advisory Panel on the Archaeology of Burials in England (APABE).

McDavid, Carol. 2014. "Community Archaeology." In *Encyclopedia of Global Archaeology,* edited by Claire Smith, 1591–1599. New York: Springer.

Morfín, Lourdes, M., and Ernesto G. Licón. 2011. "Mexico/México." In *The Routledge Handbook of Archaeological Human Remains and Legislation,* edited by Nicholas Marquez-Grant and Linda Fibiger, 543–551. London: Routledge.

National Park Service. n.d. Native American Graves Protection and Repatriation Act 1990. https://www.nps.gov/subjects/nagpra/index.htm (accessed June 27, 2024).

Nederlandse Vereniging voor Fysische Antropologie (NVFA). 2023. "Ethical Guidelines on Human Remains." https://nvfanl.files.wordpress.com/2023/03/nvfa_ethical_guidelines_en.pdf (accessed June 27, 2024).

Nieves-Colón, María A., Kelly E. Blevins, Miguel Á. Contreras-Sieck, and Miriam B. López. 2021. "Paleogenómica y Bioarqueología En México." *Cuicuilco. Revista de Ciencias Antropológicas* 28(81): 187–223.

Ortega Muñoz, Allan. 2011. "Los Restos de Nuestros Antepasados En La Construcción Del Patrimonio Cultural Tangible y La Identidad de México." In *Colecciones Esqueléticas Humanas En México: Excavación, Catalogación y Aspectos Normativos,* edited by Lourdes Márquez Morfin and Allan Ortega Muñoz, 29–50. Tlalpan: Instituto Nacional de Antropología e Historia.

Overholtzer, Lisa, and Juan R. Argueta. 2017. "Letting Skeletons out of the Closet: The Ethics of Displaying Ancient Mexican Human Remains." *International Journal of Heritage Studies* 24(5): 508–530.

Penados, Lourdes. 2011. "Guatemala." In *The Routledge Handbook of Archaeological Human Remains and Legislation,* edited by Nicholas Marquez-Grant and Linda Fibiger, 552–559. London: Routledge.

Petersen, Kai, Robert Feldt, Shahid Mujtaba, and Michael Mattsson. 2008. "Systematic Mapping Studies in Software Engineering." In *12th International Conference on Evaluation and Assessment in Software Engineering (EASE),* 2008, 1–10.

République Française. 2023. "Loi n° 2023–1251 du 26 décembre 2023 relative à la restitution de restes humains appartenant aux collections publiques." https://www.legifrance.gouv.fr/jorf/id/JORFTEXT000048668800 (accessed June 27, 2024).

Schutkowski, Holger, Elizabeth Popescu, Joseph Elders, Simon Mays, Margaret Clegg, and Rekha Gohil. 2017. Guidance for Best Practice for the Treatment of Human Remains Excavated from Christian Burial Grounds in England. Advisory Panel on the Archaeology of Burials in England (APABE).

Siegel, Peter E., and Elizabeth Righter. 2011. *Protecting Heritage in the Caribbean.* Tuscaloosa: University of Alabama Press.

Society for American Archaeology (SAA). 2021. "Statement Concerning the Treatment of Human Remains." http://www.concernedhistorians.org/content_files/file/et/265.pdf (accessed June 27, 2024).

Springer. 2020. "Are Any of Your Titles Available in Other Languages?" September 29, 2020. https://support.springer.com/en/support/solutions/articles/6000219817-are-any-of-your-titles-available-in-other-languages (accessed June 27, 2024).

Springer Nature Limited. 2024. "Authorship: Inclusion & Ethics in Global Research." Nature Portfolio. https://www.nature.com/nature-portfolio/editorial-policies/authorship#authorship-inclusion-and-ethics-in-global-research (accessed June 28, 2024).

Squires, Kirsty, Thomas Booth, and Charlotte A. Roberts. 2019. "The Ethics of Sampling Human Skeletal Remains for Destructive Analyses." In *Ethical Approaches to Human Remains: A Global Challenge in Bioarchaeology and Forensic Anthropology,* edited by Kirsty Squires, David Errickson, and Nicholas Márquez-Grant, 265–297. New York: Springer.

Squires, Kirsty, Charlotte A. Roberts, Marina L. Sardi, and Nicholas Márquez-Grant. 2022. "Ética, Bioarqueología y Publicaciones Científicas." *Runa* 43(2): 245–263.

Strecker, Amy. 2017. "Indigenous Land Rights and Caribbean Reparations Discourse." *Leiden Journal of International Law* 30(3): 629–646.

Tsosie, Krystal S., Rene L. Begay, Keolu Fox, and Nanibaa Garrison. 2020. "Generations of Genomes: Advances in Paleogenomics Technology and Engagement for Indigenous People of the Americas." *Current Opinion in Genetics and Development* 62: 91–96.

United Nations Educational, Scientific and Cultural Organization (UNESCO). 2023. "UNESCO Database of National Cultural Heritage Laws Updated." https://www.unesco.org/en/articles/unesco-database-national-cultural-heritage-laws-updated (accessed June 27, 2024).

Van Stipriaan, Alex, Luc Alofs, and Francio Guadeloupe. 2023. *Caribbean Cultural Heritage and the Nation: Aruba, Bonaire and Curaçao in a Regional Context.* Leiden: Leiden University Press.

Wagner, Jennifer. K., Chip Colwell, Kathrina G. Claw, Anne C. Stone, Deborah A. Bolnick, John Hawks, Kyle B. Brothers, and Nanibaa A. Garrison. 2020. "Fostering Responsible Research on Ancient DNA." *American Journal of Human Genetics* 107(2): 183–195.

Yáñez, Bernardo, Agustín Fuentes, Constanza P. Silva, Gonzalo Figueiro, Lumila P. Menéndez, Vivette García-Deister, Constanza de la Fuente-Castro, Columba González-Duarte, Camila Tamburrini, and Juan Manuel Argüelles. 2022. "Pace and Space in the Practice of aDNA Research: Concerns from the Periphery." *American Journal of Biological Anthropology* 180(3): 417–422.

6

Considering the Journey toward Equitable Bioarchaeological Research Practices

An Example in the South Atlantic

ANDREANA S. CUNNINGHAM

Although the colonial legacies of archaeology, and particularly bioarchaeology, have long been critiqued by some scholars, the topic has gained mainstream significance in more recent discourses (Blakey 2020; Flewellen et al. 2021; Franklin et al. 2020; Fricke and Hoerman 2022; Mills and Kawelu 2013). These critiques have demonstrated that when archaeologists fail to challenge the power dynamics and presumed roles of researcher and community, their work espouses inequitable research programs that can actively harm cultural heritage and living communities. And as Fricke and Hoerman (2022) argue, some of these power dynamics can be heavily magnified in island spaces. They argue that some of these core issues in archaeology in island spaces include the positioning of islands as frontiers where an archaeologist can thrive as a dominant force in a "small pond," local epistemic erasure/ displacement, and overall lack of transparency (Fricke and Hoerman 2022: 485–486). To combat these pervasive ideas, the lens of archipelagic studies as conceptualized by Roberts and Stephens (2013, 2017) offers an important shift that reframes the complexity and roots of islands. Namely, the notion of islands as archipelagic frames island experiences as connected, complex, and dynamic ones.

Part of the unjust archaeological engagements in island spaces is likely rooted in the predominant framing of islands in the Western imagination. In this framing, islands are a paradise to escape to, and are also largely interchangeable with one another (i.e., are synonymous with a vaguely "exotic" culture). In this framing, islanders become static recipients in this cycle of paradise-seeking, positioned as "needing" touristic generosity (Nwankwo 2017: 392). This dynamic ultimately reifies ideas that islanders are not agents of their own cultural and economic production (Roberts and Stephens 2017). In contrast, an archipelagic approach envisions islands as archipelagic chains linked by both land and sea, through which they are connected to one another by their overlapping migration histories, geographic or geological positioning, and cultural formation. And while islands are clearly connected and mutually shape one another, each island is a distinct unit. Archipelagic thinking also decenters the importance of continents (which envision islands as isolated peripheries of large landmasses), in favor of the linked land and sea being considered as sites of uncharted possibilities (Roberts and Stephens 2017; Hauʻofa 1993). Through this lens, islands can be a vector for unique biosocial negotiations and connecting island worlds. In this vein, I introduce a case study discussing evolving stakeholder dynamics in the British overseas territory of St. Helena.[1] Although St. Helena is not a Caribbean island, many of the same dynamics described above ring true for St. Helena, and placing it in conversation with the Caribbean can expand notions of what identity and cultural production can look like in island spaces. In this chapter, I discuss St. Helena as it relates to fraught claims to cultural heritage and the impact of researchers as sources of harm or repair, and I conclude by forwarding archipelagic thinking as a productive framing for the island's future.

St. Helena as an "Isolated" Island

St. Helena is a mountainous British overseas territory located in the South Atlantic Ocean. St. Helena's historical significance lay in its geographical position at the center of several currents in the South Atlantic, which made it an ideal location for cargo and slave ships making Atlantic journeys to replenish their supplies (Pearson et al. 2011; Pearson 2016). Thus, it became an important site during the slave trade as both a provisioning source for these ships, and as a direct supporter of the slave trade as enslavement on the island increased. The modern population of St. Helena thus descends from a series of voluntary, forced, and military-led migrations to the island. Namely, the English settlers, enslaved Africans and South Asians, and South and East Asian indentured laborers who historically migrated to the island have produced the island's culturally and biologically diverse population (Encyclopedia Britannica 2022; Gosse 1938; Kitching 1937).

With a population of 4,388 as of January 2024, and the island itself being 703 miles from the nearest land, the notion of "isolation" is commonly used to frame St. Helena (St. Helena Government 2023; Gosse 1938). It remains a difficult tourist destination to access, as the airport (active since 2017) has limited flight schedules. The island's geographic distance from other lands in some ways magnifies the colonial dynamics observed in Caribbean spaces. For example, the notion of the island as an "untouched" escape from modernity is pervasive, and shows up in some of the language of the island's tourism initiatives (Samuels 2018: 8–9). Scholars such as Yon (2007) have resisted the notion of isolation as a key feature of St. Helena, arguing that the island is a key site of convergence between the Atlantic and Indian Ocean worlds, particularly as it relates to the slave trade as well as on-island demography. This centrality produces ongoing acts of "Atlantic cosmopolitanism," in which St. Helenians (locally known as "Saints") make and remake their identities relative to other diasporic communities. One example of this is in descriptions of St. Helenians who lived in apartheid South Africa during the twentieth century, in which they resisted the racial oppression they faced by invoking their "identification with an elsewhere, namely an oceanic world with its openness, its mystic and unknown qualities, its movement with 'the island' at its centre" (Yon 2007: 160). This framing is archipelagic in nature, positioning Saints and the island more broadly as producers and mediators of racial, ethnic, and cultural identity.

These evolving ways that Saints have positioned themselves against the British, other diasporic communities, and distant "elsewheres" also apply to the ways that they have engaged with the island's past, as well as how they want to represent it. This grappling with the past was clearest in the emergence of what is now referred to as the "Liberated African" burial ground in the public consciousness. I outline the way that these discourses unfolded against a landscape of non-Saint archaeologists and other researchers studying the skeletal remains and material culture of the site. I explore the troubling role of the external researcher in this context, and I argue that these dynamics in St. Helena can be a window into more broadly articulating a reframing of archaeological engagement with Caribbean spaces.

The "Liberated African" Burial Ground

In 1809, following the abolition of the British slave trade two years prior, the British Royal Navy established the West Africa Squadron, which was tasked with seizing illegal slave ships across the Atlantic and emancipating the enslaved persons on board (Burroughs 2015). Once emancipated, these formerly enslaved persons were referred to as "Liberated Africans." Despite what his term implies, these Liberated Africans often had little to no power to decide where and when they would permanently settle, and in most cases they were transported to parts of the Caribbean or South America (Jackson 1905; Pearson et al. 2011). Approximately 500–1,000 of the more than 27,000 Liberated Africans brought to the island remained there and integrated into the community (Pearson 2016; St. Helena Island Info, n.d.; Sandoval-Velasco et al. 2019). During this period, St. Helena became a widely used site for temporarily housing and administering medical aid to formerly enslaved Africans before they embarked on their final journeys across the Atlantic (Pearson 2016; Schulenburg 1999). However, St. Helena lacked the infrastructure to adequately support the rapid influx of people who arrived on the island, resulting in high mortality rates among the Liberated Africans. Rupert's Valley, St. Helena, is the site of approximately 8,000 of their burials.

The British Department for International Development funded archaeological investigations of the burial ground in 2007–2008, following proposals to construct an airport on the island and ensuing environmental studies (Pearson et al. 2011). The excavation yielded the skeletal remains of 325 decedents, along with artifacts and organic material (e.g., nails, hair). After more than a decade of research, debates, and stalled progress related to the burials, the excavated materials from the site were reburied in Rupert's Valley in coffins in August 2022 with a community-led commemoration ceremony. Leading up to the reburial in 2022, the site elicited passionate responses from the Saint community, researchers, and other advocates. Among these responses were critiques levied against the St. Helenian government about the lack of support and action for reburying decedents. Although an exhaustive analysis of all stakeholders and dialogues surrounding this site is beyond the scope of this chapter, I pull out some key discourses that impacted perceptions of the site, particularly as it related to defining who this cultural heritage "belonged" to and who should speak for it. I outline three parties who loosely qualify as stakeholders, in the sense that they "have an interest in, are affected by, and have a contribution to make to an issue" (Bauer-Clapp 2016: 11): Saints, prominent non-Saint Black advocates, and researchers. Further, given that external parties have the capacity to exacerbate harm or reify colonial dynamics, I explore the roles archaeologists should have in forming and preserving heritage in ethically sound ways.

The Problem of Stakeholders

There are two key issues to consider in situating islanders' responses to the excavations at Rupert's Valley in 2008: racial formation and economic constraints. For identifications of race and nationality on the island, the existing Saint population is a combination of several ancestries, and off-island most Saints would be categorized as "non-white." However, Saints mainly forgo identifications with explicit racial categories in favor of a forged Saint identity. Further, as a result of their colonial history and influences, Saints often identify as British, which Yon (2007: 158) argues that some Saints have historically invoked as a means of resisting racialized othering they experienced overseas. Unfolding alongside these identity claims are economic ones; St. Helena relies heavily on recurrent subsidy from the United Kingdom, most recently reported as funding 60 percent–70 percent of the budget in St. Helena (Loft and Brien 2023). This reliance on UK financial aid is due in part to the island's location (well outside of the sphere of tourist-heavy circuits in the Caribbean), as well as its narrow economy and high proportion of imported goods. Even with these subsidies, Saints still grapple with the challenges of limited educational and career opportunities and growth (UK Government 2023). These factors clashed amid the excavations of Rupert's Valley, particularly in the ways that Saints identified with and took a vested interest in the site.

The excavation was funded by the British government and led by British archaeologists, with Andrew Pearson serving as the project director and Ben Jeffs as codirector. While the site was undergoing excavation, some Saints felt connected to the people buried there early on. These sentiments came across in interviews conducted by Heidi Bauer-Clapp, a then University of Massachusetts Amherst doctoral student studying heritage development, as these dialogues about Rupert's Valley unfolded. One Saint respondent in her interviews cautioned archaeologists at the site to "be careful, [because] these are my people" (Bauer-Clapp 2016: 105). Similarly, other Saints described themselves as direct or symbolic descendants of the Liberated Africans: "We are descended from these people, some of us, even if we don't think about it. These people were treated horribly and we need to make these things known" (Bauer-Clapp 2016: 110). But other islanders, while seeing the site as a sobering one, did not necessarily consider Rupert's Valley to be the site of their ancestors. Different still, some Saints did not identify as descendants of the site but still advocated for respectful treatment of the burials and expedient reburial. This problem of identification was apparent to Andrew Pearson, who remarked on an atmosphere of avoidance around the topic of slavery and enslaved ancestry on the island. It is a topic that is clearly understood by Saints to be part of their history, but at the time of the excavation there seemed to be a discomfort, particularly from elders, in speaking about their enslaved ancestors openly (Pearson and Jeffs 2016: 102). The heavily religious (mainly Christian) culture on the island may have also informed Saints' ties to the excavation, as the excavation team learned that many residents believed the dead should never be disturbed, and that doing so would have consequences. For example, some Saints associated the excavation team with haunting or bad luck, and others deliberately avoided the excavation site altogether (Pearson and Jeffs 2016: 108).

These differences in identification with the site all held impacts for both the level of urgency in which decision-making occurred and for conceptions of what comprised a "respectful" burial. The results of a compiled survey of islanders' suggested outcomes for the Rupert's Valley human remains and associated material culture determined that approximately 65 percent of the respondents favored a permanent reburial, with the rest favoring construction of an ossuary that could accommodate future access. And even among those favoring reburial, there was disagreement around the reburial location, as well as whether further research should be permitted prior to the reburial (Bauer-Clapp 2016: 116–117).

The additional layer of complication to these considerations of respect and identity was the notion of cultural heritage posing a conflict to the use and growth of the already limited economic resources on the island. For example, discussions around the future of Rupert's Valley unfolded contemporaneously with the construction of the island's airport, which was seen as a necessity to increase opportunities and quality of life on the island. Similarly, the limited funds available from UK subsidies could be used to maintain and strengthen education, housing, and medical infrastructure on the island. A recent instance of the gravity of this issue was in community discussions about medical malpractice and ineffective healthcare at the island: "It got to the point that most people neglect pains and illness because the waiting list to see an appropriate professional takes too long. . . . The elderly simply say they are getting old . . . modern medicine and treatment could afford us all a better life" (Castell 2023).[2] Although this quote occurred long after the reburial, it is emblematic of a problem that Saints have been navigating for years, and it also captures the idea that improving social infrastructure is seen as a priority by the Saint community. While this pursuit is not necessarily contradictory with aims of cultural heritage preservation, the idea of significant funds being diverted from livelihoods to fund the reburial may have been unpalatable to some in this atmosphere. Bauer-Clapp described this response as an indifference rooted in feelings that they had "bigger things to worry about" (Bauer-Clapp 2016: 137). And, like the differing degrees of identification with Rupert's Valley, this inadvertent perception of conflict between investments in the living and dead held significant impacts for the degree of urgency the Rupert's Valley decedents were treated with.

With these complex factors all unfolding in St. Helena in the years following the excavation, it is apparent that Saints were no monolith in their associations with the site. The complex racial formation on the island had a role in shaping these degrees of association with the site. This aspect is interesting when placed in comparison to the roles of non-Saint advocates of the Rupert's Valley site. A significant force of advocacy for the site emerged early on from a Namibian resident on St. Helena, Annina van Neel, who explicitly held a Black identity and mobilized action around the site. Her unequivocal claim of a Black heritage is significant, as it is a connection shared by many Afro-descendants who see themselves and their ancestors in diasporic heritage sites, even if they do not have a direct attachment to them (Agbe-Davies 2010; Blakey 2022; Fleskes et al. 2023; Flewellen et al. 2022). Although it was clear that some Saints shared her sentiment of urgent protection of the site, she remarked on setbacks and slow movement to gain momentum on commemorating the burials (Curran and de Vere 2022). Other non-local Black-identifying advocates such as Peggy King Jorde have sought to build a community around the site's advocacy, and during discussions around the site's future offered recommendations in line with other significant diasporic projects (e.g., the New York African Burial Ground). As King Jorde wrote in a response to the reburial at Rupert's Valley in August 2022: "There can be no rest until the thousands buried in Rupert's and Lemon Valleys are properly honored and memorialized with the utmost respect . . . and until the diaspora of descendants of the enslaved are held as meaningful participants and leaders in remembrance on St. Helena" (King Jorde 2022).

This sentiment draws a clear link between the decedents at Rupert's Valley and Afro-descendants across the diaspora. Further, as this quote frames this as an unmet goal, it seems to suggest that the people who should be empowered to have a meaningful claim to this site are beyond the borders of St. Helena. This claim (that Afro-descendants off-island should be decision-makers for this diasporic space) can be considered a mode of calling on the forms of racial stratification that figures clearly in prominent diasporic spaces (e.g., the United States, the Caribbean, Brazil). In those spaces, the notion of Blackness emerges as not only a tool of racialization and oppression, but also a tool of subversive Black mobility and community building. Thus, identifying with Blackness (and seeing the victims of forced displacement and generational enslavement as ancestors to venerate) is vital in building diasporic community, in which Afro-descendants can foster connections across borders (Tsagarousianou 2017). More recently, van Neel and King Jorde have advocated for transporting the ancestors at Rupert's Valley to the African continent as a means of restitution, which seems to further highlight their framing of which stakeholders should be empowered to determine the future of the site (Siddique 2024).

It is possible that quotes like King Jorde's suggest that St. Helenians' claims to the site are more tenuous, due to both the community's earlier relationship with the site's commemoration and the distance that many Saints hold from Black identity. However, despite the complicated identifications Saints have had toward the site, they ultimately conducted a community-led effort to construct coffins on the island, oversee meticulous placement of all skeletal remains into these coffins, and organize a commemorative reburial ceremony with community reflections, song, and placing flowers on the reburial site. The reburial in 2022 represents the culmination of all the abovementioned stakeholders' voices over the past decade, which saw the formation of the Liberated African Advisory Council and the creation of the Trans-Atlantic Slave Memorial Master Plan. The latter provided key guidelines for reburial (e.g., feasible location, recordkeeping, future commemoration plans) (St. Helena National Trust 2020). Further, while many Saints may not share direct ancestry with the ancestors of Rupert's Valley, their lands and histories are intertwined with the Liberated Africans, and they live and die in the same grounds. These geographies of St. Helena have given life and transformation to many phases of migration, and Saints' direct ancestors were racialized and subject to British enslavement and colonialism in many of the same ways that are present in majority Afro-descendant enslavement spaces. At least one Saint, Elsie Hughes, has traced archival records and confirmed a direct ancestral connection to the Liberated African community, which further confirms the enmeshment of living Saints with this historic community. At the reburial ceremony, Elsie made a speech that reflected on this sentiment: "As one of 11 children, we were all made aware by my parents and grandmother that we were descended from the Rupert's Bay slaves. . . . I like to think that the little of them I have within me now has given me their strength, their courage, and made me who I am today. May they rest in peace and be remembered always" (History Reclaimed 2023).

While the work that has been done by Saints, van Neel, King Jorde, and other advocates is unfinished, the collective effort in recent years by the Saint community toward reburial and identification signals a clear change and perception of responsibility on the part of Saints. Notably, during my own research in St. Helena in the summer of 2022, I spoke to a Saint who referenced the decedents at Rupert's Valley as "*our* ancestors, after all." It is likely that the increasing exposure to the site and ongoing advocacy for the site influenced the growing attachment Saints had to the site. But it is also true that Saints have been members of the diaspora from the beginning, giving them a clear stake in how slave trade heritage sites are interpreted and commemorated, especially the ones they live among.

The Fraught Role of Researchers

As described at the start of this chapter, archaeological projects (especially when carried out by non-native researchers) have the capacity to create harm for both local communities and cultural heritage. Examples of this may look like extractive research that does not benefit communities, lack of transparency, or discrediting local knowledge and collaboration. In considering the complicated stakeholder dynamics described in the previous section, these dialogues all unfolded along a backdrop of research projects at Rupert's Valley. I will highlight some of the research projects that involved direct contact with the decedents buried at Rupert's Valley to assess success in these endeavors, culminating in my own research on the island in 2022.

The original excavation team, led by Andrew Pearson, did some level of community engagement during the excavation, such as regular informal contact in public spaces, public talks, and consultations with the St. Helena government, the local expatriate community, and Saints invested in the island's history (Pearson and Jeffs 2016). They also held an "Open Day" that invited members of the public to view the excavation site and ask questions, which approximately 400 people attended (Bauer-Clapp 2016: 71; Pearson and Jeffs 2016). Pearson related problems of effective community engagement in the early years of the project to the lack of a clear descendant community to consult with on the island, borne of uncertainties among Saints about who should guide these processes. This posed problems for the team regarding who they should "answer to" and take guidance from. However, this does not mean the original excavation proceeded without critique. Advocates such as King Jorde have critiqued initiatives such as the temporary export of material culture from Rupert's Valley to the International Slavery Museum in Liverpool for an exhibit in 2014–2015 (King Jorde 2022). Further, some Saints opposed the excavation on the grounds that the burials should be left undisturbed. But because the excavation was done to remove burials from paths of future construction, as opposed to being a product of mere archaeological research interest, it seems that Saints (if uneasily) saw the project as valuable (Pearson and Jeffs 2016: 106).

Since the original excavation at Rupert's Valley, which yielded insight about the demography, patterns of health, and material culture associated with the burials of the "Liberated Africans," there have been many other researchers who have worked with the site and had varying levels of engagement with the community (Bauer-Clapp 2016; MacQuarrie and Pearson 2016; Pearson et al. 2011; Wesp and Sandoval-Velasco 2020). One prominent research initiative was EUROTAST, hosted by the Marie Curie Initial Training Network, which funded slave trade–related research at European universities. Three PhD students (Erna Jóhannesdóttir and Judy Watson of the University of Bristol, and Marcela Sandoval-Velasco of the University of Copenhagen) conducted research with the decedents of Rupert's Valley, doing dental modification, isotope, and aDNA analyses, respectively. The community engagement for the EUROTAST projects was limited. However, the researchers held a webinar open to the St. Helena community upon the project's completion to their share findings. Additionally, a Saint stakeholder and director of the island's National Trust, Helena Bennett, was included as a coauthor on a recent publication about the aDNA project (St. Helena Government 2020; Sandoval-Velasco et al. 2023). An impactful dissertation project was conducted by Heidi Bauer-Clapp (first introduced in the previous section), her on-island research spanning July 2013–May 2015. Notably, her study did not involve direct study of the skeletal remains at the site, but instead studied the decision-making process that shaped heritage development around St. Helena's "Liberated Africans" (Bauer-Clapp 2016: 78). Prior to my own project, the most recent work done at Rupert's Valley was an ancient/modern DNA study in 2018 by Gretchen Johnson, a PhD candidate at Howard University (Johnson and Jackson 2017; National Geographic 2020).

Looking at these projects collectively, their impacts on the St. Helenian community and the island's cultural heritage are mixed. The work of scholars such as Bauer-Clapp (2016) or Sandoval-Velasco et al. (2023) can be considered largely successful, in the sense that they achieved the outlined goals of their projects and made efforts to feature the perspectives of Saints in their analyses. However, more problematic outcomes have emerged from some other projects conducted at the site. For example, two of the dissertations from these projects have not been shared with St. Helenian stakeholders, nor have they been recoverable from these researchers' degree-granting institutions. And, more troubling, as I witnessed when I assessed the preservation of the skeletal remains from the site, one of these projects sampled significantly more skeletal fragments than needed for their analyses, leading to many parts of decedents being carried off-island. I came to intimately learn about these projects' impacts on Saints as I navigated my own research application and fieldwork on the island.

When I began the process of applying to conduct research at Rupert's Valley in 2018, I was cautioned by the St. Helena Research Council that embarking on this process would be long, and without any guarantee of success. I later came to realize that this caution was in large part due to island stakeholders' deep-seated distrust of outside researchers following some of the abovementioned projects. The lack of transparency and destructive displacement present in some of these projects were a rude awakening for the research oversight committees, prompting them to reinforce their protections of the decedents from further harm. I was encouraged to contact and consult key stakeholders related to Rupert's Valley, and to critically consider how I could leverage my resources and skills to yield tangible impacts to the St. Helenian community. More specifically, my research application, beyond clearly communicating the aims and significance of my research to a broader audience, needed to also describe the details and timeline of community engagement. To accommodate this, I presented preliminary engagement ideas to island stakeholders and advocates for feedback, and structured my grant applications to include support for these aims that received stakeholder approval. This process of consultation and application review took approximately three years, years which I believe were necessary to establish relationships and receive valuable feedback on my project. My research project was approved in February 2022, and I conducted my research project on-island two months later to accommodate the site's reburial schedule (St. Helena Government 2022).

Ultimately, my research and community engagement activities took place in tandem with the reburial process. The approval of my research project was contingent on the agreement that my work would not disrupt the set reburial schedule, and that I would be supervised by and work directly with members of the Liberated African Advisory Committee. I was also expected to be transparent with all stages of my project, to make all data produced from the project accessible to community stakeholders, and to establish a tentative timeline for these tasks. The community benefits I cocreated with St.

Helenian stakeholders (some completed, others in progress) include: sharing all 3D scans, raw data, and ensuing dissertation and publications; mentoring and compensating a student intern, who I instructed in digitization and basic osteology methods; conducting hands-on workshops in biological anthropology at primary and secondary schools; public presentations and interviews; and a collaborative facial approximation project. These efforts are ones that have fundamentally changed the way I approach research, particularly in how I emphasize research transparency, data accessibility, and research formation (i.e., learning what is valued and of interest to communities rather than forming questions and approaches in isolation and bringing them to communities afterward). But most importantly, I have come to embrace that my approaches are evolving, and that is key to continually strengthening ethical approaches.

As much of my work in St. Helena began while I was still a graduate student, I have since critically considered how I can expand the scope of future projects, specifically toward creating sustainable collaborations with the island that decenter myself (a non-Saint researcher). This is especially the case in grappling with how to support meaningful commemoration at Rupert's Valley. Pathways toward this could look like expanding collaborations with the St. Helena National Trust to envision and fund a memorial space to honor Rupert's Valley. It can also look like seeking accountability for the skeletal remains from the site that still exist beyond the island's borders, which is a problem that prevents restitution and continues to fuel mistrust of scientists. I mention these possibilities to underscore the fact that my own understanding of ethics is still undergoing change and exploration, both of which are crucial for identifying systems that work for a particular community.

Conclusion

As introduced at the start of this chapter, St. Helena is not a Caribbean island. However, St. Helena's process and challenges with heritage preservation echo many of the issues that emerge in the Caribbean, most clearly in the issues of lacking data transparency and accountability in some of the projects conducted with the ancestors of Rupert's Valley. Another feature St. Helena shares with the Caribbean is the problem of defining stakeholders, particularly in how conflict among stakeholders can muddle paths forward. As observed in the St. Helena case, the lack of a "built in" descendant community meant that a symbolic community of care had to be forged rather than consulted, which took time to gain traction and translate into fundamental changes in personal identifications with the site. For researchers to approach island worlds with an ethically grounded approach, they must embrace these possible challenges, and critically consider how they are defining, consulting, and (when appropriate) mediating communities.

I conclude by offering a vision of archipelagic thinking that extends to researchers. In my view, a researcher thinking archipelagically:

1. Leverages their proximity to various institutions and other researchers to investigate and bring closure and continued benefit to the communities they serve
2. Frames islands as not remote or isolated, but as places with globalized connections that can and should be regarded with complexity

These principles are not prescriptive, nor are they exhaustive. I include them as a means of prompting reflection on the way that archaeologists understand, define, and implement ethical approaches into their work.

Acknowledgments

Thank you to the St. Helena National Trust, St. Helena Government, and the Liberated African Advisory Committee for facilitating and supporting my research on island and for our continued dialogues. Thank you also to Delande Justinvil, whose insight inspired the archipelagic foundation of this chapter.

Notes

1 The island's name typically appears as "St Helena" in island-circulated formal and informal print. In this chapter, "Saint" has been abbreviated in accordance with American English style: St. Helena.
2 I quote comments to Facebook posts in this piece to reference a thriving and active mode of communication that St. Helenians use to stay connected. Given that there are many Saints who live off-island, Facebook groups like "St. Helena News" continue to be a source of news and dialogue.

References Cited

Agbe-Davies, Anna S. 2010. "Concepts of Community in the Pursuit of an Inclusive Archaeology." *International Journal of Heritage Studies* 16(6): 373–389.

Bauer-Clapp, Heidi J. 2016. "A Conflict of Interest? Negotiating Agendas, Ethics, and Consequences Regarding the Heritage Value of Human Remains." PhD dissertation, University of Massachusetts.

Blakey, Michael L. 2020. "Archaeology under the Blinding Light of Race." *Current Anthropology* 61(S22): S183–S197.

Blakey, Michael L. 2022. "Walking the Ancestors Home: On the Road to an Ethical Human Biology." *Anthropology Now* 14(1–2): 1–20.

Burroughs, Robert. 2015. "Suppression of the Atlantic Slave Trade: Abolition from Ship to Shore." In *The Suppression of the Atlantic Slave Trade: British Policies, Practices and Representation of Naval Coercion,* edited by Robert Burroughs and Richard Huzzey, 1–14. Manchester: Manchester University Press.

Castell, Christian. 2023. "Dr. Soto's Departure Sparks Questions about Professional Standards." Saint Helena Island News Facebook group. https://www.facebook.com/groups/439261969891154/permalink/1670785156738823/ (accessed June 25, 2024).

Curran, Joseph, and Dominic Aubrey de Vere. 2022. *A Story of Bones.* Documentary. Archer's Mark.

Encyclopedia Britannica. 2022. "Saint Helena." https://www.britannica.com/place/Saint-Helena-island-South-Atlantic-Ocean (accessed June 25, 2024).

Fleskes, Raquel E., Graciela S. Cabana, Joanna K. Gilmore, Chelsey Juarez, Emilee Karcher, La'sheia Oubré, Grant Mishoe, Ade A. Ofunniyin, and Theodore G. Schurr. 2023. "Community-Engaged Ancient DNA Project Reveals Diverse Origins of 18th-Century African Descendants in Charleston, South Carolina." *Proceedings of the National Academy of Sciences of the United States of America* 120(3): e2201620120.

Flewellen, Ayana Omilade, Justin P. Dunnavant, Alicia Odewale, Alexandra Jones, Tsione Wolde-Michael, Zoë Crossland, and Maria Franklin. 2021. "'The Future of Archaeology Is Antiracist': Archaeology in the Time of Black Lives Matter." *American Antiquity* 86(2): 224–243.

Flewellen, Ayana Omilade, Alicia Odewale, Justin Dunnavant, Alexandra Jones, and William White III. 2022. "Creating Community and Engaging Community: The Foundations of the Estate Little Princess Archaeology Project in St. Croix, United States Virgin Islands." *International Journal of Historical Archaeology* 26(1): 147–176.

Franklin, Maria, Justin P. Dunnavant, Anaya Omilade Flewellen, and Alicia Odewale. 2020. "The Future Is Now: Archaeology and the Eradication of Anti-Blackness." *International Journal of Historical Archaeology* 24(4): 753–766.

Fricke, Felicia, and Rachel Hoerman. 2022. "Archaeology and Social Justice in Island Worlds." *World Archaeology* 54(3): 484–489.

Gosse, Philip. 1938. *St. Helena: 1502–1938.* London: Cassell.

Hau'ofa, Epeli. 1993. "Our Sea of Islands." In *A New Oceania: Rediscovering Our Sea of Islands,* edited by Eric Waddell, Vijay Naidu, and Epeli Hau'ofa. School of Social and Economic Development, the University of the South Pacific in association with Beake House, Suva, Fiji.

History Reclaimed. 2023. "The Proudly British Descendants of Slaves Liberated by the Royal Navy." *History Reclaimed,* June 20, 2023. https://historyreclaimed.co.uk/the-proudly-british-descendants-of-slaves-liberated-by-the-royal-navy/ (accessed June 25, 2024).

Jackson, E. L. 1905. *St. Helena: The Historic Island from Its Discovery to the Present Date.* New York: Thomas Whittaker.

Johnson, Gretchen, and Fatimah Jackson. 2017. "Proposal: Reconstruction of Early Population History of Africans in the Americas through St. Helena Island (South Atlantic) and New York City." https://www.sainthelena.gov.sh/wp-content/uploads/2017/09/Appendix-4-Proposal-St-Helena-6-19-17-003.pdf (accessed June 25, 2024).

King Jorde, Peggy. 2022. "An Opportunity to Leave a Comment on the Contribution Board at the Memorial Site." https://www.facebook.com/groups/1210985019283487/permalink/1718786335170017/ (accessed June 25, 2024).

Kitching, G. C. 1937. *A Handbook and Gazetteer of the Island of St. Helena including a Short History of the Island under the Crown, 1834–1902.* St. Helena: G. C. Kitching.

Loft, Philip, and Philip Brien. 2023. "UK Aid and the Overseas Territories." House of Commons Library. https://commonslibrary.parliament.uk/research-briefings/cbp-9758/ (accessed June 25, 2024).

MacQuarrie, Helen, and Andrew Pearson. 2016. "Prize Possessions: Transported Material Culture of the Post-Abolition Enslaved—New Evidence from St. Helena." *Slavery & Abolition* 37(1): 45–72.

Mills, Peter R., and Kawelu, Kathleen L. 2013. "Decolonizing Heritage Management in Hawaiʻi." *Advances in Anthropology* 3(3): 127–132.

National Geographic. 2020. Juneteenth May Be Over, but Explorer Gretchen Johnson Is Moving Forward with a Powerful Mantra. *National Geographic* blog. June 25, 2020. https://news.nationalgeographic.org/juneteenth-may-be-over-but-explorer-gretchen-johnson-is-moving-forward-with-a-powerful-mantra/ (accessed June 25, 2024).

Nwankwo, Ifeoma Kiddoe. 2017. "Living the West Indian Dream: Archipelagic Cosmopolitanism and Triangulated Economies of Desire in Jamaican Popular Culture." In *Archipelagic American Studies,* edited by Brian Russell Roberts and Michelle Ann Stephens, 496. Durham, North Carolina: Duke University Press.

Pearson, Andrew. 2016. *Distant Freedom: St. Helena and the Abolition of the Slave Trade, 1840–1872.* Oxford: Oxford University Press.

Pearson, Andrew, and Ben Jeffs. 2016. "Slave-Trade Archaeology and the Public: The Excavation of a 'Liberated African' Graveyard on St. Helena." In *Archaeologists and the Dead: Mortuary Archaeology in Contemporary Society,* edited by Howard Williams and Melanie Giles, 97–112. Oxford: Oxford University Press.

Pearson, Andrew, Ben Jeffs, Annsofie Witkin, and Helen MacQuarrie. 2011. *Infernal Traffic: Excavation of a Liberated African Graveyard in Rupert's Valley, St. Helena.* Reading, United Kingdom: Council for British Archeology.

St. Helena Government. "2020 EUROTAST Doctoral Training Network." November 18, 2020. https://www.sainthelena.gov.sh/2020/public-announcements/eurotast-doctoral-training-network-26-november-2020/ (accessed June 25, 2024).

St. Helena Government. 2022. "Scientific Research Being Conducted on St. Helena." May 2, 2022. https://www.sainthelena.gov.sh/2022/news/scientific-research-being-conducted-on-st-helena/ (accessed June 25, 2024).

St. Helena Government. 2023. "Population and Demography." https://www.sainthelena.gov.sh/st-helena/statistics/st-helena-in-figures/demography/ (accessed June 25, 2024).

St. Helena Island Info. n.d. "Slavery and the Enslaved: Part of What Makes Us Who We Are." https://sainthelenaisland.info/slaves.htm (accessed April 20, 2024).

St. Helena National Trust. 2020. Trans-Atlantic Slave Memorial—St. Helena: Master Plan. October 2020. https://www.trust.org.sh/wp-content/uploads/2022/06/LAAC -Reburial-and-Memorialisation-Plan-Exco-Approved-Oct-2020.pdf.

Roberts, Brian Russell, and Michelle Ann Stephens. 2013. "Archipelagic American Studies and the Caribbean." *Journal of Transnational American Studies* 5(1).

Roberts, Brian Russell, and Michelle Ann Stephens. 2017. "Archipelagic American Studies: Decontinentalizing the Study of American Culture." In *Archipelagic American Studies,* edited by Brian Russell Roberts and Michelle Ann Stephens. Durham, NC: Duke University Press.

Samuels, Damian. 2018. "Cape-Helena: An Exploration of Nostalgia and Identity through the Cape Town–St. Helena Migration Nexus." https://etd.uwc.ac.za/handle/ 11394/6542 (accessed June 25, 2024).

Sandoval-Velasco, Marcela, Anuradha Jagadeesan, María C. Ávila-Arcos, Shyam Go- palakrishnan, Jazmín Ramos-Madrigal, J. Víctor Moreno-Mayar, Gabriel Renaud, et al. 2019. "The Genetic Origins of Saint Helena's Liberated Africans." *BioRxiv.* https://doi.org/10.1101/787515.

Sandoval-Velasco, Marcela, Anuradha Jagadeesan, Jazmín Ramos-Madrigal, María C. Ávila-Arcos, Cesar A. Fortes-Lima, Judy Watson, Erna Johannesdóttir, et al. 2023. "The Ancestry and Geographical Origins of St. Helena's Liberated Africans." *American Journal of Human Genetics* 110(10): 1825.

Schulenburg, Alexander Hugo. 1999. "Transient Observations: The Textualizing of St. Helena through Five Hundred Years of Colonial Discourse." University of St Andrews. https://research-repository.st-andrews.ac.uk/handle/10023/3419 (accessed June 25, 2024).

Siddique, Haroon. 2024. "St. Helena Urged to Return Remains of 325 Formerly Enslaved People to Africa." *Guardian,* March 27, 2024.

Tsagarousianou, Roza. 2017. "Rethinking the Concept of Diaspora: Mobility, Connectivity and Communication in a Globalised World." *Westminster Papers in Communication and Culture* 1(1).

UK Government. 2023. "UK–St. Helena Development Partnership Summary." https:// www.gov.uk/government/publications/uk-st-helena-development-partnership -summary/uk-st-helena-development-partnership-summary-july-2023 (accessed June 25, 2024).

Wesp, Julie K., Marcela Sandoval-Velasco, and Maraa Avila-Arcos. 2020. "Ethno-Geographic Origins and Genomic Diversity of Afro-Descendants in Colonial Mexico City." *American Journal of Physical Anthropology* 171: 305.

Yon, Daniel A. 2007. "Race-Making/Race-Mixing: St. Helena and the South Atlantic World." *Social Dynamics* 33(2): 144–163.

7

Research Ethics in Caribbean Archaeogenomics

KATHRIN NÄGELE, JADA BENN TORRES,
AND MARIA A. NIEVES-COLÓN

Archaeogenomics as a tool to add a genomic perspective to the reconstruction of the past is now a widely accepted and deployed line of evidence, and has produced a wealth of data, insights, and corroborations (Jones and Bösl 2021; Liu et al. 2021; Llamas, Rada, and Collen 2020; Nägele et al. 2022; Roca-Rada et al. 2020; Willerslev and Meltzer 2021). For the majority of its application, ancient DNA (aDNA) studies were mostly centered around temperate regions, with the highest data generation in Europe. While economic factors and Eurocentric worldviews played an important role in setting this focus, DNA preservation was the most determining factor in the feasibility of studies in tropical and subtropical regions like the Caribbean. However, through the combination of sampling elements with high preservation, laboratory protocols designed to retrieve shorter molecules, targeted enrichment approaches, and plummeting costs in sequencing, tropical and subtropical regions have become a burgeoning area of interest for aDNA studies.

One commonality of these regions, beyond poor preservation conditions for DNA, is the impact of European colonialism. Throughout the Caribbean, almost all island nations and associated territories have experienced, and partly continue to experience, some form of colonial occupation and influence (Albert, O'Brien, and Wheatle 2020). As a result of hegemonic colonial and postcolonial agendas, the broader ethical frameworks applied to aDNA work have not always been attentive to the needs and desires of descendants or local communities. Consequently, there have been recent lively discussions around ethical considerations for how aDNA research aligns (or not) with cultural heritage, the treatment of Ancestors[1] (Fox and Hawks 2019; Sirak and Sedig 2019; de Tienda Palop and Currás 2019), inclusion of local scholars, living communities, and Indigenous perspectives (Ávila-Arcos et al. 2022; Kowal et al. 2023; Tsosie, Fox, and Yracheta 2021; Wagner et al. 2020; Gibbon, Thomson, and Alves, 2024). These considerations are also broadly applicable to the Caribbean.

As highlighted in this chapter, Caribbean archaeogenomic research is not straightforward because the Caribbean is a political mosaic, with each island nation or territory having various forms of sovereignty and self-governance. While some island nations have been independent for centuries, others continue to be under colonial influence or even rule. These circumstances have also led to a great variation in the protection of national heritage. Some countries have cultural heritage legislation, while others have no such laws. Some Caribbean islands have recognized Indigenous groups; other island communities do not formally acknowledge any contemporary residents as autochthonous to the Caribbean. As a result, there can be no "one-size-fits-all" solution when conducting aDNA research in the Caribbean. Instead, we contend that researchers need a deep understanding of the political situation, demography, and societal dynamics at play to adequately navigate local sensitivities and concerns on each individual island. Similar considerations should be made when working with communities that may not self-identify as Indigenous, but also have long-term ties to the region and are deeply affected by colonial impacts, such as Afro-descendant and Maroon communities (Benn Torres, Stone, and Kittles 2013; Finneran and Welch 2019; St. Eustatius Afrikan Burial Ground Alliance 2024).

While some scholars have proposed and critiqued globally applicable ethical approaches to aDNA (Alpaslan-Roodenberg et al. 2021; Kowal et al. 2023), it should be the most basic consensus that researchers need to be knowledgeable of the relevant laws and regulations in the regions in which they intend to work. However, when colonial structures dictate the laws or lead to a lack thereof, this simple goal might not be achievable, and abiding by the laws applying to a certain nation or territory might not necessarily equate to an ethical research approach. In addition to the varying political circumstances that impact archaeogenomic research, whether intended or not, aDNA research can impact local identities, and be (mis)used in political agendas and discussions about land rights (Gannon 2019). To minimize adverse outcomes and/or experiences for descendant communities and other interested parties, aDNA researchers must also consider who benefits from an understanding of genetic signals of past societies. Are such studies just scholarly endeavors in a Western scientific method, or can they serve a broader meaning or purpose for living communities?

In response to these complexities, in this chapter we outline how colonial legacies have shaped and continue to shape the ways in which researchers engage in Caribbean archaeogenetics. Additionally, we discuss ethical aspects surrounding the destructive sampling of cultural heritage and contribute to the discussion around the curation of the data produced through archaeogenomic methods. Relying on community engagement principles derived from public health fields as well as the concept of intersectionality drawn from Black feminist scholarship, we offer alternative perspectives for engaging in ethical research within Caribbean contexts. We conclude that ultimately, conducting ethical archaeogenomic research requires forethought, intentionality, and mindfulness of the broader historical and political circumstances as it applies to the research question as well as the potential impacts for descendant communities and other implicated parties.

In writing this piece we acknowledge our positionality as researchers primarily trained in genetics, archaeogenomics, and biological anthropology within the Western scientific tradition. Consequently, we recognize and grapple with our privileges as scientists affiliated with academic and research institutions in the Global North. Because of our varying connections to the ancient and modern peoples of the Caribbean, we see value in bringing our disparate identities and experiences together to encourage a holistic conversation about conducting ethical anthropological genetic research.

Colonialism, History, and Science in the Caribbean

The Caribbean has a long and complex history of extractive colonialism. Starting in the fifteenth century, invasion and conquest, the establishment of mercantilist trade networks, and the institutionalization of forced and racialized labor systems catalyzed the large-scale extraction of wealth and resources in the service of European imperial power (Galeano 1971; Rogoziński 1999). The colonial experience shaped the development of scientific research in the Caribbean. For example, as detailed in Jim Downs's (2021) book *Maladies of Empire,* public health population-based disciplines like epidemiology grew into their characteristic reliance on large-scale data as a result of physicians' and military leaders' collection of health and hygiene information from enslaved persons, soldiers, and other communities implicated in settler-colonial expansion. These data were later used to understand the relationships between environment and disease as well as disease processes. Moreover, colonial goals, mentalities, and infrastructures often dictated who was able to conduct research, guided which questions were asked, and influenced how they were addressed (Curet 2011; McClellan III 2010; Mohammed et al. 2022; Rivera-Collazo 2011b; Sued-Badillo 1992). This legacy is especially notable in the study and management of cultural heritage and deserves consideration in Caribbean archaeogenomics research.

Colonial Narratives and Caribbean Peoples

Historical narratives about Caribbean islanders are strongly influenced by colonial biases and perspectives. The written accounts of early chroniclers, including explorers, missionaries, and colonial officials, molded the perceptions of Indigenous Caribbean peoples that linger into the present day among both academics and the public (Pagán-Jiménez 2004; Reid 2009). These descriptions were often permeated by Western ideas of racial hierarchy and motivated by the goals of the colonizing project (Curet 2014; Grunberg 2011; Rivera-Pagán 2003; Ulloa Hong 2016). For example, the term "Taíno" first appears in the writings of early chroniclers defined as an adjective meaning "good" or "good person," while the opposing term "Caribe" or "Caniba" appears in reference to peoples described as "man eaters" who engaged in kidnapping raids against the "Taíno" (Curet 2006; Lenik 2012; Whitehead 2011; de la Luz Rodríguez 2010). These dichotomized ethnonyms paved the way for the development of the concept of the "Noble Savage" in the Western imagination (Ellingson 2001) and justified the subjugation and exploitation of Native peoples who did not fit this essentialized archetype (Keegan 1996; Sued-Badillo 2020).

Although there is no evidence that Indigenous Caribbean communities referred to themselves as "Taíno" or "Caribe," the use of these terms in the writings of nineteenth-century scholars and their wide-scale adoption as analytical categories in historiography and anthropology resulted in a homogenized view of precolonial Caribbean cultural diversity (Herrera Malatesta 2022). This simplified perspective collapses an array of diverse communities with a variety of worldviews, subsistence strategies, and social and political systems into two dichotomous and opposing groups primarily defined by their relationship to the colonial enterprise (Curet 2006, 2014; Lenik 2012). Because these groupings are not well supported by emerging archaeological evidence, and they perpetuate a reductive and colonialist lens of Caribbean history, many scholars are deemphasizing their use today (Curet 2014; Keegan and Hofman 2017; Oliver 2009; Rodríguez Ramos 2010; Sued-Badillo 2007; Ulloa Hong 2016). However, the omnipresence of the Taíno versus Caribe dichotomy in educational materials, museum exhibits, and national heritage narratives has popularized these ethnonyms, and their essentialized meanings, among the general public (Berman, Febles, and Gnivecki 2005; Feliciano-Santos 2017; Herrera Malatesta, Aguilar, and Alvarez 2024; Martínez-San Miguel 2011; Rodríguez Ramos and Pagán-Jiménez 2016; Yaremko 2009).

Colonial perspectives also fostered historical narratives about the "extinction" of Indigenous Caribbean peoples and minimized their contributions to broader Caribbean history (Pagán-Jiménez 2004). Early colonial sources describe the rapid disappearance of Indigenous communities due to disease, overwork, and conflict in the first decades after European contact (Anderson-Córdova 2017). These ideas were later extrapolated and perpetuated in historical and archaeological scholarship and eventually became institutionalized in Caribbean historical memory, especially in the Greater Antilles (Benn Torres 2014; Laguer Díaz 2013; Ulloa Hong 2016). The extinction narrative ignores the complex and diverse ways in which Indigenous Caribbean communities reacted to, resisted, and were transformed by colonization (Pešoutová 2019). For instance, documentary and archaeological evidence suggests that small Indigenous communities persisted in rural areas of the Greater Antilles until well after the sixteenth century (Anderson-Córdova 2017; Valcárcel Rojas 2016). In some islands, Indigenous peoples, along with self-liberated Africans and Afro-descendants, engaged in marronage and actively resisted colonial encroachment well into the nineteenth century (Beckles 1992; Fuller and Benn Torres 2018; Schwaller 2018). Today, Indigenous and Maroon descendant communities of these groups exist all across the Caribbean. Moreover, many islanders carry Indigenous genetic ancestries (Benn Torres et al. 2019; Madrilejo, Lombard, and Benn Torres 2015; Moreno-Estrada et al. 2013; Schurr et al. 2016; Winful et al. 2023), some of which have been traced to precontact Caribbean communities through aDNA (Fernandes et al. 2020; Forbes-Pateman et al. 2022; Nieves-Colón et al. 2020).

The extinction narrative also minimizes the impact of Indigenous communities on island ecological landscapes, perpetuating the "pristine myth" of the Americas as a "virgin wilderness" (Denevan 1992; Mohammed et al. 2022). There is extensive archaeological evidence that Indigenous peoples shaped the ecological diversity of the Caribbean prior to European arrival and continued to do so after European colonization (Kemp et al. 2020; LeFebvre, Giovas, and Laffoon 2019; Rivera-Collazo 2011a). Traditional knowledge systems passed down from Indigenous and African ancestors (Le Gall 2012) continue to mediate the relationship of modern Caribbean peoples with island ecosystems and to inform modern subsistence practices. For instance, Maroon communities in Jamaica draw upon Indigenous and African knowledge of medicinal plants and hillside farming (Connell 2020; Picking and Vandebroek 2019). In the Greater Antilles, agricultural techniques recorded in the precontact archaeological record such as *conuco* farming, cassava cultivation and preparation, and guinea pig husbandry are still in use today (Rodríguez Ramos and Pagán-Jiménez 2016). As demonstrated by these findings, Indigenous communities did not "vanish without a trace" or become marginal to Caribbean history. Instead, they continued to be active participants in island societies, influencing the creolization process, and leaving an important biocultural legacy for present-day island communities. For this reason, scholars of the Caribbean past, including archaeogenomicists, must exercise caution not to perpetuate the extinction narrative by uncritically adopting, or privileging, colonial perspectives when drawing interpretations about the legacies of pre- and post-contact Indigenous Caribbean societies. For instance, while Western scientific research relies on measurable data, such as the percentage of genetic ancestry, ancestral ties may go much deeper than just the genetic segments inherited from an ancestor. Because for some, genetic continuity would be a measure of the connection to the past and proof of Indigenous survival, the lack of a specific genetic ancestry is not proof of a disruption (or extinction) of the ancestral community. In other words, an individual's ties to a community can be understood as more than only biological (genetic); rather, people may ascribe to cultural, spiritual, and other ways of belonging. Consequently, connecting to a community cannot be only measured in genetic continuity, but cultural and identity continuity also need to be considered.

Legacies of Extractive and Imperial Science

During the colonial period, spaces such as the Caribbean were seen by imperial scientists as exotic, distant, and peripheral—places useful for making observations, collecting specimens, and testing novel research methodologies. For naturalists and collectors, the infrastructure of colonial extraction could be leveraged in service of these research goals (Craciun and Terrall 2019; Cummins, Farmer, and Russell 2013; McClellan III 2010). For example, in the eighteenth century, the largest natural history collection in London was put together by leveraging the networks of the transatlantic slave trade, requesting specimens from slave ship surgeons or captains, and exploiting enslaved peoples as collectors in colonized territories. As described by historian Kathleen Murphy (2013: 648): "In 1716, the naturalist requested . . . 'lend my flycatchers to some of your blacks whilst your on the Island' [of Jamaica] 'to take & kill whatever butterflies & Moths they meet.'" This collection eventually became part of the Natural History Museum of London, where it is still used in active research (Trustees of the Natural History Museum n.d.). This example highlights the importance of the colonial enterprise and enslaved labor for the development of European scientific capabilities and the legacy of extractivism placed on colonized spaces such as the Caribbean (Kean 2019).

Just as the growth of natural history in the eighteenth and nineteenth centuries was made possible by the networks and power structures of European colonization, the growth of Caribbean anthropology and archaeology corresponded with US expansionism toward the region in the late nineteenth and early twentieth century (Armstrong and Hauser 2009; Berman, Febles, and Gnivecki 2005; Dacal Moure and Watters 2005; Rivera-Collazo 2011b; Siegel 2013). After the Spanish-American War, the United States acquired Cuba, Puerto Rico, and the Philippines as colonial possessions (Rogoziński 1999). The incorporation of these territories and the expansion of American interests abroad opened novel research opportunities for US scholars (Baatz 1996). Many of these scientific efforts were shaped by American imperial interests and reproduced contemporary Western views about racial inferiority, exoticism, and "otherness" (Berman, Febles, and Gnivecki 2005; Curet 2011; Rivera-Collazo 2011b). For example, a 1912 scientific survey of Puerto Rico including archaeological studies was proposed to the New York Academy of Sciences. As described by historian Simon Baatz (1996: 4), the proposal was successful because it "dovetailed nicely with the rhetoric used to justify the annexation of the island, namely, to spread North American values to supposedly less enlightened areas of the Americas."

Although archaeological research had been conducted in the Caribbean by both local and foreign scholars for decades, US and European researchers working in the region from the late nineteenth to the early twentieth century developed the intellectual scaffolding that became the backbone of modern Caribbean archaeology (Berman, Febles, and Gnivecki 2005; Curet 2011; Dacal Moure and Watters 2005; Haviser and Hofman 2015; Rostain 2007; Siegel 2013; Ulloa Hong 2016). These ideas and frameworks had a long-lasting impact on the study of the Caribbean past, defining the tendencies and approaches that dominated the field until the late twentieth century. Some of these ideas—such as an emphasis on the identification and classification of cultures, and in tracing "waves of migration" to reconstruct the settlement of the archipelago (Rouse 1992; 1987)—still influence the field today. Additionally, many of the cultural categories and ethnic identifiers still used in Caribbean archaeology and anthropology (e.g., Archaic and Ceramic; Saladoid and Ostionoid; Classic and Lucayan Taíno) were defined in the studies conducted by American scholars between the early and mid-twentieth century (Curet 2011; Keegan and Hofman 2017). These ethnonyms and intellectual frameworks became so ingrained within the study of Caribbean archaeology that they continue to be deployed—often uncritically—by scholars from other fields seeking to frame their interpretations of biological and genetic data (Lalueza-Fox et al. 2001, 2003; Ross et al. 2020) and have also permeated into educational and public discourse (Benn Torres 2014; Curet 2015; Feliciano-Santos 2017; Martínez-San Miguel 2011; Rodriguez Ramos and Pagán-Jiménez 2016). More recent scholarship—especially the research produced by a new generation of Caribbean scholars—has started to move away from these frameworks as it has become evident that they tend to reproduce colonialist and simplistic interpretations of Caribbean precontact history, and there is poor empirical support for some of their central tenets (Dacal Moure and Watters 2005; Pagán-Jiménez and Rodríguez Ramos 2008; Pestle et al. 2013; Rodríguez Ramos 2010; Siegel et al. 2013; Valcárcel Rojas 2016).

Another legacy of the colonial context in which Caribbean archaeology developed is that many archaeological materials and Ancestors' remains have been exported abroad. In a continuation of the collecting and exporting tradition set by early naturalists, the largest collections of Caribbean archaeological and ethnographic materials are found in museums in the United States and Europe (Cummins, Farmer, and Russell 2013; Curet 2018, 2011; Dacal Moure and Watters 2005; DaRos and Colten 2009; Françozo and Strecker 2017). Some of these remains and objects have also made their way to private collections and commercial auction houses (Brito 2021; Zornosa 2021). Although these collections are sometimes available for research, they present important challenges, and their uncritical use may perpetuate colonial biases. For example, historical collections that precede the development of systematic excavation methods are often biased toward objects that are aesthetically pleasing but not necessarily the most informative about ancient lifeways (Curet 2018). Plus, due to the diverse circumstances of their collection and export, the extent and quality of provenience information that accompanies these archaeological materials can vary widely. Consequently, the legality and ethics of the object's ownership or transfer history are often obscure and difficult to trace. This complexity also extends to ancestral human remains, especially as many of them were removed from the islands before the enactment of local heritage legislation (Françozo and Strecker 2017). Whether the remains of human Ancestors are subject to local heritage management guidelines or consulting about structures—especially in the case of destructive aDNA research—can be difficult to ascertain (Ávila-Arcos et al. 2022). Lastly, despite ongoing efforts to digitize museum databases, access to these collections is often difficult for communities in the Caribbean, a barrier that limits the pursuit of novel research questions by Caribbean scholars and reduces engagement by the Caribbean public (Françozo and Strecker 2017). For this reason, scholars of the Caribbean past, including archaeogenomicists, must critically review the history of collections they are working on, and seek consent not only from the museum curators, but also the appropriate institutions in the country or island of origin.

Lessons from the Living for Respectful Work with the Ancestors

Beyond obtaining the appropriate work and export permits, currently, there is little to no ethical oversight for aDNA research involving Ancestors in the Caribbean. This lack of some type of systematic review has not gone unnoticed by scholars (Fleskes et al. 2022; Tamburrini et al. 2023). Undoubt-edly, the development of a broadly applicable ethical framework for aDNA research will be complex and challenging to create and then implement. However, looking at how DNA research with living populations has histori-cally developed, and accompanying advances in bioethics, can potentially be instructive for developing guidelines for aDNA research.

The history of bioethics is often traced to antiquity and highlights how underlying philosophies about research on humans have changed in re-sponse to ethical and moral violations such as those seen in the Tuskegee Syphilis Study and the Jewish Chronic Disease Hospital cancer experiment (McWhirter 2012). More recently, following the 1999 death of gene therapy research participant Jesse Gelsinger, there has been more emphasis on regula-tory oversight and informed consent for research with living people (Rinde 2019). Within the United States, the Department of Health and Human Services (HHS) implemented policies known as the "Common Rule." This federal law set standards for institutional review boards (IRBs)[2] and made explicit regulations surrounding protections for participants involved in research as well as for participants who are members of vulnerable com-munities such as pregnant people, fetuses, children, and prisoners (Protec-tions [OHRP] 2009). Based on previous reports and ethical codes (e.g., the Belmont report, Declaration of Helsinki, and the Nuremberg Code [Emanuel 2008]) the main principles of how participants should be incorporated into research are autonomy, non-maleficence/benevolence, and justice. The ethics surrounding population genetic studies have also changed in response to critique (Harry et al. 2000; Reardon 2011; TallBear 2001). "Helicopter" or "parachute" science, an extractive practice that involves a researcher dropping in to collect samples from a community and then never returning or providing any feedback (Haelewaters, Hofmann, and Romero-Olivares 2021), is no longer generally viewed as an acceptable research approach by anthropologists. Rather, researchers are encouraged to use more community-engaged practices inclusive of identifying and involving descendant communities (Turner, Wagner, and Cabana 2018).

In addition, there is a broader recognition that ethical norms developed within North American contexts are not necessarily applicable nor appropriate in other global settings (Alpaslan-Roodenberg et al. 2021; George et al. 2020; Kowal et al. 2023). As a result, the development and implementation of protocols dictating ethical research have emanated from a variety of impacted communities, such as San communities in South Africa and Māori communities in Aotearoa/New Zealand (Callaway 2017; Chennells and Steenkamp 2018; Tauri 2014). Since at least 1990, clinical researchers have developed research consultation services that are designed to aid researchers across different settings with study design, proposal review, project execution, and advice when ethical dilemmas might arise during and after a study (Beskow et al. 2009). In addition, there are also standalone companies that explicitly provide services related to ethical review of protocols, consent forms, and record-keeping. For researchers involved in international studies, HHS has compiled a list of IRBs or IRB consultation services across the globe that can aid in reviewing research that seeks to involve living people (US Department of Health and Human Services 2010).

For genetic anthropologists, all federal and local institutional regulations are applicable for research involving the collection and use of genetic material from living people. Typically, projects that propose to collect genetic (or any biological) samples from study participants are ineligible for exempt or expedited reviews and, instead, must be reviewed and approved by a fully convened IRB prior to the commencement of the research. These types of reviews usually involve an evaluation of the proposed project's protocol, consent form, and recruitment materials. Once approved, no changes may be made to approved protocols or materials without prior review and authorization from the IRB. In addition, approved projects are subject to, at a minimum, annual continuing reviews. The revised post-2018 regulations no longer require continuing reviews for projects that have moved into data analysis (US Code of Federal Regulations 2024: § 46.109[f][1][iii][A]).

For researchers using genetic/genomic data that are archived in databases or biorepositories (see below), there is a suite of other reviews and practices that dictate data sharing and sample reuse (Knoppers and Joly 2018; Rahimzadeh, Dyke, and Knoppers 2016; Tsosie et al. 2020; Turner and Mulligan 2019). Typically, projects using samples from a biorepository are subject to review by a designated panel in charge of sample stewardship. In addition, there are global consortiums such as the Global Alliance for Genomics and Health or UNESCO's International Bioethics Committee that have weighed in on ethical data usage (Global Alliance for Genomics and Health 2023; International Bioethics Committee 2023). Given the nature of genetic anthropological work that involves data collection from living populations, all investigators are expected to obtain IRB review or equivalent reviews and, increasingly, review and approval from local institutions or the relevant community groups involved in the research. In addition to these types of reviews, some academic journals now require authors to include explicit descriptions of ethical approaches for the peer-review process or included as part of the published manuscript (Kiefer 2022).

In archaeogenomic research, consent for sampling genomic material is also complex, and the IRB protocols used for living human research participants are not completely transferable. Notwithstanding, anthropologists, related scholars, and activists have agitated for explicit ethical research standards surrounding studies of human Ancestors' remains for decades, inclusive of and preceding the development of the Native American Graves Protection and Repatriation Act of 1990 (NAGPRA) (Office of Secretary of the Interior, Department of Interior 1990; Riding In 1996; Trope and Echo-Hawk 1992; Ubelaker and Guttenplan Grant 1989). Many scholars and community activists contributed to debates on best practices for studying Ancestors throughout the turn of the twenty-first century. However, the controversy within North America was reignited in 2021 through an online course by a Princeton University professor. In her course, the professor displayed the remains of Delisha and Katricia "Tree" Africa without their families' knowledge or consent.[3] In the aftermath of this incident becoming more widely known, anthropology departments, museums, professional organizations, and funding organizations began to more proactively consider how Ancestors are used in scholarly research and teaching.

Among professional organizations, there was a concerted effort to reconsider how research that involves human-derived materials should be conducted. Two anthropological flagship organizations, the American Anthropological Association (AAA) and the American Association for Biological Anthropology (AABA), created task forces/committees designed to address issues pertaining to the ethical treatment of Ancestors. The AAA commission, known as the Commission for the Ethical Treatment of Human Remains (TCETHR), was composed of scholars working in bioarchaeology, archaeology, cultural anthropology, anatomy, bioethics, and other biological anthropology subdisciplines (e.g., genetic anthropology). The AAA commission was asked to "coordinate with work that is contemplated or underway in sister societies; complete a comprehensive survey of the current status of legislative, policy, and professional society standards and guidelines, as well as the ethical, legal, social, and scientific issues involved in eliminating the gap between the current status and model standards of institutional and professional accountability; and develop a proposed model of standards for adoption" (TCETHR 2023). The commission's final report was published by the AAA in summer 2024 (Agarwal et al 2024), and AAA is currently seeking public feedback regarding the recommendations presented in the report. There are complementary efforts in the AABA's "Task Force for the Ethical Study of Human Remains," which is charged to "assess and develop guidance concerning the study and disposition of human remains in universities, laboratories, and museums, especially those of underrepresented and marginalized communities, as well as those that are the product of colonialism" (Auerbach and Jackson 2022; Clinton and Jackson 2021). The expected outcomes of these task forces are sets of guidelines to help institutions and individual researchers develop research protocols that are more attentive to contemporary ethical expectations of handling Ancestors. While the outcomes of the renewed momentum to revisit ethical norms around the use of Ancestors are yet to be realized, there are still considerable open questions about how existing and developing techniques in archaeogenomics may fit into the new perspectives on ethical research (Alpaslan-Roodenberg et al. 2021; Bader et al. 2023).

Unlike the recovery of modern DNA, aDNA recovery is still highly invasive. Sampling a skeletal element can lead to the partial or complete destruction of Ancestors' remains (for details on destructive sampling for aDNA, see Nägele et al. 2022), despite efforts to minimize or avoid destruction (Harney et al. 2021; Sirak and Sedig 2019; Sirak et al. 2017). Ideally, destructive aDNA sampling should be considered in close consultation with local communities, scholars, curators, and under the oversight of a governmental entity regulating access (see Figure 7.1). The need to minimize the destruction of cultural heritage has led to a search for alternative sources of aDNA. Apart from bony and soft tissues, aDNA has been extracted from bone pendants

Problem	Possible Solution	Realized by

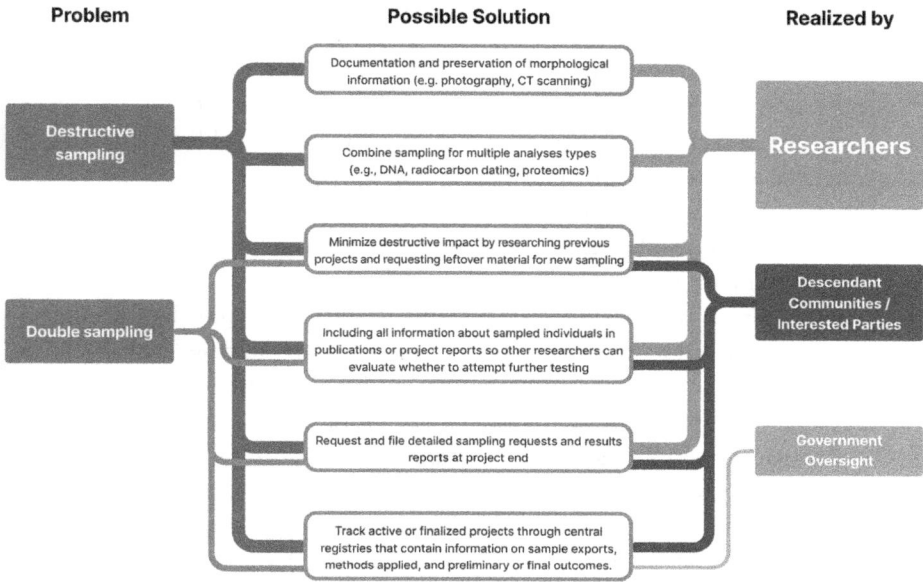

Figure 7.1. Summary of aDNA problems to consider, possible solutions, and the responsible entities to ensure ethical conduct of aDNA studies. Box and line thickness illustrate the relative responsibility of each entity, where larger boxes and thicker lines represent greater obligation of the entity for addressing the problem. Illustration by Kathrin Nägele and Gilberto C. Martinez Vicentini.

(Essel et al. 2023), birch tar and mastics (Jensen et al. 2019), lice nit cement (Pedersen et al. 2022), and soil, which has proven to be a rich source of environmental DNA (Vernot et al. 2021). But, in addition to the DNA of the ecosystem, soil samples can also include human DNA, both from Ancestors and from contemporary communities. As soil is not typically recognized as archaeological or cultural heritage per se, current ethical and regulatory regimes leave archaeological sediments as a possible gray area. Though these types of studies do not directly incorporate skeletal remains, they can still have important implications and consequences for local communities.

Data Sharing, Access, and Curation/Stewardship

The data produced in archaeogenomic research not only has to be analyzed and communicated, but also stored and curated. The genomes retrieved from Ancestors are immortalized in the lab through synthetic copies, and in silico through the digital signature of their genomic code. Today, the vast majority of aDNA data is openly available (Anagnostou et al. 2015). This astounding and often praised fact is the result of history of reproducibility issues in aDNA (Hebsgaard, Phillips, and Willerslev 2005; Pääbo et al. 2004) and a more general agreement to increase collaboration in genomic science (Contreras 2011). With increased data production, other problems emerged, which led to the definition of the FAIR principles, stating that scholarly data should be Findable and Accessible, Interoperable and Reusable in an effort to enhance reproducibility and allow equal access (Huston, Edge, and Bernier 2019; Wilkinson et al. 2016).

However, while there are vast benefits to data sharing, calls for open data have also led to arguments against repatriation (Halcrow et al. 2021). Additionally, the "fairness" of open data has been questioned because accessibility varies between stakeholders, decisions on permitting access can lack transparency, and access to data are dependent on institutional support (Powell 2021). Moreover, human genomic data—both modern and ancient—is often inaccessible to a large fraction of the population, including Indigenous peoples, due to a variety of reasons (e.g., lack of the appropriate computing resources, technical knowledge) (Bowrey and Anderson 2009). To address these significant shortcomings, the CARE principles of Indigenous data governance were proposed to complement the FAIR principles by ensuring equity through Collective benefit (especially for the communities), Authority to control data access and its use, Responsibility in curation and interpretation, and Ethics in Indigenous data governance (Carroll et al. 2020).

Open data policies are also in conflict with several United Nations (UN) declarations and in some places national law. The UN Declaration on the Rights of Indigenous Peoples emphasizes Indigenous peoples' right to control and protect traditional knowledge and cultural heritage, and ensures their right to decide about matters affecting their communities (United Nations 2007: Article 18). The sustainable development goals defined by the UN aim to ensure that the benefits of genetic resources are shared (United Nations 2015: Solutions Network Target 15.6) and the UN Convention on Biological Diversity (CBD)—a matter of international law (United Nations 1992)—protects Indigenous peoples' rights to determine the use and mode of sharing Indigenous resources, which include data. Unrestricted open access to data effectively removes the need for ongoing consultation with Indigenous communities and, therefore, their opportunity to mitigate harms, discuss benefits, or address issues of equity and autonomy (Garrison et al. 2019).

Currently, genomic databases have an increasing bias toward European and Euro-descendant genomes (Mills and Rahal 2019), creating a "genetic divide." The origins of this divide are in European and North American institutions that have misled Indigenous communities into participating in research in violation of modern ideas of informed consent (Hiraldo et al. 2020). Institutional ethics review boards (especially in the Global North) lack representation from Indigenous and underrepresented communities and are therefore not necessarily fit to decide on the ethical aspects of data collection and use. As exemplified by the historical experience of many Indigenous and underrepresented communities, unclear and varying rules can lead—and have led—to exploitations such as the appropriation or repurposing of genetic material without consent (i.e., Henrietta Lacks's cancer cells [Pratt 2020], the case of the Havasupai Tribe [Garrison 2013], and Native Hawaiians [Chang and Lowenthal 2001]). These cases have led to a rejection of genetic research in the affected communities. The understandable concerns and their consequences, however, lead to the unintentional exclusion of many minoritized communities from research-derived benefits (McCartney et al. 2022).

The destructive and finite nature of aDNA data production calls for a meticulous data archive (Bergström 2023), but when considering who benefits in the context of global inequitable infrastructures, it is natural that affected or related communities are cautious about fully openly available data of their relatives and Ancestors. The archive and curation of genomic datasets requires resources and creates a potential for appropriation through the gathering, reprocessing, and offering of the curated data (Mallick et al. 2023). In this process, it might be more difficult for researchers to identify restrictions imposed not by the data, but by the cultural, political, and societal context of individual populations. Ignoring the histories of colonialism and oppression, fully open data can increase the risk of harming communities with potential stigma emerging from results. While aDNA currently does have the limitations of much missing data, the increased strength and accuracy of imputation methods already overcomes these issues in many applications (i.e., IBD analyses; Fernandes et al. 2020; Ringbauer et al. 2023), and might lead to unforeseeable applications and implications for the descendant communities.

Today, human genomic data, whether from modern or ancient sources, is curated in various forms. Most data are stored in openly available databases accessible by anyone with an account such as the European Nucleotide Archive (ENA) or the National Center for Biotechnology Information (NCBI) GenBank. Other databases, such as the European Genome-phenome Archive (EGA) or the Database of Genotype and Phenotype (dbGaP) maintained by the US National Institutes of Health (NIH), provide restricted data access pending on approval by a data access committee. However, these committees can consist of only one person, and do not necessarily have to include representatives of the relevant donor or descendant communities. The person responsible for curating the dataset is then tasked with assuring that future use requests comply with the original consented purposes agreed upon during data collection. Moreover, most of these genomic databases are located in institutions in Europe or North America, highlighting inequities in data access and control between researchers and participants in the Global North versus South (Geary, Reay, and Bubela 2019). Commercial DNA testing is rapidly gaining significance, and companies are able to offer their customers ancestry testing (de Groot, van Beers, and Meynen 2021; Udesky 2010) at a low price. This is achieved by the drop in costs of genomic data generation, but perhaps also aided by subsequent commercialization of customer data (i.e., by selling to GlaxoSmithKline and Almirall [Dodson and Williamson 1999; Fox 2020]), thereby raising questions about the commodification of customer genomes. This is especially problematic when such genomes come from Indigenous or underprivileged communities, perpetuating historical marginalization and disempowerment of Indigenous peoples' agency surrounding the use of their data (Garrison et al. 2019).

Regardless of the positive and negative aspects of open data sharing, it is now enforced by some publications. Journals have varying policies on data sharing, including strongly encouraging (i.e., *Nature*) to demanding (i.e., *Genome Research*) public availability upon publication, or adhering to the Joint Data Archiving Policy (Dryad 2020). So how can this field of friction be navigated? As shown in Table 7.1, several possible solutions and alternative approaches can be considered. In the case of archaeogenomic research some particular complexities arise though, as there might not be a particular community related to the individuals under study, and consent might be necessary from a superordinate institution. It also might be difficult to establish who speaks for the community, and how many individuals should consent to genomic sampling of Ancestors.

While the approaches detailed in Table 7.1 provide hope for a more inclusive and just research landscape, they also come with inherent problems of accessibility and economic considerations. Many of these approaches require digital literacy and access to the digital world, which cannot be expected, and might even be rejected by some communities. Additionally, reviewing researchers' proposals on a community level requires time, which for the communities in charge may represent unpaid labor. Examples of Indigenous data ownership and databases already exist in the Te Mana Raraunga Māori Data Sovereignty Network, the US Indigenous Data Sovereignty Network,

Table 7.1. Alternative Approaches toward Consent for Genetic Research Conducted with Human Participants or Descendant Communities

Approach	Description	References
DNA on loan	DNA is only collected and consented for a particular study or research question. To address new questions, participants (or descendant communities in the case of aDNA) must consent to the newly proposed research methods and goals, resulting in more agency and access control over resulting data, as well as increased community trust and collective interest.	(Hudson et al. 2020; Arbour and Cook 2006)
Fractional ownership	Communities or individual participants keep ownership of the data, granting these people full agency over what questions can be investigated, but also allowing them to reap the resulting benefits, economic or otherwise.	(Fox 2020)
Dynamic consent	The consent process prioritizes ongoing communication between researchers and participants or descendant community members, allowing for revisiting and changing previous decisions.	(Prictor, Teare, and Kaye 2018; Tiffin 2018)

and the Maiam nayri Wingara Indigenous Sovereignty Collective and Torres Strait Islander Data Sovereignty Group in Australia (Caron et al. 2020). In these cases, Indigenous peoples have taken data curation into their own hands, providing templates for future efforts to work with Indigenous and traditional community data.

While Western-trained scientists understand and accept the risks of unregulated DNA data use for modern populations, the relationship becomes more difficult, and epistemological differences more pronounced, when considering aDNA from Ancestors. In a Western scientific context, the relation between past societies and modern peoples is one defined by history and genetic ancestry. Arguably, the conception of genetic ancestry to connect people from millennia ago to people today is a problem, as mathematically, most of the earth's population is similarly related to people in the distant past (Coop 2013; Huff et al. 2011). However, in today's political and social global landscape, "it is human history, therefore all have a right to study everyone" disregards the power imbalances between European or Euro-descendant researchers and Indigenous and traditional communities. Additionally, different communities' conceptions may vary from Western understandings of ancestry, connections to land, cultural attributes, or language (Blanchard et al. 2019; TallBear 2013; Turner, McDonald Perrurle, and Perrurle Dobson

2010). For many researchers trained in a Western scientific tradition, DNA is often seen as just a molecule, a chemical structure transporting "objective" information. In other communities, views about DNA and its broader meanings can be substantially different than the perspective of Western-trained researchers.

As ancient (and modern) DNA are used to construct history, interpretations emerging through aDNA research can have profound social, psychological, legal, and political consequences for individuals, families, and communities, especially if they interpret DNA results through epistemologies different from those used by Western researchers (Blanchard et al. 2019; TallBear 2013). Data should be considered a responsibility, not an entitlement (Tsosie, Fox, and Yracheta 2021), and centering Indigenous peoples and their experiences, knowledges, and beliefs, as well as their stakes in research, can make sure that unforeseen future applications and risks are not detrimental to the goal of global equity. As Frank Dukepoo, a Laguna and Hopi geneticist, explains: "To us, any part of ourselves is sacred. Scientists say it's just DNA. For an Indian, it's not just DNA, it's part of a person, it is sacred, with deep religious significance. It is part of the essence of a person" (Petit 1998). Centering and foregrounding Western perceptions of DNA as the only measure of ancestry discussions on how to produce, analyze, communicate, and curate genetic data imposes Western worldviews and conceptions on others, risking an "epistemicide" (Hall and Tandon 2017), and a biased construction of the past.

Sustainability, Equitability, and Capacity Building

Caribbean archaeogenomics, like other forms of scientific knowledge production, cannot be divorced from the social and historical context of the communities it studies. As stated by archaeologist Mary Jane Berman (2005: 41), research into the Caribbean past is necessarily shaped by "the interconnectedness and interdependency of political ideology, cultural climate, social context, and archaeological practice." For archaeogenetic researchers working in the Caribbean today it is important to keep in mind that colonial legacies continue to shape not just the way scientific research is conducted, but also the daily lives of island and diasporic communities (Gahman, Thongs, and Greenidge 2021). As seen in recent controversies surrounding the uncritical use of terms such as "extinct peoples" to describe Caribbean Indigenous communities (Hawks 2011; Kowal et al. 2023), it is imperative that researchers consider the possible ramifications of their findings and how their results will be interpreted against this historic backdrop. To do otherwise is to risk perpetuating biased understandings of the Caribbean past in which the contributions of non-European communities are viewed as marginal to a broader history focused on colonial protagonists (Siegel et al. 2013).

The Caribbean's colonial history has also created major challenges for the development of local scientific capacities. As is the case in many Global South countries with recent histories of colonization, Caribbean nations and territories face significant challenges in funding, setting up, and maintaining scientific infrastructure and educational programs (Brusi and Godreau 2021; Ferreyra et al. 2017; Siegel et al. 2013). The legacy of extractive sampling combined with chronic underfunding of local museums and universities means that many Caribbean islands lack comprehensive, and well-maintained, reference collections for archaeological, anthropological, or natural history research. The skeletal remains of human Ancestors in particular require specific preservation and storage conditions, which are often challenging to implement for underfunded heritage institutions in the region (Crespo-Torres, Mickleburgh, and Rojas 2013; Cummins, Farmer, and Russell 2013; Mickleburgh 2015). Thus, to conduct research on questions about Caribbean cultural history, local researchers must often travel abroad to visit collections housed in Europe or the United States. This presents important financial and logistical barriers for locally led research projects, especially when these are conducted by students or early career scientists (Ávila-Arcos et al. 2022; Mohammed et al. 2022). The economic factors are especially significant for ancient DNA research. Recovering ancient DNA requires a highly sterile lab that cannot be used for other types of genetic analysis. The infrastructure to build a cleanroom and the consumables needed are not easily accessible everywhere, and are often much more expensive when delivered to Global South or island locations (Ávila-Arcos et al. 2022). While ideas to overcome the problems of creating a sterile environment for aDNA processing are being developed (Jaramillo-Valverde et al. 2022; Utge, Sévêque et al. 2020), the lack of locally based trained personnel to work in them remains an issue.

A lack of well-supported institutions for higher education means that many Caribbean students do not have access to specialized training programs in fields such as anthropology, archaeology, and paleogenomics, especially at the graduate level. Trainees must often travel abroad to complete their studies and may find few opportunities for local employment upon their return (Curet 2011; Dacal Moure and Watters 2005). The lack of locally based trained professionals in these fields creates a vicious cycle of "brain drain" emigration that contributes to existing gaps in local expertise and training opportunities and can lead to the reproduction of colonial and extractive interactions through unequal research collaborations (Ávila-Arcos et al. 2022; Mohammed et al. 2022; Yáñez et al. 2023). To break with the extractive and colonialist origins of Caribbean research, foreign and local researchers should work together to improve local scientific and educational capacities. This can be achieved by creating opportunities for local student training and by engaging in horizontal partnerships where Caribbean researchers are not considered solely as sample providers or "intermediaries" (Argüelles, Fuentes, and Yáñez 2022) but instead as equal partners in the design, conduct, interpretation, and publication of research studies that involve and impact them, and their home communities.

Finally, colonial legacies of inequality make Caribbean infrastructure, scientific or otherwise, extremely vulnerable to climate change impacts (Ficek 2018; Gahman, Thongs, and Greenidge 2021; Perdikaris et al. 2021). Just in the past decade, high-intensity hurricanes destroyed museums and art galleries in the Bahamas (Kurin 2019; Mohammed et al. 2022), and damaged research facilities, museum collections, and archaeological sites in Puerto Rico (López Lloreda 2022; Rivera-Collazo 2020). The challenges posed by climate change strain already precarious island economies and divert resources away from heritage management, basic scientific research, education, and training that could benefit island communities and the study of their past.

Decolonizing Caribbean Archaeogenomics

Without being prescriptive, it is useful to consider how an equitable, sustainable research relationship that builds capacity might look in the context of an aDNA study in the Caribbean. Inspired by community-based participatory research approaches (Jagosh et al. 2015; Lemke et al. 2022; Minkler 2004), as a baseline, we hold that an equitable and sustainable study is purposeful in its intent to both address research questions and engage in reciprocal activity that either addresses the needs and/or builds the capacity of local collaborators, descendant communities, or other interested parties (DCIPs). Researchers might consider, for example, whether and in what ways local investigators and DCIPs are involved in various aspects of the aDNA project. Does the research collaboration empower or enable local researchers to have more prominent roles in ongoing or future aDNA research in their home communities? Has the potential for reciprocity to the local researchers and communities been fully explored within the context of the project? Are there ways to disseminate protocols, technological knowledge, equipment, or other project-related materials to local researchers, students, or DCIPs

Table 7.2. Give-Get Grid, a Framework for Establishing an Equitable Research Relationship

Expected Contributions	Expected Benefits
What local collaborator/DCIP plans to "give" to partnership:	What local collaborator/DCIP hopes to "get" from the partnership:
What academic partner plans to "give" to partnership:	What academic partner hopes to "get" from the partnership:

Note: Adapted from Behringer 1996.

involved in the aDNA project? These and related questions may be useful to consider upon entering collaborative research relationships as well as during study design. The Give-Get Grid is a simple tool developed and used among public health researchers to systematically consider how communities can be involved, beyond participation, in research projects (Behringer 1996). This grid visualizes the roles of both researchers and local collaborators/DCIPs in establishing an equitable working relationship (Table 7.2).

While we do not intend to promote this particular approach as a panacea for creating sustainable, equitable research projects, it is intended to help more systematically consider the broader implications of conducting aDNA work for all those involved, and similar approaches have already been implemented in at least two aDNA studies (Fleskes et al. 2023; Harney et al. 2023). Both studies focused on African American Ancestors and, in different ways, involved DCIPs such as historical societies and community grassroots organizations in the inception, design, and dissemination of the work. These studies illustrate the importance and broader impacts of seeking and sustaining equitable collaborative relationships with DCIPs.

Toward an Ethical Framework for Ancestors

While community-researcher collaborative approaches described here hold promise for advancing more ethical ways of conducting aDNA studies, they are by no means universally applied nor expected. Overall, ethical oversights mandated for genetic research involving living people do not apply to research involving Ancestors. For the most part, aDNA analysis is unregulated as a separate process beyond seeking the appropriate permits to conduct the adjacent (bio)archaeological research. The lack of a separate, standardized ethical review protocol for aDNA projects can result in a myriad of ethical issues that can negatively impact relationships with DCIPs (Kowal et al.

2023; Mega 2023). Arguably, in some contexts under-involvement from DCIPs may be less problematic due to the age or particular history of the Ancestors under study. In other cases, a lack of involvement from DCIPs may be extremely troubling, because it can inflict further harm or trauma for already disempowered communities. Regardless of the lack of a standardized protocol, similar to research involving living people, the onus of acting ethically sits with the investigator (see Figure 7.1). Ethical behavior results in accountability and trust, and enhances possibilities for future growth and understanding. Unethical research can sow mistrust between involved parties and hinder future opportunities to expand knowledge bases. Consequently, the ethics of archaeogenomic research extends beyond any individual investigator but also has implications for DCIPs, impacts relationships between the living and the nonliving, and has repercussions for the discipline itself.

Due to the importance of ethical research, investigators should make concerted efforts to conduct their studies in ways that are cognizant of and responsive to potentially harmful outcomes. However, given the varying contexts where archaeogenomic work can be done, there is not one approach that is likely to be suitable for all research contexts. In response to this, we propose that the concept of intersectionality, initially described by Kimberlé Crenshaw (1989), and expounded upon by other Black feminist scholars (Davis 1983; Hill Collins 2022; hooks 1981), is a useful foundation for developing ethical archaeogenomic research regardless of the research site. Originally proposed within legal scholarship, intersectionality acknowledges how social identities, including race, class, gender, sexuality, ability status, et cetera, in conjunction with broader political systems of oppression, overlay and intersect to shape unique lived experiences. The recognition of broader systems of oppression is a critical part of this concept because it aids in providing the necessary context for making sense of how individuals are able to operate within a given environment.

In the context of the Caribbean, the recognition of oppressive systems is especially relevant given the role of colonialism in shaping the region and, consequently, the conditions in which Caribbean archaeogenomics is practiced. Deploying intersectionality as a foundation for ethical archaeogenomics demands the acknowledgment of the full range of intersecting social identities of both the living and the nonliving, in addition to the systems of oppressions impacting DCIPs and the investigators conducting research. With cognizance of these broader factors, investigators might consider how their positionality, privilege, and worldview shape the ways in which they approach and conduct aDNA research. For example, having clarity about one's ideas about appropriate ways to engage (or not) with Ancestors would be critical for developing an aDNA study design as it will inform how Ancestors are handled throughout the duration of the research. Having awareness of how one's professional status (e.g., a student, a postdoctoral researcher, a senior scholar, etc.) figures into interpersonal relationships with collaborators or DCIPs has utility for developing a fair system for the distribution of labor within the research project. In the end, the application of intersectionality for framing ethical aDNA research forces engagement with the historical, political, and social dynamics that impact the research. Furthermore, use of this concept helps to understand how existing hierarchies and power dynamics influence some of the most critical aspects of a project (e.g., appropriate central study questions or the distribution of project-related labor). Considering the intersecting broader contexts of all those involved in the project, including Ancestors, centralizes the most vulnerable elements involved in conceiving, executing, and disseminating the research. Ideally, reliance on the concept of intersectionality can help mitigate potential harms as a result of research and can work toward ensuring the development of a comprehensive ethical framework that is appropriately suited to the specific study area.

Looking Forward for the Discipline: Ideas for What Ethical Review Might Look Like in Caribbean Contexts

Regarding ethical archaeogenomic research in Caribbean contexts, it bears repeating that no single approach will be appropriate for all research contexts. While arguably, there are some broad historical and cultural similarities across Caribbean nation-states, there are enough differences to warrant a more individualized approach to ethical aDNA research. Many of these differences within the region emerged as a result of differences in colonial histories. As discussed elsewhere in this chapter, colonial histories are deeply intertwined and entrenched with the development and practice of science. These histories influence the types of research questions that are asked and investigated and ultimately impact how archaeogenomics work is done. For example, research done where communities assert a deep relationship to the autochthonous peoples of the Caribbean and have strong political footing is likely to look very different from other areas without a significant Indigenous resurgence movement or in places where Indigenous peoples are not recognized as such by the state or the broader community. In the former, there are DCIPs that may potentially be involved in aDNA projects about First Peoples of the island nation/community and want to see such work completed as it may be useful for regaining a sense of their ancestors. In the latter case, there may be a lack of perceived continuity between Indigenous Ancestors and contemporary populations and less interest in aDNA projects involving Indigenous Ancestors or different motivations for engaging in archaeogenomic research (e.g., to enhance general knowledge). While what has been described here represents two ends of a spectrum, many research contexts lie somewhere between these poles. Accordingly, approaching each research context with the knowledge of historical and political contexts, and being mindful of a researcher's own position within this context, is critical to developing and implementing ethical archaeogenomic approaches in the Caribbean and beyond.

Notes

1 "Human remains," "skeletal elements," and "archaeological specimens" are all terms used in this context. However, these terms are viewed by many as reductive, disrespectful, and sometimes even dehumanizing. In this chapter, we attempt to preserve the humanity of the deceased individuals under study by using the term "Ancestors" to refer to deceased individuals and to distinguish from living individuals (see also Wagner et al. 2020).

2 Institutional review boards (IRBs) are boards that provide ethical review of all research involving living human study participants. In the United States, IRBs must exist at institutions that receive federal funds, and the composition and functions of these boards are mandated by the Code of Federal Regulations.

3 In April 2021, an op-ed published online in the *Philadelphia Inquirer* and reprinted on onamove.com (Muhammad 2021) revealed that the remains of two children, Delisha and Katricia "Tree" Africa, aged 12 and 14 respectively, were housed by researchers at Penn Museum and subsequently used in an online Princeton University course (Muhammad 2021). The children were killed in their Philadelphia home by a state-sanctioned bombing of their residence in 1985. The family was unaware that the remains of the children had been retained and were used as a case study in the online course. Subsequent independent investigations by two law firms highlighted disagreement regarding the identification of the remains between the Medical Examiner's Office and forensic anthropologists at the University of Pennsylvania that had been called on to assist with the identification of the remains. The law firm investigations also detailed the (mis)handling of the remains, their usage within the online course, and the lack of institutional policy guiding normative ethical handling of human remains (DECHERT LLP 2022; Tucker Law Group 2021).

References Cited

Albert, Richard, Derek O'Brien, and Se-shauna Wheatle, eds. 2020. *The Oxford Handbook of Caribbean Constitutions*. Oxford: Oxford University Press.

Alpaslan-Roodenberg, Songül, David Anthony, Hiba Babiker, Eszter Bánffy, Thomas Booth, Patricia Capone, Arati Deshpande-Mukherjee, et al. 2021. "Ethics of DNA Research on Human Remains: Five Globally Applicable Guidelines." *Nature* 599(7883): 41–46.

Anagnostou, Paolo, Marco Capocasa, Nicola Milia, Emanuele Sanna, Cinzia Battaggia, Daniela Luzi, and Giovanni Destro Bisol. 2015. "When Data Sharing Gets Close to 100%: What Human Paleogenetics Can Teach the Open Science Movement." *PloS One* 10(3): e0121409.

Anderson-Córdova, Karen Frances. 2017. *Surviving Spanish Conquest: Indian Fight, Flight, and Cultural Transformation in Hispaniola and Puerto Rico*. Caribbean Archaeology and Ethnohistory. Tuscaloosa: University of Alabama Press.

Agarwal, S. C., M. L. Blakey, T. H. Champney, C. dela Cova, J. L. Davis, D. L. Martin, K. Supernant, D. A. Thomas, R. Watkins, and T. Weik. 2024. "Final Report." The Commission for the Ethical Treatment of Human Remains (TCETHR). American Anthropological Association. https://americananthro.org/about/committees-and-task-forces/tcethr/.

Arbour, Laura, and Doris Cook. 2006. "DNA on Loan: Issues to Consider When Carrying Out Genetic Research with Aboriginal Families and Communities." *Public Health Genomics* 9(3): 153–160.

Argüelles, Juan Manuel, Agustín Fuentes, and Bernardo Yáñez. 2022. "Analyzing Asymmetries and Praxis in aDNA Research: A Bioanthropological Critique." *American Anthropologist* 124(1): 130–140.

Armstrong, Douglas V., and Mark W. Hauser. 2009. "A Sea of Diversity: Historical Archaeology in the Caribbean." In *International Handbook of Historical Archaeology*, edited by David Gaimster and Teresita Majewski, 583–612. New York: Springer.

Auerbach, Benjamin M., and Fatimah L. C. Jackson. 2022. *Preliminary Report: Results of the AABA Taskforce on the Ethical Study of Human Remains Surveys of Members of the African American Community and of Biological Anthropologists*. AABA Task Force for the Ethical Study of Human Remains. American Association of Biological Anthropologists.

Ávila-Arcos, Maria C., Constanza de la Fuente Castro, Maria A. Nieves-Colón, and Maanasa Raghavan. 2022. "Recommendations for Sustainable Ancient DNA Research in the Global South: Voices from a New Generation of Paleogenomicists." *Frontiers in Genetics* 13: 880170.

Baatz, Simon. 1996. "Imperial Science and Metropolitan Ambition: The Scientific Survey of Puerto Rico, 1913–1934." *Annals of the New York Academy of Sciences* 776(1): 1–16.

Bader, Alyssa C., Aimée E. Carbaugh, Jenny L. Davis, Krystiana L. Krupa, and Ripan S. Malhi. 2023. "Biological Samples Taken from Native American Ancestors Are Human Remains under NAGPRA." *American Journal of Biological Anthropology* 181(4): 527–534.

Beckles, Hilary M. 1992. "Kalinago (Carib) Resistance to European Colonisation of the Caribbean." *Caribbean Quarterly* 38(2/3): 123–124.

Behringer, B. 1996. "The Nature of Communities." In *Building Partnerships: Educating Health Professionals for the Communities They Serve,* edited by Ronald W. Richards, 91–104. San Francisco: Jossey-Bass.

Benn Torres, Jada. 2014. "Prospecting the Past: Genetic Perspectives on the Extinction and Survival of Indigenous Peoples of the Caribbean." *New Genetics and Society* 33(1): 21–41.

Benn Torres, Jada, Victoria Martucci, Melinda C. Aldrich, Miguel G. Vilar, Taryn MacKinney, Muhammad Tariq, Jill B. Gaieski, et al. 2019. "Analysis of Biogeographic Ancestry Reveals Complex Genetic Histories for Indigenous Communities of St. Vincent and Trinidad." *American Journal of Physical Anthropology* 169(3): 482–497.

Benn Torres, Jada, Anne C. Stone, and Rick Kittles. (2013). "An Anthropological Genetic Perspective on Creolization in the Anglophone Caribbean." *American Journal of Physical Anthropology* 151(1): 135–143.

Bergström, Anders. 2023. "Improving Data Archiving Practices in Ancient Genomics." *bioRxiv,* 2023.05.15.540553.

Berman, Mary Jane, Jorge Febles, and Perry L. Gnivecki. 2005. "The Organization of Cuban Archaeology: Context and Brief History." In *Dialogues in Cuban Archaeology,* edited by L. Antonio Curet, Shannon L. Dawdry, and Gabino La Rosa Corzo, 41–61. Tuscaloosa: University of Alabama Press.

Beskow, Laura M., Christine Grady, Ana S. Iltis, John Z. Sadler, and Benjamin S. Wilfond. 2009. "Points to Consider." *IRB: Ethics and Human Research* 31(6): 1–9.

Blanchard, Jessica W., Simon Outram, Gloria Tallbull, and Charmaine D. M. Royal. 2019. "'We Don't Need a Swab in Our Mouth to Prove Who We Are': Identity, Resistance, and Adaptation of Genetic Ancestry Testing among Native American Communities." *Current Anthropology* 60(5): 637–655.

Bowrey, Kathy, and Jane Anderson. 2009. "The Politics of Global Information Sharing: Whose Cultural Agendas Are Being Advanced?" *Social & Legal Studies* 18(4): 479–504.

Brito, Christopher. 2021. "Christie's Is Auctioning off Ancient Taino Items. This Native Group Wants to Stop Them." CBS News. https://www.cbsnews.com/news/christies-taino-auction/ (accessed June 26, 2024).

Brusi, Rima, and Godreau, Isar. 2021. "Public Higher Education in Puerto Rico: Disaster, Austerity, and Resistance." *AAUP Journal of Academic Freedom* 12: 19.

Callaway, Ewen. 2017. "South Africa's San People Issue Ethics Code to Scientists." *Nature* 543: 7646.

Caron, Nadine Rena, Meck Chongo, Maui Hudson, Laura Arbour, Wyeth W. Wasserman, Stephen Robertson, Solenne Correard, and Phillip Wilcox. 2020. "Indigenous

Genomic Databases: Pragmatic Considerations and Cultural Contexts." *Frontiers in Public Health* 111.

Carroll, Stephanie Russo, Ibrahim Garba, Oscar L. Figueroa-Rodríguez, Jarita Holbrook, Raymond Lovett, Simeon Materechera, Mark Parsons, et al. 2020. "The CARE Principles for Indigenous Data Governance." *Data Science Journal* 19(43): 7–12.

Chang, R. M., and Philip H. Lowenthal. 2001. "Genetic Research and the Vulnerability of Native Hawaiians." *Pacific Health Dialog* 8(2): 364–367.

Chennells, Roger, and Andries Steenkamp. 2018. "International Genomics Research Involving the San People." In *Ethics Dumping: Case Studies from North-South Research Collaborations,* edited by Doris Schroeder, Julie Cook, François Hirsch, Solveig Fenet, and Vasantha Muthuswamy, 15–22. Cham: Springer International Publishing.

Clinton, Carter K., and Fatimah L. C. Jackson. 2021. "Historical Overview, Current Research, and Emerging Bioethical Guidelines in Researching the New York African Burial Ground." *American Journal of Physical Anthropology* 175(2): 339–349.

Connell, Robert. 2020. "Maroon Ecology: Land, Sovereignty, and Environmental Justice." *Journal of Latin American and Caribbean Anthropology* 25(2): 218–234.

Contreras, Jorge L. 2011. "Bermuda's Legacy: Policy, Patents, and the Design of the Genome Commons." *Minnesota Journal of Law Science & Technology* 12: 61.

Coop, Graham. 2013. "How Many Genetic Ancestors Do I Have?" *Gcbias* (blog). November 11, 2013. https://gcbias.org/2013/11/11/how-does-your-number-of-genetic-ancestors-grow-back-over-time/ (accessed June 26, 2024).

Craciun, Adriana, and Mary Terrall, eds. 2019. *Curious Encounters: Voyaging, Collecting, and Making Knowledge in the Long Eighteenth Century.* Toronto: University of Toronto Press.

Crenshaw, Kimberlé. 1989. "Demarginalizing the Intersection of Race and Sex: A Black Feminist Critique of Antidiscrimination Doctrine, Feminist Theory and Antiracist Politics." *University of Chicago Legal Forum* 1989: 139.

Crespo-Torres, Edwin F., Hayley L. Mickleburgh, and Roberto Valcárcel Rojas. 2013. "The Study of Pre-Columbian Human Remains in the Caribbean Archipelago: From Descriptive Osteology to a Bioarchaeological Approach." In *The Oxford Handbook of Caribbean Archaeology,* edited by William F. Keegan, Corinne L. Hofman, and Reniel Rodríguez Ramos, 436–51. Oxford: Oxford University Press.

Cummins, Alissandra, Kevin Farmer, and Roslyn Russell, eds. 2013. *Plantation to Nation: Caribbean Museums and National Identity.* Chicago: Common Ground Research Networks.

Curet, L. Antonio. 2011. "Colonialism and the History of Archaeology in the Spanish Caribbean." In *Comparative Archaeologies,* edited by Ludomir R. Lozny, 641–72. New York: Springer.

Curet, L Antonio. 2006. "Las Crónicas en la Arqueología de Puerto Rico y del Caribe." *Caribbean Studies* 34(1): 163–199.

Curet, L. Antonio. 2015. "Indigenous Revival, Indigeneity, and the Jíbaro in Borikén." *Centro Journal* 28(1): 206–247.

Curet, L. Antonio. 2014. "The Taino: Phenomena, Concepts, and Terms." *Ethnohistory* 61(3): 467–495.

Curet, L. Antonio. 2018. "Theodoor De Booy in Puerto Rico: An Untold Story in the History of Caribbean Archaeology." *Caribbean Studies* 46(1): 3–32.

Dacal Moure, Ramón, and David Watters. 2005. "Three Stages in the History of Cuban Archaeology." In *Dialogues in Cuban Archaeology,* edited by L. Antonio Curet, Shannon L. Dawdry, and Gabino La Rosa Corzo, 29–40. Tuscaloosa: University of Alabama Press.

DaRos, Maureen, and Roger H. Colten. 2009. "A History of Caribbean Archaeology at Yale University's Peabody Museum of Natural History." *Bulletin of the Peabody Museum of Natural History* 50(1): 49–62.

Davis, Angela Y. 1983. *Women, Race & Class.* New York: Vintage Books.

De Groot, Nina F., Britta C. van Beers, and Gerben Meynen. 2021. "Commercial DNA Tests and Police Investigations: A Broad Bioethical Perspective." *Journal of Medical Ethics* 47(12): 788–795.

De la Luz Rodríguez, Gabriel. 2010. "Taino as a Romantic Term: Notes on the Representation of the Indigenous in Puerto Rican Archaeology and Ethnohistory." In *Bridging the Divide: Indigenous Communities and Archaeology into the 21st Century,* edited by Caroline Phillips and Harry Allen, 93–106. Walnut Creek: Left Coast Press.

Denevan, William M. 1992. "The Pristine Myth: The Landscape of the Americas in 1492." *Annals of the Association of American Geographers* 82(3): 369–385.

De Tienda Palop, Lydia, and Brais X. Currás. 2019. "The Dignity of the Dead: Ethical Reflections on the Archaeology of Human Remains." In *Ethical Approaches to Human Remains,* edited by Kirsty Squires, David Errickson, and Nicholas Márquez-Grant, 19–37. Cham: Springer International Publishing.

Dodson, Michael, and Robert Williamson. 1999. "Indigenous Peoples and the Morality of the Human Genome Diversity Project." *Journal of Medical Ethics* 25(2): 204–208.

Downs, Jim. 2021. *Maladies of Empire: How Colonialism, Slavery, and War Transformed Medicine.* Cambridge: Belknap Press of Harvard University.

Dryad. 2020. "Joint Data Archiving Policy." https://datadryad.org/docs/JointDataArchivingPolicy.pdf (accessed June 28, 2024).

Ellingson, Ter. 2001. *The Myth of the Noble Savage.* Berkeley: University of California Press.

Emanuel, Ezekiel J. 2008. *The Oxford Textbook of Clinical Research Ethics.* Oxford: Oxford University Press.

Essel, Elena, Elena I. Zavala, Ellen Schulz-Kornas, Maxim B. Kozlikin, Helen Fewlass, Benjamin Vernot, Michael V. Shunkov, et al. 2023. "Ancient Human DNA Recovered from a Palaeolithic Pendant." *Nature* 618(7964): 328–332.

Feliciano-Santos, Sherina. 2017. "How Do You Speak Taíno? Indigenous Activism and Linguistic Practices in Puerto Rico." *Journal of Linguistic Anthropology* 27(1): 4–21.

Fernandes, Daniel M., Kendra A. Sirak, Harald Ringbauer, Jakob Sedig, Nadin Rohland, Olivia Cheronet, Matthew Mah, et al. 2020. "A Genetic History of the Pre-Contact Caribbean." *Nature* 590: 103–110.

Ferreyra, María Marta, Javier Botero Álvarez, Francisco Haimovich Paz, and Sergio Urzúa. 2017. *At a Crossroads: Higher Education in Latin America and the Caribbean.* Washington, DC: World Bank Group.

Ficek, Rosa E. 2018. "Infrastructure and Colonial Difference in Puerto Rico after Hurricane María." *Transforming Anthropology* 26(2): 102–117.

Finneran, Niall, and Christina Welch. 2019. "Out of the Shadow of Balliceaux: From Garifuna Place of Memory to Garifuna Sense of Place in Saint Vincent and the Grenadines, Eastern Caribbean." *Journal of African Diaspora Archaeology and Heritage* 8(3): 226–251.

Fleskes, Raquel E., Alyssa C. Bader, Krystal S. Tsosie, Jennifer K. Wagner, Katrina G. Claw, and Nanibaa' A. Garrison. 2022. "Ethical Guidance in Human Paleogenomics: New and Ongoing Perspectives." *Annual Review of Genomics and Human Genetics* 23(1): 627–652.

Fleskes, Raquel E., Graciela S. Cabana, Joanna K. Gilmore, Chelsey Juarez, Emilee Karcher, La'Sheia Oubré, Grant Mishoe, Ade A. Ofunniyin, and Theodore G. Schurr. 2023. "Community-Engaged Ancient DNA Project Reveals Diverse Origins of 18th-Century African Descendants in Charleston, South Carolina." *Proceedings of the National Academy of Sciences* 120(3): e2201620120.

Forbes-Pateman, Vanessa, Aram Yardumian, Miguel Vilar, Tanya M. Simms, Michael P. Pateman, and William Keegan. 2022. "A Population History of Indigenous Bahamian Islanders: Insights from Ancient DNA." *American Journal of Biological Anthropology* 177(4): 630–643.

Fox, Keolu. 2020. "The Illusion of Inclusion—The 'All of Us' Research Program and Indigenous Peoples' DNA." *New England Journal of Medicine* 383(5): 411–413.

Fox, Kelou, and John Hawks. 2019. "Use Ancient Remains More Wisely." *Nature* 572: 581–83.

Françozo, Mariana, and Amy Strecker. 2017. "Caribbean Collections in European Museums and the Question of Returns." *International Journal of Cultural Property* 24(4): 451–477.

Fuller, Harcourt, and Jada Benn Torres. 2018. "Investigating the 'Taíno' Ancestry of the Jamaican Maroons: A New Genetic (DNA), Historical, and Multidisciplinary Analysis and Case Study of the Accompong Town Maroons." *Canadian Journal of Latin American and Caribbean Studies / Revue Canadienne Des Études Latino-Américaines et Caraïbes* 43(1): 47–78.

Gahman, Levi, Gabrielle Thongs, and Adaeze Greenidge. 2021. "Disaster, Debt, and 'Underdevelopment': The Cunning of Colonial-Capitalism in the Caribbean." *Development (Society for International Development)* 64(1–2): 112–118.

Galeano, E. 1971. "Lust for Gold, Lust for Silver." *Open Veins of Latin America,* 2–58.

Gannon, Megan. 2019. "When Ancient DNA Gets Politicized." *Smithsonian.* July 12, 2019. https://www.smithsonianmag.com/history/when-ancient-dna-gets-politicized-180972639/ (accessed June 26, 2024).

Garrison, Nanibaa' A. 2013. "Genomic Justice for Native Americans: Impact of the Havasupai Case on Genetic Research." *Science, Technology, & Human Values* 38(2): 201–223.

Garrison, Nanibaa'A., Māui Hudson, Leah L. Ballantyne, Ibrahim Garba, Andrew Martinez, Maile Taualii, Laura Arbour, Nadine R. Caron, and Stephanie Carroll Rainie. 2019. "Genomic Research through an Indigenous Lens: Understanding the Expectations." *Annual Review of Genomics and Human Genetics* 20: 495–517.

Geary, Janis, Trish Reay, and Tania Bubela. 2019. "The Impact of Heterogeneity in a Global Knowledge Commons: Implications for Governance of the DNA Barcode Commons." *International Journal of the Commons* 13(2): 909–930.

George, Lily, Lindsey Te Ata o Tū Macdonald, and Juan Tauri. 2020. "An Introduction to Indigenous Research Ethics." In *Indigenous Research Ethics: Claiming Research Sovereignty Beyond Deficit and the Colonial Legacy,* edited by Lily George, Juan Tauri, and Lindsey Te Ata o Tū MacDonald, 1–15. Leeds, UK: Emerald Publishing Limited.

Gibbon, Victoria E., Jessica C. Thompson, and Sianne Alves. 2024. "Informed Proxy Consent for Ancient DNA research." *Communications Biology* 7(1): 815.

Global Alliance for Genomics and Health. 2023. "Global Alliance for Genomics and Health." 2023. https://www.ga4gh.org/ (accessed June 26, 2024).

Grunberg, Bernard. 2011. "An Ethnohistorical Approach of the Carib through Written Sources: The Example of the Relation by Jacques Bouton." In *Communities in Contact: Essays in Archaeology, Ethnohistory, and Ethnography of the Amerindian Circum-Caribbean,* edited by Corinne L. Hofman and Anne van Duijvenbode, 327–342. Leiden: Sidestone Press.

Haelewaters, Danny, Tina A. Hofmann, and Adriana L. Romero-Olivares. "Ten Simple Rules for Global North Researchers to Stop Perpetuating Helicopter Research in the Global South." *PLOS Computational Biology* 17(8): e1009277.

Halcrow, Siân, Amber Aranui, Stephanie Halmhofer, Annalisa Heppner, Norma Johnson, Kristina Killgrove, and Gwen Robbins Schug. 2021. "Moving beyond Weiss and Springer's Repatriation and Erasing the Past: Indigenous Values, Relationships, and Research." *International Journal of Cultural Property* 28(2): 211–220.

Hall, Budd L., and Rajesh Tandon. 2017. "Decolonization of Knowledge, Epistemicide, Participatory Research and Higher Education." *Research for All* 1(1): 6–19.

Harney, Éadaoin, Olivia Cheronet, Daniel M. Fernandes, Kendra Sirak, Matthew Mah, Rebecca Bernardos, Nicole Adamski, et al. 2021. "A Minimally Destructive Protocol for DNA Extraction from Ancient Teeth." *Genome Research* 31(3): 472–483.

Harney, Éadaoin, Steven Micheletti, Karin S. Bruwelheide, William A. Freyman, Katarzyna Bryc, Ali Akbari, Ethan Jewett, et al. 2023. "The Genetic Legacy of African Americans from Catoctin Furnace." *Science* 381(6657): eade4995.

Harry, Debra, Stephanie Howard, and Brett Lee Shelton. 2000. "Biopiracy and Globalization: Indigenous Peoples Face a New Wave of Colonialism." *Indigenous People, Genes, and Genetics: What Indigenous People Should Know about Biocolonialism.* Wadsworth, Nevada: Indigenous Peoples Council on Biocolonialism.

Haviser, Jay B., and Corinne L. Hofman. 2015. "A Review of Archaeological Research in the Dutch Caribbean." In *Managing our Past into the Future: Archaeological Heritage Management in the Dutch Caribbean,* edited by Corinne L. Hofman and Jay B. Haviser, 37–70. Leiden: Sidestone Academic Press.

Hawks, John. 2011. "Watch Who You Call _Extinct_!" *John Hawks* (blog). 2011. johnhawks.net/weblog/topics/race/taino-extinct-1000-genomes-2011.html.

Hebsgaard, Martin B., Matthew J. Phillips, and Eske Willerslev. 2005. "Geologically Ancient DNA: Fact or Artefact?" *Trends in Microbiology* 13(5): 212–220.

Herrera Malatesta, Eduardo. (2022). "The Transformation of Indigenous Landscape in the First Colonized Region of the Caribbean." *Land* 11(4): 509.

Herrera Malatesta, Eduardo, Eldris con Aguilar, and Arlene Alvarez. 2024. "Revising Biased Representations of Past Indigenous People in School Settings in the Dominican Republic." In *Local Voices, Global Debates: The Uses of Archaeological Heritage in the Caribbean,* edited by Joseph Sony Jean and Eduardo Herrera Malatesta, 32–55. Leiden: Brill.

Hill Collins, Patricia. 2022. *Black Feminist Thought: Knowledge, Consciousness, and the Politics of Empowerment.* New York: Routledge.

Hiraldo, Danielle, Miriam Jorgensen, Stephanie Russo Carroll, Dominique M. David-Chavez, and Mary Beth Jäger. 2020. "Native Nation Rebuilding for Tribal Research and Data Governance." NNI Policy Brief Series. Tucson: Native Nations Institute, University of Arizona.

hooks, bell. 1981. *Ain't I a Woman: Black Women and Feminism.* Boston: South End Press.

Hudson, Maui, Nanibaa' A. Garrison, Rogena Sterling, Nadine R. Caron, Keolu Fox, Joseph Yracheta, Jane Anderson, et al. 2020. "Rights, Interests and Expectations: Indigenous Perspectives on Unrestricted Access to Genomic Data." *Nature Reviews Genetics* 21(6): 377–384.

Huff, Chad D., David J. Witherspoon, Tatum S. Simonson, Jinchuan Xing, W. Scott Watkins, Yuhua Zhang, Therese M. Tuohy, Deborah W. Neklason, Randall W. Burt, and Stephen L. Guthery. 2011. "Maximum-Likelihood Estimation of Recent Shared Ancestry (ERSA)." *Genome Research* 21(5): 768–774.

Huston, P., V. L. Edge, and E. Bernier. 2019. "Open Science/Open Data: Reaping the Benefits of Open Data in Public Health." *Canada Communicable Disease Report* 45(11): 252.

International Bioethics Committee. 2023. "International Bioethics Committee (IBC)." UNESCO. https://www.unesco.org/en/ethics-science-technology/ibc (accessed June 26, 2024).

Jagosh, Justin, Paula L. Bush, Jon Salsberg, Ann C. Macaulay, Trish Greenhalgh, Geoff Wong, Margaret Cargo, Lawrence W. Green, Carol P. Herbert, and Pierre Pluye. 2015. "A Realist Evaluation of Community-Based Participatory Research: Partnership Synergy, Trust Building and Related Ripple Effects." *BMC Public Health* 15: 725–736.

Jaramillo-Valverde, Luis, Andrés Vásquez-Domínguez, Kelly S. Levano, Rony Castrejon-Cabanillas, Pedro Novoa-Bellota, Marco Machacuay-Romero, Ruth Garcia-de-la-Guarda, Raul J. Cano, Ruth Shady Solis, and Heinner Guio. 2022. "A Mobile Lab for Ancient DNA Extraction in Peru." *Bioinformation* 18(12): 1114.

Jensen, Theis Z. T., Jonas Niemann, Katrine Højholt Iversen, Anna K. Fotakis, Shyam Gopalakrishnan, Åshild J. Vågene, Mikkel Winther Pedersen, et al. 2019. "A 5700

Year-Old Human Genome and Oral Microbiome from Chewed Birch Pitch." *Nature Communications* 10(1): 5520.

Jones, Elizabeth D., and Elsbeth Bösl. 2021. "Ancient Human DNA: A History of Hype (Then and Now)." *Journal of Social Archaeology* 2(2).

Kean, Sam. 2019. "Historians Expose Early Scientists' Debt to the Slave Trade." *Science* (blog). April 4, 2019. https://www.sciencemag.org/news/2019/04/historians-expose-early-scientists-debt-slave-trade (accessed June 26, 2024).

Keegan, William F. 1996. "Columbus Was a Cannibal: Myth and the First Encounters." In *The Lesser Antilles in the Age of European Expansion,* edited by Robert L. Paquette and Stanley L. Engerman, 17–32. Gainesville: University Press of Florida.

Keegan, William F., and Corinne L. Hofman. 2017. *The Caribbean before Columbus.* Oxford: Oxford University Press.

Kemp, Melissa E., Alexis M. Mychajliw, Jenna Wadman, and Amy Goldberg. 2020. "7000 Years of Turnover: Historical Contingency and Human Niche Construction Shape the Caribbean's Anthropocene Biota." *Proceedings of the Royal Society B: Biological Sciences* 287(20200447): 1–10.

Kiefer, Philip. 2022. "Anthropologists Are Still Wrestling with Their Obligations to the Living and Dead." *Popular Science* (blog). April 13, 2022. https://www.popsci.com/science/anthropology-human-remains-guidelines/ (accessed June 26, 2024).

Knoppers, B. M., and Joly, Yann. 2018. "Introduction: The Why and Whither of Genomic Data Sharing." *Human Genetics* 137(8): 569–574.

Kowal, Emma, Laura S. Weyrich, Juan Manuel Argüelles, Alyssa C. Bader, Chip Colwell, Amanda Daniela Cortez, Jenny L. Davis, et al. 2023. "Community Partnerships Are Fundamental to Ethical Ancient DNA Research." *Human Genetics and Genomics Advances* 4(2): 100161.

Kurin, Richard. 2019. "Rescuing Bahamian Culture from Dorian's Wrath." *Smithsonian,* November 22, 2019. https://www.smithsonianmag.com/smithsonian-institution/rescuing-bahamian-culture-dorians-wrath-180973588/ (accessed June 26, 2024).

Laguer Díaz, Carmen A. 2013. *The Construction of an Identity and the Politics of Remembering.* Oxford: Oxford University Press.

Lalueza-Fox, C., F. L. Calderon, F. Calafell, B. Morera, and J. Bertranpetit. 2001. "MtDNA from Extinct Tainos and the Peopling of the Caribbean." *Annals of Human Genetics* 65(2): 137–151.

Lalueza-Fox, C., M. T. P. Gilbert, A. J. Martínez-Fuentes, F. Calafell, and J. Bertranpetit. 2003. "Mitochondrial DNA from Pre-Columbian Ciboneys from Cuba and the Prehistoric Colonization of the Caribbean: mtDNA From Extinct Ciboneys from Cuba." *American Journal of Physical Anthropology* 121(2): 97–108.

LeFebvre, Michelle J., Christina M. Giovas, and Jason E. Laffoon. 2019. "Advancing the Study of Amerindian Ecodynamics in the Caribbean: Current Perspectives." *Environmental Archaeology* 24(2): 107–114.

Le Gall, Sharon. 2012. "Defining Traditional Knowledge: A Perspective from the Caribbean." *Caribbean Quarterly* 58(4): 62–68.

Lemke, Amy A., Edward D. Esplin, Aaron J. Goldenberg, Claudia Gonzaga-Jauregui, Neil A. Hanchard, Julie Harris-Wai, Justin E. Ideozu, et al. 2022. "Addressing

Underrepresentation in Genomics Research through Community Engagement." *American Journal of Human Genetics* 109(9): 1563–1571.

Lenik, Stephan. 2012. "Carib as a Colonial Category: Comparing Ethnohistoric and Archaeological Evidence from Dominica, West Indies." *Ethnohistory* 59(1): 79–107.

Lewis, Dawn A., Rebecca Simpson, Azure Hermes, Alex Brown, and Bastien Llamas. 2023. "More than Dirt: Sedimentary Ancient DNA and Indigenous Australia." *Molecular Ecology Resources.* DOI: 10.1111/1755-0998.13835.

Liu, Yichen, Xiaowei Mao, Johannes Krause, and Qiaomei Fu. 2021. "Insights into Human History from the First Decade of Ancient Human Genomics." *Science* 373(6562): 1479–1484.

Llamas, Bastien, Xavier Roca Rada, and Evelyn Collen. 2020. "Ancient DNA Helps Trace the Peopling of the World." *Biochemist* 42(1): 18–22.

López Lloreda, Claudia. 2022. "Researchers in Puerto Rico Struggle to Adapt in the Aftermath of Hurricane Fiona." *Science.* https://www.science.org/content/article/researchers-puerto-rico-struggle-adapt-aftermath-hurricane-fiona (accessed June 26, 2024).

Madrilejo, Nicole, Holden Lombard, and Jada Benn Torres. 2015. "Origins of Marron-age: Mitochondrial Lineages of Jamaica's Accompong Town Maroons: Maternal Ancestries of Jamaican Maroons." *American Journal of Human Biology* 27(3): 432–437.

Mallick, Swapan, Adam Micco, Matthew Mah, Harald Ringbauer, Iosif Lazaridis, Iñigo Olalde, Nick Patterson, and David Reich. 2023. "The Allen Ancient DNA Resource (AADR): A Curated Compendium of Ancient Human Genomes." *bioRxiv,* April 6, 2023.

Martínez-San Miguel, Yolanda. 2011. "Taino Warriors? Strategies for Recovering Indigenous Voices in Colonial and Contemporary Hispanic Caribbean Discourses." *Centro Journal* 23(1): 197–215.

McCartney, Ann M., Jane Anderson, Libby Liggins, Maui L. Hudson, Matthew Z. Anderson, Ben TeAika, Janis Geary, Robert Cook-Deegan, Hardip R. Patel, and Adam M. Phillippy. 2022. "Balancing Openness with Indigenous Data Sovereignty: An Opportunity to Leave No One behind in the Journey to Sequence All of Life." *Proceedings of the National Academy of Sciences* 119(4): e2115860119.

McClellan III, James E. 2010. *Colonialism and Science: Saint Domingue in the Old Regime.* Chicago: University of Chicago Press.

McWhirter, R. E. 2012. "The History of Bioethics: Implications for Current Debates in Health Research." *Perspectives in Biology and Medicine* 55(3): 329–338.

Mega, Emiliano Rodríguez. 2023. "Navigating the Ethics of Ancient Human DNA Research." *Knowable Magazine,* January 1, 2023. https://knowablemagazine.org/content/article/society/2023/navigating-ethics-ancient-human-dna-research (accessed July 21, 2025).

Mickleburgh, Hayley L. 2015. "Skeletons in the Closet: Future Avenues for the Curation of Archaeological Human Skeletal Remains in the Dutch Caribbean and the Rest of the Region." In *Managing Our Past into the Future: Archaeological Heritage Management in the Dutch Caribbean,* edited by Corinne L. Hofman and Jay B. Haviser, 113–30. Leiden: Sidestone Press.

Mills, Melinda C., and Charles Rahal. 2019. "A Scientometric Review of Genome-Wide Association Studies." *Communications Biology* 2(1): 9.

Minkler, M. 2004. "Ethical Challenges for the 'Outside' Researcher in Community-Based Participatory Research." *Health Education & Behavior: The Official Publication of the Society for Public Health Education* 31: 684–97.

Mohammed, Ryan S., Grace Turner, Kelly Fowler, Michael Pateman, Maria A. Nieves-Colón, Lanya Fanovich, Siobhan B. Cooke, et al. 2022. "Colonial Legacies Influence Biodiversity Lessons: How Past Trade Routes and Power Dynamics Shape Present-Day Scientific Research and Professional Opportunities for Caribbean Scientists." *American Naturalist* 20(1): 140–155.

Moreno-Estrada, Andrés, Simon Gravel, Fouad Zakharia, Jacob L. McCauley, Jake K. Byrnes, Christopher R. Gignoux, Patricia A. Ortiz-Tello, et al. 2013. "Reconstructing the Population Genetic History of the Caribbean." *PLoS Genetics* 9(11): e1003925.

Muhammad, Adbul-Aliy. 2021. "Penn Museum Owes Reparations for Previously Holding Remains of a MOVE Bombing Victim." (Philadelphia) *Inquirer.* April 21, 2021. https://onamove.com/penn-museum-owes-reparations-for-previously -holding-remains-of-a-move-bombing-victim-opinion/ (accessed June 27, 2024).

Murphy, Kathleen S. 2013. "Collecting Slave Traders: James Petiver, Natural History, and the British Slave Trade." *William and Mary Quarterly* 70(4): 637.

Nägele, Kathrin, Maite Rivollat, He Yu, and Ke Wang. 2022. "Ancient Genomic Research—From Broad Strokes to Nuanced Reconstructions of the Past." *Journal of Anthropological Sciences* 100: 193–230.

Nieves-Colón, Maria A., William J. Pestle, Austin W. Reynolds, Bastien Llamas, Constanza de la Fuente, Kathleen Fowler, Katherine M. Skerry, Edwin Crespo-Torres, Carlos D. Bustamante, and Anne C. Stone. 2020. "Ancient DNA Reconstructs the Genetic Legacies of Precontact Puerto Rico Communities." *Molecular Biology and Evolution* 37(3): 611–626.

Office of Secretary of the Interior, Department of the Interior. 1990. *Native American Graves Protection and Repatriation Regulations* 43: CFR Part 10.

Oliver, José R. 2009. *Caciques and Cemí Idols: The Web Spun by Taíno Rulers between Hispaniola and Puerto Rico.* Tuscaloosa: University of Alabama Press.

Pääbo, Svante, Hendrik Poinar, David Serre, Viviane Jaenicke-Després, Juliane Hebler, Nadin Rohland, Melanie Kuch, Johannes Krause, Linda Vigilant, and Michael Hofreiter. 2004. "Genetic Analyses from Ancient DNA." *Annual Review of Genetics* 38(1): 645–679.

Pagán-Jiménez, Jaime R. 2004. "Is All Archaeology at Present a Postcolonial One? Constructive Answers from an Eccentric Point of View." *Journal of Social Archaeology* 4(2): 200–213.

Pagán-Jiménez, Jaime, and Reniel Rodríguez Ramos. 2008. "Sobre arqueologías de liberación en una 'colonia postcolonial' (Puerto Rico)." *Revista de Ciencias Sociales,* 34.

Pedersen, Mikkel W., Catia Antunes, Binia de Cahsan, J. Víctor Moreno-Mayar, Martin Sikora, Lasse Vinner, Darren Mann, Pavel B. Klimov, Stuart Black, and Catalina Teresa Michieli. 2022. "Ancient Human Genomes and Environmental DNA from the Cement Attaching 2,000-Year-Old Head Lice Nits." *Molecular Biology and Evolution* 39(2): msab351.

Perdikaris, Sophia, Rebecca Boger, Edith Gonzalez, Emira Ibrahimpašić, and Jennifer D. Adams. 2021. "Disrupted Identities and Forced Nomads: A Post-Disaster Legacy of Neocolonialism in the Island of Barbuda, Lesser Antilles." *Island Studies Journal* 16(1): 115–134.

Pešoutová, J. 2019. *Indigenous Ancestors and Healing Landscapes: Cultural Memory and Intercultural Communication in the Dominican Republic and Cuba.* Leiden: Sidestone Press.

Pestle, William J., L. Antonio Curet, Reniel Rodríguez Ramos, and Miguel Rodríguez López. 2013. "New Questions and Old Paradigms: Reexamining Caribbean Culture History." *Latin American Antiquity* 24(3): 243–261.

Petit, Charles. 1998. "Trying to Study Tribes While Respecting Their Cultures / Hopi Indian Geneticist Can See Both Sides." *SFGate,* February 19, 1998. https://www.sfgate.com/news/article/Trying-to-Study-Tribes-While-Respecting-Their-3012825.php (accessed June 24, 2025).

Picking, David, and Ina Vandebroek. 2019. "Traditional and Local Knowledge Systems in the Caribbean: Jamaica as a Case Study." In *Traditional and Indigenous Knowledge for the Modern Era,* edited by David R. Katerere, Wendy Applequist, Oluwaseyi M. Aboyade, and Chamunorwa Togo, 89–115. Boca Raton: CRC Press.

Powell, Kendall. 2021. "The Broken Promise That Undermines Human Genome Research." *Nature* 590(7845): 198–202.

Pratt, Elizabeth. 2020. "The Medical Ethics of HeLa Cells (2020–2021)." SUNY College Cortland Digital Commons. https://digitalcommons.cortland.edu/cgi/viewcontent.cgi?article=1007&context=rhetdragonsresearchinquiry (accessed June 26, 2024).

Prictor, Megan, Harriet J. A. Teare, and Jane Kaye. 2018. "Equitable Participation in Biobanks: The Risks and Benefits of a 'Dynamic Consent' Approach." *Frontiers in Public Health* 6: 253.

Protections (OHRP), Office for Human Research. 2009. "Federal Policy for the Protection of Human Subjects ('Common Rule')." June 23, 2009. https://www.hhs.gov/ohrp/regulations-and-policy/regulations/common-rule/index.html (accessed June 26, 2024).

Rahimzadeh, Vasiliki, Stephanie O. M. Dyke, and Bartha M. Knoppers. 2016. "An International Framework for Data Sharing: Moving Forward with the Global Alliance for Genomics and Health." *Biopreservation and Biobanking* 14(3): 256–259.

Reardon, Jenny. 2011. "Human Population Genomics and the Dilemma of Difference." In *Reframing Rights: Bioconstitutionalism in the Genetic Age,* edited by Sheila Jasanoff, 217–38. Cambridge: MIT Press.

Reid, Basil A. 2009. *Myths and Realities of Caribbean History.* Tuscaloosa: University of California Press.

Riding In, James. 1996. "Repatriation: A Pawnee's Perspective." *American Indian Quarterly* 20(2): 238–250.

Rinde, Meir. 2019. "The Death of Jesse Gelsinger, 20 Years Later." Science History Institute. June 4, 2019. https://www.sciencehistory.org/distillations/the-death-of-jesse-gelsinger-20-years-later (accessed June 26, 2024).

Ringbauer, Harald, Yilei Huang, Ali Akbari, Swapan Mallick, Nick Patterson, and David Emil Reich. 2023. "ancIBD-Screening for Identity by Descent Segments in Human Ancient DNA." bioRxiv, March 9, 2023.

Rivera-Collazo, Isabel C. 2011a. "Paleoecology and Human Occupation during the Mid-Holocene in Puerto Rico: The Case of Angostura." In Communities in Contact: Essays in Archaeology, Ethnohistory, and Ethnography of the Amerindian Circum-Caribbean, edited by Corinne L. Hofman and Anne Van Duijvenbode, 407–20. Leiden: Sidestone Press.

Rivera-Collazo, Isabel C. 2011b. "The Ghost of Caliban: Island Archaeology, Insular Archaeologists, and the Caribbean." In Islands at the Crossroads: Migration, Seafaring, and Interaction in the Caribbean, edited by L. Antonio Curet and Mark W. Hauser, 22–40. Tuscaloosa: University of Alabama Press.

Rivera-Collazo, Isabel C. 2020. "Severe Weather and the Reliability of Desk-Based Vulnerability Assessments: The Impact of Hurricane Maria to Puerto Rico's Coastal Archaeology." Journal of Island and Coastal Archaeology 15(2): 244–263.

Rivera-Pagán, Luis N. 2003. "Freedom and Servitude: Indigenous Slavery and the Spanish Conquest of the Caribbean." In General History of the Caribbean: Volume I: Autochthonous Societies, edited by Jalil Sued-Badillo, 316–62. New York: Palgrave Macmillan.

Roca-Rada, Xavier, Yassine Souilmi, João C. Teixeira, and Bastien Llamas. 2020. "Ancient DNA Studies in Pre-Columbian Mesoamerica." Genes 11(11): 1346.

Rodríguez Ramos, Reniel. 2010. Rethinking Puerto Rican Precolonial History. Tuscaloosa: University of Alabama Press.

Rodríguez Ramos, Reniel, and Jaime R. Pagán-Jiménez. 2016. "Sobre nuestras indigenidades Boricuas." In Indígenas e Indios En El Caribe: Presencia, Legado y Estudio, edited by Jorge Ulloa Hong and Roberto Valcárcel Rojas, 97–114. Santo Domingo, Dominican Republic: Editora Búho.

Rogoziński, Jan. 1999. A Brief History of the Caribbean. New York: Plume.

Ross, Ann H., William F. Keegan, Michael P. Pateman, and Colleen B. Young. 2020. "Faces Divulge the Origins of Caribbean Prehistoric Inhabitants." Scientific Reports 10(1): 147.

Rostain, S. 2007. "L'archéologie des départements français d'Amérique." Les nouvelles de l'archéologie 108/109: 5–6.

Rouse, Irving. 1987. Migrations in Prehistory. Inferring Population Movement from Cultural Remains. New Haven, Connecticut: Yale University Press.

Rouse, Irving. 1992. The Tainos. New Haven, Connecticut: Yale University Press.

Schurr, Theodore G., Jada Benn Torres, Miguel G. Vilar, Jill B. Gaieski, and Carlalynne Melendez. 2016. "An Emerging History of Indigenous Caribbean and Circum-Caribbean Populations: Insights from Archaeological, Ethnographic, Genetic and Historical Studies." In New Directions in Biocultural Anthropology, edited by Molly

K. Zuckerman and Debra L. Martin, 385–402. Hoboken, New Jersey: John Wiley & Sons.

Schwaller, Robert C. 2018. "Contested Conquests: African Maroons and the Incomplete Conquest of Hispaniola, 1519–1620." *Americas* 75(4): 609–638.

Siegel, Peter E. 2013. "Caribbean Archaeology in Historical Perspective." In *The Oxford Handbook of Caribbean Archaeology*, edited by William F. Keegan, Corinne L. Hofman, and Reniel Rodríguez Ramos. Oxford: Oxford University Press.

Siegel, Peter E., Corinne L. Hofman, Benoît Bérard, Reg Murphy, Jorge Ulloa Hung, Roberto Valcárcel Rojas, and Cheryl White. 2013. "Confronting Caribbean Heritage in an Archipelago of Diversity: Politics, Stakeholders, Climate Change, Natural Disasters, Tourism, and Development." *Journal of Field Archaeology* 38(4): 376–390.

Sirak, Kendra A., Daniel M. Fernandes, Olivia Cheronet, Mario Novak, Beatriz Gamarra, Tímea Balassa, Zsolt Bernert, Andrea Cséki, János Dani, and József Zsolt Gallina. 2017. "A Minimally-Invasive Method for Sampling Human Petrous Bones from the Cranial Base for Ancient DNA Analysis." *BioTechniques* 62(6): 283–289.

Sirak, Kendra A., and Jakob W. Sedig. 2019. "Balancing Analytical Goals and Anthropological Stewardship in the Midst of the Paleogenomics Revolution." *World Archaeology* 51(4): 560–573.

St. Eustatius Afrikan Burial Ground Alliance. 2024. Main page. https://steustatiusafrikanburialground.org/ (accessed June 26, 2024).

Sued-Badillo, Jalil. 2020. "Cristobal Colón y la esclavitud de los Amerindios en el Caribe." In *Caribe Taíno: Ensayos Históricos Sobre El Siglo XVI*, edited by Jalil Sued Badillo, 217–56. San Juan, Puerto Rico: Editorial Luscinia C.E.

Sued-Badillo, Jalil. 1992. "Facing up to Caribbean History." *American Antiquity* 57(4): 599.

Sued-Badillo, Jalil. 2007. "Guadalupe: ¿Caribe o Taína? La isla de Guadalupe y su cuestionable identidad Caribe en la época pre-colombina: Una revisión etnohistórica y arqueológica preliminar." *Caribbean Studies* 35(1): 50.

TallBear, Kim. 2013. *Native American DNA: Tribal Belonging and the False Promise of Genetic Science*. Minneapolis: University of Minnesota Press.

TallBear, Kimberly. 2001. "The Tribal Specific Approach to Genetic Research and Technology." Paper presented at R&D Management Conference, Wellington, New Zealand, February 9, 2001. https://citeseerx.ist.psu.edu/document?repid=rep1&type=pdf&doi=22206ffdff13352d83a702ef470fed72b27ff2ea (accessed July 21, 2025).

Tamburrini, Camila, Silvia Lucrecia Dahinten, Rubén Ricardo Romero Saihueque, María C. Ávila-Arcos, and María Laura Parolin. 2023. "Towards an Ethical and Legal Framework in Archeogenomics: A Local Case in the Atlantic Coast of Central Patagonia." *American Journal of Biological Anthropology* 182(2): 161–176.

Tauri, Juan Marcellus. 2014. "Resisting Condescending Research Ethics in Aotearoa New Zealand." *AlterNative: An International Journal of Indigenous Peoples* 10(2): 134–150.

TCETHR, AAA. 2023. "The Commission for the Ethical Treatment of Human Remains (TCETHR)—Participate & Advocate." April 18, 2023. https://americananthro .org/about/committees-and-task-forces/tcethr/ (accessed June 26, 2024).

Tiffin, Nicki. 2018. "Tiered Informed Consent: Respecting Autonomy, Agency and Individuality in Africa." *BMJ Global Health* 3(6): e001249.

Trope, Jack F., and Walter R. Echo-Hawk. 1992. "Native American Graves Protection and Repatriation Act: Background and Legislative History." *Arizona State Law Journal* 24(1): 35–78.

Trustees of the Natural History Museum. N.d. "Historical Collections—Natural History Museum." https://www.nhm.ac.uk/our-science/collections/entomology -collections/historical-collections.html (accessed June 26, 2024).

Tsosie, Krystal S., Keolu Fox, and Joseph M. Yracheta. 2021. "Genomics Data: The Broken Promise Is to Indigenous People." *Nature* 591(7851): 529–530.

Tsosie, Krystal S., Joseph M. Yracheta, and Donna Dickenson. 2019. "Overvaluing Individual Consent Ignores Risks to Tribal Participants." *Nature Reviews Genetics* 20(9): 497–498.

Tsosie, Krystal S., Joseph M. Yracheta, Jessica Kolopenuk, and R. A. Smith. 2020. "Letter to the Editor: Indigenous Data Sovereignties and Data Sharing in Biological Anthropology." *American Journal of Physical Anthropology* 174(2): 183–186.

Turner, Margaret Kemarre, Barry McDonald Perrurle, and Veronica Perrurle Dobson. 2010. *Iwenhe Tyerrtye: What It Means to Be an Aboriginal Person.* Alice Springs, Australia: IAD Press.

Turner, Trudy R., and Connie J. Mulligan. 2019. "Data Sharing in Biological Anthropology: Guiding Principles and Best Practices." *American Journal of Physical Anthropology* 170(1): 3–4.

Turner, Trudy R., Jennifer K. Wagner, and Graciela S. Cabana. 2018. "Ethics in Biological Anthropology." *American Journal of Physical Anthropology* 165(4): 939–951.

Ubelaker, Douglas H., and Lauryn Guttenplan Grant. 1989. "Human Skeletal Remains: Preservation or Reburial?" *American Journal of Physical Anthropology* 32(S10): 249–287.

Udesky, Laurie. 2010. "The Ethics of Direct-to-Consumer Genetic Testing." *Lancet* 376(9750): 1377–1378.

Ulloa Hong, Jorge. 2016. "Colonialismo, Indigenismo, y arqueología en República Dominicana: Silencios confusos y encubrimientos diversos." In *Indígenas e Indios En El Caribe: Presencia, Legado y Estudio,* edited by Jorge Ulloa Hong and Roberto Valcárcel Rojas, 203–46. Santo Domingo, Dominican Republic: Editora Búho.

United Nations. 1992. "Convention on Biological Diversity." 1992. https://www.cbd.int/ doc/legal/cbd-en.pdf (accessed June 26, 2024).

United Nations. 2015. "Transforming our World: The 2030 Agenda for Sustainable Development." https://sdgs.un.org/2030agenda (accessed June 28, 2024).

United Nations. 2007. "United Nations Declaration on the Rights of Indigenous Peoples." 2007. https://social.desa.un.org/issues/indigenous-peoples/united-nations -declaration-on-the-rights-of-indigenous-peoples (accessed June 26, 2024).

US Code of Federal Regulations. 2024. "IRB Review of Research." National Archives. https://www.ecfr.gov/current/title-45/subtitle-A/subchapter-A/part-46/subpart-A/section-46.109 (accessed June 28, 2024).

US Department of Health and Human Services. 2010. "International Compilation of Human Research Standards." October 15, 2010. https://www.hhs.gov/ohrp/international/compilation-human-research-standards/index.html (accessed June 26, 2024).

Utge, José, Noémie Sévêque, Anne-Sophie Lartigot-Campin, Agnès Testu, Anne-Marie Moigne, Régis Vézian, Frédéric Maksud, Robert Begouën, Christine Verna, Sylvain Soriano, and Jean-Marc Elalouf. 2020. "A Mobile Laboratory for Ancient DNA Analysis." *PLoS One* 15(3): e0230496.

Valcárcel Rojas, Roberto. 2016. "El mundo colonial y los indios en las Antillas Mayores: Repensando su estudio arqueológico." *Boletín del Museo del Hombre Dominicano* 47: 359–376.

Vernot, Benjamin, Elena I. Zavala, Asier Gómez-Olivencia, Zenobia Jacobs, Viviane Slon, Fabrizio Mafessoni, Frédéric Romagné, et al. 2021. "Unearthing Neanderthal Population History Using Nuclear and Mitochondrial DNA from Cave Sediments." *Science* 372(6542): eabf1667.

Wagner, Jennifer K., Chip Colwell, Katrina G. Claw, Anne C. Stone, Deborah A. Bolnick, John Hawks, Kyle B. Brothers, and Nanibaa' A. Garrison. 2020. "Fostering Responsible Research on Ancient DNA." *American Journal of Human Genetics* 107(2): 183–195.

Whitehead, Neil L. 2011. *Of Cannibals and Kings.* University Park: Pennsylvania State University Press.

Wilkinson, Mark D., Michael Dumontier, Ijsbrand Jan Aalbersberg, Gabrielle Appleton, Myles Axton, Arie Baak, Niklas Blomberg, Jan-Willem Boiten, Luiz Bonino da Silva Santos, and Philip E. Bourne. "The FAIR Guiding Principles for Scientific Data Management and Stewardship." *Scientific Data* 3(1): 1–9.

Willerslev, Eske, and David J. Meltzer. 2021. "Peopling of the Americas as Inferred from Ancient Genomics." *Nature* 594(7863): 356–364.

Winful, Taiye, Katie McCormack, Elsa Mueller, Lijuan Chen, La Corporación Piñones Se Integra (COPI), Maricruz Rivera Clemente, and Jada Benn Torres. 2023. "Exploring the Legacy of African and Indigenous Caribbean Admixture in Puerto Rico." *American Journal of Biological Anthropology* 182(2): 194–209.

Yáñez, Bernardo, Agustín Fuentes, Constanza P. Silva, Gonzalo Figueiro, Lumila P. Menéndez, Vivette García-Deister, Constanza de la Fuente-Castro, Columba González-Duarte, Camila Tamburrini, and Juan Manuel Argüelles. 2023. "Pace and Space in the Practice of aDNA Research: Concerns from the Periphery." *American Journal of Biological Anthropology* 180(3): 417–422.

Yaremko, Jason M. 2009. "'Obvious Indian'—Missionaries, Anthropologists, and the 'Wild Indians' of Cuba: Representations of the Amerindian Presence in Cuba." *Ethnohistory* 56(3): 449–477.

Zornosa, Laura. 2021. "Taíno People Want to Stop Christie's Sale of Artifacts." *New York Times,* November 9, 2021. https://www.nytimes.com/2021/11/09/arts/design/taino-artifacts-christies-sale.html (accessed June 24, 2025).

8

Boxing and Re-Boxing Artifacts

Rethinking Archaeological Collections in the Caribbean

JOHN ANGUS MARTIN AND JOSEPH SONY JEAN

There has long been a standing demand for reparations, reparative justice, and repatriation on multiple levels to address the evils of colonialism (slavery, invasion, discrimination, exploitation, banditry, and outright genocide). However, few thought that the struggle would be realized in such short order, due to the continuing rejection by some former colonial powers, for example the United Kingdom (Beckles 2013, 2021; Hicks 2020). A few decades ago it would have been unthinkable to envision the repatriation of looted and removed objects from countries as a result of colonialism and imperialism, but in the past few years several former colonial powers, among them Germany and the Netherlands, have taken the lead in correcting these egregious wrongs. This has emboldened former colonies to push harder for the return of their cultural heritage—an important part of their citizens' history, and thus education and identity.

This chapter, in discussing the ethics of Caribbean archaeology, will explore the current state of repatriation of objects (excluding human remains or biological samples) excavated legally, looted, or otherwise illegally removed from the region and why it is imperative that Caribbean peoples demand the return of their cultural heritage. It will also examine how current power imbalances between some international archaeological projects and Caribbean governments and local heritage institutions need to change. As a way of illustrating the complexities of the historical and current state of archaeological collections in the Caribbean, this paper will present two examples from the region: Haiti in the Greater Antilles, and Grenada and Carriacou in the Lesser Antilles. By examining the status of archaeological artifacts in these islands, this chapter addresses some of the important issues surrounding the ethics of archaeological artifacts, their ownership, and responsibility for their storage and care, as well as critically envisioning solutions on moving forward. Excavated artifacts have often served scientific and educational purposes and have been exhibited to the general public in museums. Our position is that Caribbean countries have the right to reclaim their artifacts currently housed abroad, and this process should not merely involve packing artifacts into boxes and returning them to their countries of origin. Instead, it should emphasize establishing a commitment to the artifacts' long-term care and preservation.

Approaching Returns and Implications for Archaeological and Heritage Practices

Discussions about returning artifacts to countries of origin have increased recently in popular culture and in academia. These discussions, particularly concerning artifacts looted or removed in colonial contexts, are critical in archaeology and heritage debates (e.g. Agostinho 2024; Amo-Agyemang 2024; Sarr and Savoy 2018; Turnbull and Pickering 2010). Recent decolonial and postcolonial critiques have also proposed further consideration of collections from past excavations (e.g., Montgomery and Supernant 2022; Nilsson Stutz 2013). These critiques give shape to the need to challenge the colonial legacies embedded within archaeological and heritage practices. Scholars consider repatriation and restitution as restorative and heritage justice (e.g., Joy 2020; Simpson 2009), which help renew traditions and promote healing in local communities (e.g., Aranui 2020; Atkinson 2010). While repatriating archaeological objects to their country of origin serves many interests, critics note the challenges of stewardship once the objects are repatriated. In a popular opinion piece entitled "Repatriation of Artefacts: A Recipe for Disaster" published in *History Reclaimed,* Elizabeth Weiss (2022) used the case of the Benin Bronzes being returned to Nigeria to express concerns about the long-term care of artifacts returned to unsecured locations. Weiss took as examples the cases of different countries in Africa, such as Tanzania, Ethiopia, and Nigeria, to illustrate issues related to improper care in museums, including destruction, vandalism, looting, and neglect in these countries. Weiss argued that when the Benin Bronzes returned to their new home, they would face theft, neglect, or destruction, as had so many other lost treasures of Africa. Indeed, arguments for rejecting return requests frequently state that the country of origin lacks adequate facilities for the storage and display of objects (see also Cuno 2014; Stack 2019). We recognize the challenges many countries face in preserving their collections; however, they have the right to claim the return of their heritage. Approaches that focus on ethical return consider a shared stewardship policy to fully engage in discussion and action for returning artifacts to the country of origin (Smithsonian Institution 2022).

Reclaiming objects is also currently causing issues in applying specific international laws, since objects housed outside the countries of origin are from diverse and unclear circumstances, which may for example involve military extraction and missionary expeditions. Conversations about the return of collections go beyond academic debates and into diplomatic and political discourses and practices, seeing repatriation as an act of reconciliation between states. In an example of a European country holding many collections that are not theirs, the Dutch government's advisory report *Colonial Collections and Recognition of Injustice* stands in favor of returning stolen collections and concludes that "there is no possibility of undoing the historical injustices that took place during the colonial period. However, a contribution can be made to redress injustices by taking responsibility for the legacy of that past when dealing with colonial cultural objects" (Raad voor Cultuur 2022: 83).

Increasingly, conversations concerning reclamation and repatriation are being amplified in the Caribbean (Françozo and Strecker 2017). When addressing archaeological practice, the return of archaeological objects goes beyond artifacts looted in colonial and imperialist circumstances. In this case, it concerns past and present stewardship of excavated collections. It raises the questions of who should and how to curate artifacts in a post-excavation context. Calling for repatriation of archaeological objects is not new in Caribbean debates (Cummins 2006), but these questions were critical at a panel discussion at the Society for American Archaeology's conference in 2016, at which presenters in the session "Caribbean Archaeological Collections: History, Museums, and Politics," discussed legal issues and possibilities surrounding the ownership and display of Caribbean archaeological objects in the context of claims for repatriation and reparations (SAA 2016). Moreover, during a 2021 online workshop entitled "Local Voices, Global Debates" about Caribbean archaeology and heritage, scholars and practitioners from the Caribbean raised concerns about the heritage missing from their countries (Jean, Herrera Malatesta, and Jacobson 2024). These issues voiced by local actors are also reflected in the challenges related to storage and curation in the Caribbean, some of the most pressing issues facing archaeological and museum practices (Kersel 2015). Addressing these issues, Schiappacasse

(2019) has highlighted the beneficial approach of training students in collection preservation and collection-based research, illustrating alternative methods for research data collection beyond excavation.

Despite the importance of collection-based research, as highlighted by Murphy (2014), many communities in the Caribbean face an ongoing challenge in managing data and collections, especially after decades of scientific research in the region. In the case of Haiti for instance, Jean et al. (2020) point out that the problems of inadequate storage spaces and poor cataloguing critically impact the conservation and preservation of archaeological heritage (see also Vendryes 2013). Combining factors like unsuitable conditions in their homeland with guarantees of stewardship at established institutions overseas creates a complex situation. When research permits have been granted, a country should retain the right to reclaim its collections from international institutions in the future. In reclaiming, one may ask, what is the ethical responsibility of research institutions toward people's culture and history? Furthermore, if repatriation is not funded, and adequate resources to sustain the collections in the future are not provided, how can we ensure these collections are preserved and protected?

In April 2022, the Smithsonian Institution adopted a policy on Shared Stewardship and Ethical Returns (Smithsonian Institution 2022). This policy addresses ethical concerns related to items in the Smithsonian's collections and considers that past historical collecting practices may not be in accordance with current ethical standards. The policy advocates for shared stewardship arrangements in which the Smithsonian and other relevant parties, such as communities, individuals, and governments, that have a role in caring for and interpreting the objects, should consider the return of collections, based on ethical considerations. While this step forward by the Smithsonian has implications for the Caribbean, other important compiled works have laid the groundwork to further address the challenges of heritage co-stewardship in the Caribbean more specifically (e.g. Cummins, Farmer, and Russell 2013; Jean and Herrera Malatesta 2024; Ostapkowicz and Hanna 2021; Siegel and Righter 2011).

Examples from the Greater and Lesser Antilles

To illustrate the current state of archaeological collections in the Caribbean, this chapter presents two examples: Haiti in the Greater Antilles, and Grenada and Carriacou in the Lesser Antilles. It looks at the conditions under which archaeological fieldwork has been carried out in these islands in the past century, leading to the accumulation of large archaeological collections and their dominance to the detriment of all other collections, including historical ones. It will show that, despite great benefits in knowledge to local museums and communities, the storage of these large collections has created outsized burdens, especially for small heritage institutions. Asymmetrical relationships between research projects and local governments/communities can lead to an untenable situation. Here, we will center potential solutions regarding the countries' cultural and heritage goals, and museum policies and their varied heritage, and not solely the interests of international institutions.

Pagán-Jiménez and Rodríguez Ramos (2008) have proposed the need to move toward an "archaeology of liberation." This pathway must untie practices of archaeology from colonialism by making the "the desired post-colonial, multivocal, multitangential, and/or polycentric conditions possible in eccentric contexts with respect to the centers of theoretical production" (Pagán-Jiménez and Rodríguez Ramos 2008: 55). This reflection conveys the historical and ongoing unequal relationship between international research projects and local governments/communities and heritage institutions. In many cases, the relations produce a power imbalance where local people are at the mercy of those who have better access to academic knowledge and financial resources. This can place local communities and institutions at a disadvantage, even when foreign researchers are well meaning. Due to the absence or limited presence of local archaeological knowledge and specific archaeological policies by governments and heritage institutions, the status quo regarding power imbalance is likely to continue until the underlying causes are addressed.

Looking beyond the Dig: Challenging the Dominance of Archaeological Collections in Grenada and Carriacou

Archaeological studies across the Caribbean have added new and fascinating dimensions to the study of the region's past (Keegan and Hofman 2017; Reid and Gilmore 2014). The discipline has the potential to complement historical sources and enhance our understanding of the diverse chronologies of Caribbean peoples. It has already transformed the study of precolonial societies' lifeways and deathways, enabling discussions on the origins of various Indigenous groups, migration and interaction patterns, chronologies, settlement patterns, and technological advancements (Boomert 1986; Bright 2011; Bullen 1964; Fitzpatrick et al. 2014; Hofman and Antczak 2019; Keegan and Hofman 2017; Rouse 1964, 1992). Additionally, these studies have pushed back the occupation date of the islands by centuries, thus negating or at least minimizing the prevailing view that Caribbean history began with the arrival of Europeans in 1492, and have thereby proven important in island and regional identities (Honychurch 2000; Lowenthal 1972).

In the case of Grenada and Carriacou, archaeological studies have provided a wealth of knowledge on Indigenous peoples, particularly in the so-called "contact period" (Hanna 2017; Holdren 1998; Hofman 2016, 2017; Hofman et al. 2022), but much remains to be done. Historical or colonial archaeology, which has the potential to provide unique insights into the lives of the enslaved, slavery, plantations, and the evolution of Creole society has until now been almost non-existent on Grenada and Carriacou because it has not been a priority for international researchers. Recent excavations at La Poterie, Saint Andrew, have revealed evidence of possible "slave huts" and remains of "Afro-Caribbean pottery" that only begin to tell this story (Hofman 2016, 2017; Hofman et al. 2022; Martin 2023).

The early twentieth century witnessed the advent of extensive archaeological investigations in Grenada, which have become even more intensive since the 1960s. Dozens of Indigenous sites have been identified across Grenada and Carriacou, dating from the Early Ceramic Age (Saladoid series) to the early colonial period (Cayo complex) (Bullen 1964; Cody 1991; Hanna 2017; Holdren 1998). In the early 1900s, collections-based studies were carried out by Holmes (1907) and Fewkes (1922), and surveys were carried out by Huckerby (1921). Four decades later, Bullen (1964) did the most comprehensive archaeological study to date in Grenada by surveying and testing sites across the island. After examining thousands of pottery sherds he developed a typology, and defined new ceramic types named after places in Grenada: Pearls and Simon, Saint Andrew; Caliviny, Saint George; and Suazey, Saint Patrick (Bullen 1964).

Professional field studies remained practically absent until Petitjean Roget (1981) conducted salvage archaeology and surveys at the construction site of the international airport at Point Salines in 1980, and at several other sites across Grenada. Banks (1988, 1993) carried out several surveys between 1986 and 1988. Keegan (1991) excavated at Pearls, Saint Andrew, between 1988 and 1991, being the most extensive examination of this important yet damaged (heavily looted) archaeological site to date (Hanna 2021; Keegan and Cody 1990). In the early 1990s, Holdren (1998) surveyed and excavated possible contact-era sites. Between 2016 and 2018, Hanna surveyed and inventoried precolonial sites, producing the most extensive study of Indigenous sites in Grenada (Hanna 2017, 2018, 2019, 2022). In the same period Hofman et al.

(2016, 2017) excavated at La Poterie, Saint Andrew, one of the few Kalinago contact sites excavated in the Lesser Antilles to date. Several archaeologists have also worked on particular materials assumed to be from the Pearls site (Boomert 2007; Breukel 2019; Byrne and Keegan 2001; Guzzo Falci et al. 2020; Harris 2001). In 2023–2024, the Grenada National Museum was the designated recipient of all of the chance finds (primarily historical) from the World Bank–funded restoration of Fort George, an eighteenth-century French and British fortification. Unfortunately, there was no funding for storage or analysis of the finds, thus adding to the already overburdened institution's limited space and management capacity.

The nearby island of Carriacou in the Grenadines did not receive serious archaeological attention until Sutty (1983, 1990, 1991, 1993) carried out archaeological research there. Between 2003 and 2014, the Carriacou Ecodynamics Archaeological Project under Scott M. Fitzpatrick, Michiel Kappers, and Quetta Kaye carried out extensive excavations at Grand Bay and Sabazan, two continuously occupied Indigenous sites from the Saladoid to post-Saladoid periods (see Fitzpatrick et al. 2009, 2014; Kaye, Fitzpatrick, and Kappers 2005).

The result of all of these surface collections and excavations in the past century is massive collections of mostly Indigenous archaeological objects, including ceramics and human and faunal remains (Figure 8.1) (see Hanna 2017, 2022, 2023). Unfortunately, the basic permissions granted by the local government/communities to international institutions to carry out archaeological excavations do not require any responsibility for collection care and management post excavations, as there is little in the way of local policies on these issues. The majority of these collections have remained in Grenada, with small collections scattered in museums and other research facilities in Martinique, the United States, and Europe; it is unclear whether proper documentation exists of the objects that were removed from Grenada. The management of these large collections of Indigenous artifacts is a huge burden on the local institutions (Grenada National Museum and Carriacou Museum) forced to maintain them at great cost (in storage, care, and the inability to acquire other necessary collections), even as they have little or no immediate use due to lack of local public or research access once they have been deposited by international researchers.

Archaeologists primarily pursue their own academic interests, which guide their own proposal writing, fieldwork, and publications. Meanwhile, underdeveloped Caribbean museums and heritage institutions are left with huge burdens that they do not have the financial and human resources to

Figure 8.1. Archaeological artifacts take up a large portion of the storage space at the Grenada National Museum. Photo by John Angus Martin, 2024.

adequately address. In some cases, this has resulted in the mistreatment/ mishandling of human remains and artifacts due to a lack of appropriate expertise in both storage and care (Hanna 2017). This situation is untenable and must be addressed if local institutions are to grow and develop as their country's primary heritage institutions.

In the case of the Carriacou Museum, the immediate problem of storage faced by many Caribbean heritage institutions was easier to address because the Carriacou Ecodynamics Archaeological Project was ongoing for almost a decade. The local community was able to get some concessions from the archaeologists in the form of a large container to house the recovered artifacts, though it can be argued that these were not enough to deal with proper collections management in the long term. The primary problem of collections care and management remains, as the small local museum struggles to even display some of these artifacts. In the case of the Grenada National Museum, the problem of collections care and management has never been confronted by the permanent staff and continues to affect the collections, although some effort has been made toward appropriate storage and cataloging (Hanna 2023). As a result of these continuing failures, it is now more urgent than ever for both institutions to develop solutions to these pressing issues of collections care and management.[1]

The cases of Grenada and Carriacou are similar to those of other countries in the Caribbean and force us to think about how these heritage institutions can foster adequate policies to establish how foreign archaeologists provide for the management of collections generated by their excavations. This management includes cataloging and digital access, which was done by the Carriacou Ecodynamics Archaeological Project in the case of Carriacou. Since 2022, consultations on how to deal with human remains can now revolve around the "International Association for Caribbean Archaeology (IACA) Code of Ethics" and "IACA Best Practice Guide" (Cunningham et al. 2022a, 2022b; also see Fricke, Giovas, Hanna, Shorter, and Victorina, this volume). With specific policies in place, Grenada's heritage institutions can better re/negotiate with international research projects to change the historically unequal situations that have been the basis of these relationships for decades. Engaging with archaeologists to share experiences before setting up excavations would help local institutions navigate their own specific goals and find possible overlap. The objective is to develop a more equal relationship between the two, so that each can achieve their goals.

Renegotiating Responsibilities in the Haitian Case

American archaeologists Irving Rouse and Froelich Rainey carried out extensive archaeological excavations at several sites in Fort Liberté, Haiti, in the 1930s, contributing to the development of the chronology of Indigenous settlements and culture later established by Rouse (1992). The objects served as a basis for stylistic and chronological study, were transported to the United States for further analysis (Rainey 1936, 1941; Rouse 1939). Since the creation in 1941 of the Bureau National d'Ethnologie, which advocates for archaeological research in Haiti, there is still no proper laboratory space in the country to conduct post-excavation work. Meanwhile, most of the material excavated by international archaeological research projects in Haiti is curated at American institutions.

Appropriate spaces are essential for storing and maintaining archaeological collections for further study and for sharing knowledge with the public. Unfortunately, the absence of such spaces in Haiti poses major challenges, for example in creating a vocation in archaeology for Haiti's young students. Beyond the legal issues relating to Haitian archaeological collections, it is difficult to advocate for an immediate return of archaeological objects from past scientific projects led by international researchers because of the lack of appropriate storage (Jean et al. 2020). There is a need to reevaluate and renegotiate the responsibilities of the institutions guarding the Haitian archaeological collections, including stewardship, communication, and knowledge sharing.

In Haiti, lack of secure space also encourages looting and illicit trafficking of archaeological objects. There are no risk mitigation strategies for heritage collections in times of crisis, which sometimes leads to illicit trafficking activities. Political and social crises, including the 2010 earthquake, have contributed to the loss of cultural patrimony. Given the uncertain context after the 2010 earthquake, the International Council of Museums (ICOM) had wisely taken the lead in communicating a "red list" to alert the public of the potential trafficking of Haiti's cultural property, including archaeological objects. The ICOM Red List stated: "The Emergency Red List of Haitian Cultural Objects at Risk is ICOM's first response to the increased risk in illicit trafficking, meeting the request of Interpol, the World Customs Organization (WCO), and UNESCO. Given the importance of cultural heritage as a unifying force among the Haitian people today, the protection of these objects and the prevention of their dispersal are essential to the ongoing reconstruction effort" (ICOM 2010, 2).

The list was a reference guide that recorded the categories of movable objects from Haiti that are most susceptible to looting, theft, and illicit heritage trafficking and was developed in response to the illegal trafficking of cultural artifacts during times of crisis. Thus during the 2010 crisis, public institutions such as the Bureau National d'Ethnologie, which maintains the archaeological collections of Haiti, were greatly damaged, and the lack of appropriate rescue plans and emergency responses to address risks and other sociopolitical crises affecting heritage care was laid bare. The humanitarian contribution to heritage was decisive, leading to the creation of the Haiti Cultural Recovery Project for the Université Quisqueya (Jean-Julien and Hornbeck 2023). In the context of humanitarian aid, the Haitian state was unable to establish the groundwork for a heritage future, which included designing and constructing public spaces that would benefit national archaeological collections, in the same way that the global humanitarian program failed. Despite the Red List highlighting endangered Haitian archaeological heritage, discussions on practical strategies for archaeological heritage futures, both at the official and grassroots level, remain limited. This lack of a comprehensive emergency plan for collections can further hinder efforts to claim repatriation of artifacts currently housed outside the country.

The case of Haiti's archaeological collections illustrates two fundamental challenges when discussing ethics related to the co-stewardship and return of archaeological objects resulting from investigations. On the one hand, how can Haiti claim and receive archaeological collections from past international investigations, considering that these artifacts come from legal research in Haiti with the permission of the Haitian government? Another concern is the maintenance of any returned objects in the future. These challenges concern the roles and responsibilities of local and foreign institutions in the future care of collections. Reclaiming Haiti's artifacts requires a trans-institutional approach that goes beyond simply shipping them back in boxes. In this case, there are two crucial aspects to consider: First, establishing the rightful ownership of these collections within Haiti. Second, acknowledging the ethical responsibility of current holders.

In 2020, the Federal Bureau of Investigation (FBI) Art Crime Team repatriated to Haiti more than 450 cultural and historical artifacts recovered at the home of an American citizen, who had taken advantage of Haiti's institutional weakness in transnational heritage trafficking to bring collections to the United States illegally during several missionary trips to Haiti. The US authorities informed Haiti of the existence of these objects, and Haiti subsequently claimed them without requesting any appropriate equipment and curation expertise to maintain them in the future. The ethical considerations surrounding the return of trafficked collections are distinct from those of objects acquired by academic institutions. Returning trafficked collections might involve diplomatic agreements and politics. Under different circumstances, universities and other research institutions may have invested significantly in preserving artifacts from other countries, and have contributed to global scientific debates. However, the countries in which objects are found often do not have access to these collections or to information related to them. This forces us to navigate possibilities of reclaiming objects while envisioning the responsibilities of actors such as archaeologists, curating institutions, and the collection's country-owner. In this case, international institutions involved in acquiring artifacts through past legal excavation must think beyond just potentially sending objects back to Haiti. Instead, they should focus on contributing to Haiti's long-term capacity for artifact conservation and knowledge sharing.

Discussion and Conclusion: Re-Boxing is Unclear—Rethinking Pathways for Heritage Co-Stewardship

Archaeological practices in the Caribbean have a long history, from the collection of artifacts in the nineteenth century to the use of archaeological methods and techniques during the twentieth century. Through Caribbean archaeology, local and international researchers have studied Indigenous and colonial Caribbean societies and their material cultures. Despite the valuable insights gained through archaeological research, a substantial number of archaeological objects and collections are currently located outside their countries of origin. When it comes to highlighting the ethical practice of archaeology and the stewardship of archaeological materials, it is fundamental to situate the return process as an act of institutional responsibility. The Smithsonian Institution, which curates objects from the Caribbean region, emphasizes shared stewardship, an ethical and respectful approach that recognizes the cultural significance of the objects for the communities from which they originated (Smithsonian Institution 2022).

Our thoughts here have echoed many interesting discussions about dealing with archaeological heritage in the Caribbean (Jean and Herrera Malatesta 2024; Ostapkowicz and Hanna 2021; Siegel and Righter 2011). We believe that the returns process for archaeological artifacts can go beyond simply re-boxing them. As a post-excavations procedure, preparing artifacts for curation includes careful sorting and labeling procedures for long-term research potential beyond the simple preservation of the objects. It involves moving the objects from their original locations to another to analyze and disseminate knowledge through academic discussion, publication, and exhibition. This requires institutional agreements between the country-owner of excavated collections and the institutions that undertake the research. The partners can establish additional parameters to foster open communication with the authorities in the source country and for collaborative research opportunities involving the collections. Post-excavation study remains fundamental for researchers to answer critical and timely questions and deepen knowledge about the past. Such study may take several years. Consequently, this involves appropriate long-term curation and conservation measures.

Figure 8.2 charts post-excavation implications regarding archaeological collections derived from archaeological investigation, focusing on respectful and sustainable actions. While "boxing artifacts" is clearly situated during and after moving them from one country to another, it can be blurry in the act of return. Re-boxing refers to the problematic practice of placing artifacts in boxes for return to their countries of origin, often done without proper communication on how to care for them in the future. Their future in communities and countries of origin may remain unclear, and re-boxing processes may not comply with the requirements of ethical repatriation. We believe that a shared stewardship policy can acknowledge the socioeconomic and political challenges of the country-owner where the research is conducted. If we start with the question of whether countries facing socioeconomic challenges

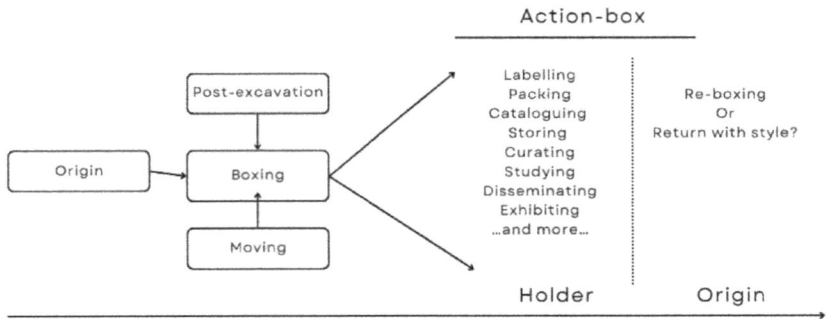

Figure 8.2. Action box with post-excavation implications and the role of each action in the collections' co-stewardship, including the ways of return. Illustration by Joseph Sony Jean.

can advocate for the return of artifacts from excavations at all, then other critical questions may follow. What is the engagement of foreign collection holders in acknowledging the socioeconomic challenges of the collection country-owner? What is the engagement of the foreign collection holder in providing long-term technical assistance to the collection's country-owner? What practical strategies can countries adopt to address logistical challenges in sustaining returned collections? Additionally, which action-box should be considered alongside the artifact return plan? We are aware of several cases from the Caribbean, such as Carriacou, where the volume of artifacts is larger than the curation space itself, and Haiti, where the absence of space impacts archaeological knowledge dissemination to the public, and a large part of its collections remain outside the country. The archaeological collection may be currently held elsewhere, but the country holds the right to pursue its return whenever circumstances allow. Returning artifacts from excavations should not be a passive gesture, but rather should involve critical responsibilities of institutions, archaeologists, heritage practitioners, and curators in maintaining the objects in the long-term. This forces us, as heritage professionals, to critically rethink our own practices and engagement with heritage in challenging times (Flewellen et al. 2022; Fricke and Hoerman 2023).

The case for repatriation of looted and other removed objects to formerly colonized countries is no longer an issue for debate. More and more governments, national museums, and heritage institutions in the West have (grudgingly) accepted that the (long overdue) time has arrived to abide by the ethical standards of our modern societies. What we need to address now, with equal voices, is the process that incorporates co-stewardship of our shared cultural heritage. This process should prioritize excavation, care, management, display, and sharing of these materials for all involved. As the debate centers around protecting these objects in collections and facilities that are currently deemed inadequate, it becomes the collective goal to ensure the necessary resources are available to achieve that objective. If countries like Grenada and Haiti lack the facilities to research, securely store, manage, analyze, and interpret their national patrimony, it should be the goal of archaeologists and institutions who work and have worked in these countries to become a part of the solution, by providing the necessary knowledge and resources to achieve this universal goal.

Acknowledgments

We would like to thank the editors for inviting us to the workshop in Copenhagen. Joseph Sony Jean gratefully acknowledges the support of the Dutch Research Council (NWO) Veni Grant (VI.Veni.211F.084), which made his contribution to cowriting this chapter possible.

Note

1   In July 2024 Carriacou was hit by Hurricane Beryl, a Category 4 hurricane that devastated the island, demolishing the first floor of the Carriacou Museum. All of its records and documentation of its artifacts were lost, further illustrating the difficult predicament these small institutions in the region are forced to contend with on a regular basis.

References Cited

Agostinho, Nathan Assunção. 2024. "The Reason for the Artifact: Paths for the Repatriation of Indigenous Cultural Assets." In *Colonial Heritage, Power, and Contestation: Negotiating Decolonisation in Latin America and the Caribbean,* edited by Camila Andrea Malig Jedlicki, Naomi Oosterman, and Rodrigo Christofoletti, 87–104. Cham: Springer International Publishing.

Amo-Agyemang, Charles. 2024. "Ghana's Demand for Restitution of Material Artifacts: A Decolonial Reflection." *African Identities* 1–21.

Aranui, Amber. 2020. "Restitution or a Loss to Science? Understanding the Importance of Māori Ancestral Remains." *Museum & Society* 18(1): 19–29.

Atkinson, Henry Dushan. 2010. "The Meanings and Values of Repatriation." In *The Long Way Home: The Meaning and Values of Repatriation,* edited by Paul Turnbull and Michael Pickering, 15–19. New York: Berghahn Books.

Banks, T. J. 1988. *Archaeological Excavation at the Grand Anse Beach Site, Grenada, W.I.* Saint George's, Grenada: Foundation for Field Research.

Banks, T. J. 1993. *Project Reports Funded by FFR on Grenada, 1993.* Saint George's, Grenada: Foundation for Field Research.

Beckles, Hilary. 2013. *Britain's Black Debt: Reparations for Caribbean Slavery and Native Genocide.* Kingston, Jamaica: University of the West Indies Press.

Beckles, Hilary. 2021. *How Britain Underdeveloped the Caribbean: A Reparation Response to Europe's Legacy of Plunder and Poverty.* Kingston, Jamaica: University of the West Indies Press.

Boomert, Arie. 1986. "The Cayo Complex of St. Vincent: Ethnohistorical and Archaeological Aspects of the Island Carib Problem." *Antropológica* 66: 3–86.

Boomert, Arie. 2007. "Exotics from Pearls, Grenada: A Preliminary Assessment." *Proceedings of the 21st Congress of the International Association for Caribbean Archaeology.* Kingston, Jamaica: IACA.

Breukel, Thomas W. 2019. "Tracing Interactions in the Indigenous Caribbean through a Biographical Approach: Microwear and Material Culture across the Historical Divide (AD 1200–1600)." PhD dissertation, Leiden University.

Bright, Alistair J. 2011. *Blood Is Thicker Than Water: Amerindian Intra- and Interinsular Relationships and Social Organization in the pre-Colonial Windward Islands.* Leiden: Sidestone Press.

Bullen, Ripley P. 1964. "Archaeology of Grenada, West Indies." Contributions of the Florida State Museum 11. Gainesville: University of Florida.

Byrne, B., and William Keegan. 2001. "Structural Analysis of Saladoid Adornos from Grenada." *Proceedings of the 18th Congress of the International Association for Caribbean Archaeology,* 21–24. Saint George's, Grenada: IACA.

Cody, Annie. 1991. "From the Site of Pearls, Grenada: Exotic Lithics & Radiocarbon Dates." In *Proceedings of the 13th Congress of the International Association for Caribbean Archaeology* (IACA), Curaçao.

Cummins, Alissandra, Kevin Farmer, and Roslyn Russell, eds. 2013. *Plantation to Nation: Caribbean Museums and National Identity.* Champaign, IL: Common Ground Research Networks.

Cummins, Alissandra. 2006. "The Role of the Museum in Developing Heritage Policy." In *Art and Cultural Heritage: Law, Policy and Practice,* edited by Barbara T. Hoffman, 47–51. New York: Cambridge University Press.

Cunningham, Andreana, Felicia J. Fricke, Christina Giovas, Jonathan A. Hanna, Tabisay Sankatsing Nava, John Shorter, and Amy Victorina. 2022a. "International Association for Caribbean Archaeology (IACA) Code of Ethics." Translated by Marianny Aguasvivas and Gérard Richard. International Association for Caribbean Archaeology (IACA).

Cunningham, Andreana, Felicia J. Fricke, Christina Giovas, Jonathan A. Hanna, Tibisay Sankatsing Nava, John Shorter, and Amy Victorina. 2022b. "International Association for Caribbean Archaeology (IACA) Best Practice Guide." Translated by Marianny Aguasvivas and Gérard Richard. International Association for Caribbean Archaeology (IACA).

Cuno, James. 2014. "Culture War: The Case Against Repatriating Museum Artifacts." *Foreign Affairs* 93(6): 119–129.

Fewkes, J. W. 1922. *A Prehistoric Island Culture Area of America, v. 34.* Annual Report of the Bureau of American Ethnology to the Secretary of the Smithsonian Institution, Washington, DC.

Fitzpatrick, Scott M., Quetta Kaye, Michiel Kappers, and Christina Giovas. 2014. "A Decade of Archaeological Research on Carriacou, Grenadine Islands, West Indies." *Caribbean Journal of Science* 48(2/3): 151–161.

Fitzpatrick, Scott M., Michiel Kappers, Quetta Kaye, Christina M. Giovas, Michelle J. LeFebvre, Mary Hill Harris, Scott Burnett, Jennifer A. Pavia, Kathleen Marsaglia, and James Feathers. 2009. "Pre-Columbian Settlements on Carriacou, West Indies." *Journal of Field Archaeology* 34(3): 247–266.

Flewellen, Ayana Omilade, Alicia Odewale, Justin Dunnavant, Alexandra Jones, and William White III. 2022. "Creating Community and Engaging Community: The Foundations of the Estate Little Princess Project in St. Croix, United States Virgin Islands." *International Journal of Historical Archaeology* 26: 147–176.

Françozo, Mariana, and Amy Strecker. 2017. "Caribbean Collections in European Museums and the Question of Returns." *International Journal of Cultural Property* 24(4): 451–477.

Fricke, Felicia, and Rachel Hoerman. 2023. "Archaeology and Social Justice in Island Worlds." *World Archaeology* 54(3): 484–489.

Guzzo Falci, Catarina, Alice C. S. Knaf, Annelou van Gijn, Gareth R. Davies, and Corinne L. Hofman. 2020. "Lapidary Production in the Eastern Caribbean: A Typo-Technological and Microwear Study of Ornaments from the Site of Pearls, Grenada." *Archaeological and Anthropological Sciences* 12, article 53.

Hanna, Jonathan A. 2017. "The Status of Grenada's Prehistoric Sites: Report on the 2016 Survey and an Inventory of Known Sites." Ministry of Tourism, Botanical Gardens, Grenada. Available at https://scholarsphere.psu.edu/resources/59f9fca4-d629-4b02-b27c-d95bda5bb694 (accessed July 12, 2024).

Hanna, Jonathan A. 2018. "Grenada and the Guianas: Mainland Connections and Cultural Resilience during the Caribbean Late Ceramic Age." *World Archaeology* 50(4): 651–675.

Hanna, Jonathan A. 2019. "Camáhogne's Chronology: The Radiocarbon Settlement Sequence on Grenada, West Indies." *Journal of Anthropological Archaeology* 55.

Hanna, Jonathan A. 2021. "Spice Isle Sculptures: Antiquities and Iconography in Grenada, West Indies: Real, Recent, or Replica?" In *Case Studies in the Amerindian (and Neo-Amerindian) Antiquities Markets of the Caribbean,* edited by Joanna Ostapkowicz and Jonathan A. Hanna. Tuscaloosa: University of Alabama Press.

Hanna, Jonathan A. 2022. *Re-Envisioning the Grenada National Museum: A Development Plan through 2026 and Beyond.* Saint George's, Grenada: Grenada National Museum.

Hanna, Jonathan A. 2023. *Overview and Status of the National Collection at the Grenada National Museum, 25 May 2023.* Saint George's, Grenada: Grenada National Museum.

Harris, P. O. B. 2001. "A Common Format for Basic Archaeological Data in Caribbean Islands: Grenada as Test Example." Proceedings of the 18th Congress of the International Association for Caribbean Archaeology (IACA), Grenada.

Hicks, Dan. 2020. *The Brutish Museums: The Benin Bronzes, Colonial Violence and Cultural Restitution.* London: Pluto Press.

Hofman, Corinne L., ed. 2016. "Fieldwork Report: Grenada 2016." Available at https://www.universiteitleiden.nl/binaries/content/assets/customsites/nexus1492/field/grenada-2016-survey-report_final.pdf (accessed March 4, 2019).

Hofman, Corinne L., ed. 2017. "Field Report from the Work Carried Out at La Poterie, Grenada in January 2017." Leiden: Leiden University, the Netherlands. Available at https://www.universiteitleiden.nl/binaries/content/assets/customsites/nexus1492/field/fieldwork-report-grenada-2017-final.pdf (accessed February 28, 2019).

Hofman, Corinne L., and Andrzej T. Antczak, eds. 2019. *Early Settlers of the Insular Caribbean: Dearchaizing the Archaic.* Leiden: Sidestone Press.

Hofman, Corinne L., John Angus Martin, Arie Boomert, Sébastien Manem, Katarina Jacobson, and Menno L. P. Hoogland. 2022. "Reimagining Creolization: The Deep History of Cultural Interactions in the Windward Islands, Lesser Antilles, through the Lens of Material Culture." *Latin American Antiquity* 33(2): 279–292.

Holdren, Anne Cody. 1998. "Raiders and Traders: Caraïbe Social and Political Networks at the Time of European Contact and Colonization in the Eastern Caribbean." PhD dissertation, University of California.

Holmes, W. H. 1907. "Report of the Chief." 25th Annual Report of the Bureau of American Ethnology to the Secretary of the Smithsonian Institution 1903/1904. Washington, DC: Government Printing Office.

Honychurch, Lennox. 2000. *From Carib to Creole: Contact and Culture Exchange.* Roseau, Dominica: Dominica Institute.

Huckerby, Thomas. 1921. "Petroglyphs of Grenada and a Recently Discovered Petroglyph in St. Vincent." *Indian Notes and Monographs (Museum of the American Indian, New York)* 1(3): 143–164.

International Council of Museums (ICOM). 2010. "Haiti Red List." Available at https://icom.museum/en/ressource/emergency-red-list-of-haitian-cultural-objects-at-risk/ (accessed July 12, 2024).

Jean, Joseph Sony, and Eduardo Herrera Malatesta, eds. 2024. *Local Voices, Global Debates: The Uses of Archaeological Heritage in the Caribbean.* Leiden: Brill.

Jean, Joseph Sony, Eduardo Herrera Malatesta, and Katarina Jacobson. 2024. "Local Voices: The Uses of Archaeological Heritage in the Caribbean." In *Local Voices, Global Debates: The Uses of Archaeological Heritage in the Caribbean,* edited by Joseph Sony Jean and Eduardo Herrera Malatesta, 1–17. Leiden: Brill.

Jean, Joseph Sony, Marc Joseph, Camille Louis, and Jerry Michel. 2020. "Haitian Archaeological Heritage: Understanding Its Loss and Paths to Future Preservation." *Heritage* 3(3): 733–752.

Jean-Julien, Olsen, and Stephanie E. Hornbeck. 2023. "Post-Disaster Cultural Recovery in Haiti, 2010–2021: Reflections on a Decade of Collaboration." In *Prioritizing*

People in Ethical Decision-Making and Caring for Cultural Heritage Collections, edited by Nina Owczarek, 140–156. London: Routledge.

Joy, Charlotte. 2020. *Heritage Justice.* Cambridge: Cambridge University Press.

Kaye, Quetta P., Scott M. Fitzpatrick, and Michiel Kappers. 2005. "Continued Archaeological Investigations at Grand Bay, Carriacou, West Indies (May 23rd–July 22, 2005), and the Impact of Hurricanes and Other Erosive Processes." *Papers from the Institute of Archaeology* 16: 108–114.

Keegan, William F. 1991. "Archaeology at Pearls, Grenada: The 1990 Field Season." Miscellaneous Project Report Number 47. Gainesville: Florida Museum of Natural History.

Keegan, William, and Annie K. Cody. 1990. "Progress Report on the Archaeological Excavations at the Site of Pearls, Grenada, August 1989." Miscellaneous Project Report Number 44. Gainesville: Florida Museum of Natural History.

Keegan, William F., and Corinne L. Hofman. 2017. *The Caribbean before Columbus.* New York: Oxford University Press.

Kersel, Morag M. 2015. "Storage Wars: Solving the Archaeological Curation Crisis?" *Journal of Eastern Mediterranean Archaeology and Heritage Studies* 3(1): 42–54.

Lowenthal, David. 1972. *West Indian Societies.* London: Oxford University Press.

Martin, John Angus. 2023. "'We Navel-String Bury Here': Landscape Biography, Representation and Identity in Grenada." PhD dissertation, University of Leiden.

Montgomery, Lindsay M., and Kishna Supernant. 2022. "Archaeology in 2021: Repatriation, Reclamation, and Reckoning with Historical Trauma." *American Anthropologist* 124(4): 800–812.

Murphy, Reginald. 2014. "Local Communities and Archaeology: A Caribbean Perspective." In *Encyclopedia of Global Archaeology,* edited by Claire Smith, 4538–4540. New York: Springer.

Nilsson Stutz, Liv. 2013. "Claims to the Past: A Critical View of the Arguments Driving Repatriation of Cultural Heritage and Their Role in Contemporary Identity Politics." *Journal of Intervention and Statebuilding* 7(2): 170–195.

Ostapkowicz, Joanna, and Jonathan A. Hanna, eds. 2021. *Real, Recent, or Replica: Precolumbian Caribbean Heritage as Art, Commodity, and Inspiration.* Tuscaloosa: University of Alabama Press.

Petitjean Roget, Henry. 1981. *Archaeology in Grenada: A Report.* Saint Michael, Barbados: Caribbean Conservation Association.

Raad voor Cultuur. 2022. "Colonial Collections and Recognition of Injustice." Available at https://www.raadvoorcultuur.nl/documenten/adviezen/2022/02/10/colonial-collection-and-a-recognition-of-injustice (accessed on July 12, 2024).

Rainey, Froelich. 1936. "A New Prehistoric Culture in Haiti." *Proceedings of the National Academy of Sciences* 22(1): 4–8.

Rainey, Froelich. 1941. *Excavations in the Ft. Liberté Region, Haiti.* Published for the Department of Anthropology, Yale University. New Haven, Connecticut: Yale University Press.

Reid, Basil A., and R. Grant Gilmore III. 2014. *Encyclopedia of Caribbean Archaeology.* Gainesville: University Press of Florida.

Rouse, Irving. 1939. *Prehistory in Haiti: A Study in Method.* New Haven, Connecticut: Yale University Press.

Rouse, Irving. 1964. "Prehistory of the West Indies." *Science* 144(3618): 499–513.

Rouse, Irving. 1992. *The Tainos: Rise and Decline of the People Who Greeted Columbus.* New Haven, Connecticut: Yale University Press.

Sarr, Felwine, and Bénédicte Savoy. 2018. "Rapport sur la restitution du patrimoine culturel africain: Vers une nouvelle éthique relationnelle." Available at https://www.culture.gouv.fr/Espace-documentation/Rapports/La-restitution-du-patrimoine-culturel-africain-vers-une-nouvelle-ethique-relationnelle (accessed July 12, 2024).

Schiappacasse, Paola A. 2019 "Excavating Repositories: Academic Research Projects Using Archaeological Collections." *Advances in Archaeological Practice* 7(3): 247–257.

Siegel, Peter. E., and Elizabeth Righter, eds. 2011. *Protecting Heritage in the Caribbean.* Tuscaloosa: University of Alabama Press.

Simpson, Moira. 2009. "Museums and Restorative Justice: Heritage, Repatriation and Cultural Education." *Museum International* 61(1–2): 121–129.

Smithsonian Institution. 2022. "Shared Stewardship and Ethical Returns." Smithsonian National Museum of Natural History. Available at naturalhistory.si.edu/research/shared-stewardship-and-ethical-returns (accessed July 12, 2024).

Society for American Archaeology (SAA). 2016. "Abstracts of the SAA 81st Annual Meeting." Available at https://www.saa.org/annual-meeting/programs/abstract-archives (accessed July 12, 2024).

Stack, Liam. 2019. "Are African Artifacts Safer in Europe? Museum Conditions Revive Debate." *New York Times,* September 4, 2019. Available at https://www.nytimes.com/2019/09/04/arts/design/germany-museum-condition-artifacts.html (accessed July 12, 2024).

Sutty, Leslie. 1983. "Liaison Arawak-Calivigny-Carib between Grenada and St. Vincent, Lesser Antilles." In *Proceedings of the 9th International Congress for the Study of Pre-Colombian Cultures in the Lesser Antilles.* Santo Domingo, Dominican Republic: International Association for Caribbean Archaeology (IACA).

Sutty, Leslie. 1990. "A Listing of Amerindian Settlements on the Island of Carriacou in the Southern Grenadines and a Report on the Most Important of These: Grand Bay." In *Proceedings of the 11th International Congress for Caribbean Archaeology,* edited by A. G. Pantel et al. San Juan, Puerto Rico: International Association for Caribbean Archaeology (IACA).

Sutty, Leslie. 1991. "Paleoecological Formations in the Grenadines of Grenada and Their Relationships to Preceramic and Ceramic Settlements: Carriacou." In *Proceedings of the 13th International Congress for Caribbean Archaeology,* edited by E. N. Ayubi and Jay B. Haviser. Willemstad, Curaçao: International Association for Caribbean Archaeology (IACA).

Sutty, Leslie. 1993. "The Use of Genital Sheaths by Insular Prehistoric Cultures: A Unique Case of an Ampullaria Genital Sheath from Carriacou, Southern Grenadines." In *Proceedings of the 14th International Congress for Caribbean Archaeology,* edited by Alissandra Cummins and P. King. Bridgetown, Barbados: International Association for Caribbean Archaeology (IACA).

Turnbull, Paul, and Michael Pickering. 2010. *The Long Way Home: The Meanings and Values of Repatriation.* New York: Berghahn Books.

Vendryes, M.-L. 2013. "Haiti, Museums and Public Collections: Their History and Development after 1804." In *Plantation to Nation: Caribbean Museums and National Identity,* edited by Alissandra Cummins, Kevin Farmer, and Roslyn Russell, 47–56. Champaign, Illinois: Common Ground Research Networks.

Weiss, Elizabeth. 2022. "Repatriation of Artefacts: A Recipe for Disaster." Available at https://historyreclaimed.co.uk/repatriation-of-artefacts-a-recipe-for-disaster/ (accessed July 12, 2024).

9

Conservation Ethics

Artifact Collection, Selection, Deposition, Storage, and Curation in the Eastern Caribbean; A Barbados Case Study

MAAIKE S. DE WAAL, MATTHEW C. REILLY,
ANNE I. BANCROFT, AND KEVIN FARMER

Worldwide, the past decades have seen an increase in studies and discussions relating to artifact collection and conservation, especially with regard to topics such as colonial heritage, contested heritage, ownership, and repatriation of artifacts. In the Caribbean, these topics are also receiving heightened attention (e.g., Françozo and Strecker 2014; Müller 2021; Welch and Finneran 2022: 196). March 2023 saw precolonial human remains excavated by Leiden University archaeologists in the 1980s being repatriated to Sint Eustatius after formal requests by the government of this island to the Dutch Heritage Agency (Leiden University 2023). In May 2023, in response to King Charles's coronation, Jamaica, Grenada, Antigua and Barbuda, Belize, Saint Kitts and Nevis, Saint Lucia, the Bahamas, and Saint Vincent and the Grenadines participated in a request to the king for a formal apology for British slavery and reparations for centuries of colonialism and human exploitation, also including repatriation of human remains and Indigenous artifacts currently at British institutions. So far, these demands have not been acknowledged.

Debates or publications about the curation of archaeology collections in local Caribbean museums are rarer, although exceptions do exist (e.g., Martin and Jean, this volume). Collection, selection, and conservation strategies strongly impact the image of the past presented and experienced. While not considered as newsworthy as debates surrounding reparations and repatriation, we suggest that collection practices and standards are inextricably linked to ethical issues in Caribbean archaeology. Ownership and stewardship of

Figure 9.1. The Caribbean and the location of Barbados. Map by Maaike S. de Waal.

the past are political topics that have practical implications when considering how collections are cared for and by, and for, whom. In this chapter, we carefully outline how curatorial challenges come to bear on the ethics of Barbadian archaeology and heritage management. By critically assessing practices and management strategies, museums can solidify the ways they reach and engage the public and how they present and preserve the past, thus instituting more ethical practices in how the past is conserved and made accessible.

This chapter concentrates on conservation ethics, in a broad sense. The term "conservation" is often reserved to denote the care and stabilization of artifacts, relating to processes of taking charge of collected materials to ensure their preservation and accessibility for future generations, whether in the context of a repository or an exhibit. In this contribution, we include the processes of collection during fieldwork, and selection during both fieldwork and processing phases, as well as deposition and storage in the facilities that were designated for that purpose. By critically discussing current best practices, guidelines, and principles, and by highlighting the everyday reality, we aim to contribute to the discussion on conservation ethics and to present a roadmap for achievable appropriate improvements within a tropical environment. Underlying these conversations is a conscious treatment of how everyday practices directly pertain to larger ethical considerations in the field. We focus in particular on the Barbados Museum and Historical Society ("Barbados Museum"), an organization playing a central role in the curation of archaeological heritage in Barbados (Figure 9.1, Figure 9.2).

Figure 9.2. Block B, the Garrison, in 2024. Photo by Maaike S. de Waal.

Relevance

In 2022, the International Association for Caribbean Archaeology (IACA; Cunningham et al. 2022a) presented a new "code of ethics," which highlights responsibilities regarding materials collected during fieldwork and prerequisites for curation and archiving (see Fricke, Giovas, Hanna, Shorter, and Victorina, this volume). These include (1) creating agreements between relevant authorities and organizations about funds needed to process and store finds, submitting digital documentation, and eventually transporting materials abroad; (2) reserving time for relevant stakeholders to adjust final reports; (3) providing all documentation to the official local archaeology organization in a timely fashion; and (4) creating signed accords for materials being transported abroad (Cunningham et al. 2022a: 4).

In Barbados and in the Caribbean more generally there is an urgency for these prerequisites. Attendees at the 2019 IACA Congress discussed the issue of archaeology projects not reserving budgetary funds for local storage and curation. Local heritage institutions, however, need funding, trained staff, facilities, logistics, and materials to guarantee the preservation of collected materials and documentation. Without consultation, researchers transfer the responsibility for artifact caretaking to local institutions without providing them with the necessary funding, thus furthering unethical, extractivist research practices. Furthermore, they often do not adequately plan for the collections management of the excavated material in their project proposals to ensure funding is available to allow for best practice curation and collections management. Such pre-planning is important and must include conversations with repositories especially in islands where heritage funding is scarce.

On the other hand, researchers may get discouraged by inadequate storage rooms, sometimes with insufficient protection against natural elements, which can be the result of a lack of trained staff, space, materials, and resources. This can raise questions related to where and how to submit artifacts. It is urgent to discuss selection, deposition, storage, and curation, and to break this vicious cycle. Without dialogue and collaboration between researchers and institutional staff, foreign-based researchers maintain authority over the past while building archaeological knowledge, relegating local institutions to secondary roles of logistical and curatorial support.

Aims

The four authors of this chapter draw from diverse experiences as archaeologists with decades of experience in Caribbean archaeology (de Waal and Reilly), as conservator at the Barbados Museum (Bancroft), and as deputy director of the Barbados Museum (Farmer). Additionally, with such countries of origin as the Netherlands, the United States, Barbados, and England, we bring our own positionalities to bear on discussions of local practices and disciplinary ethics. With these professional and personal backgrounds in mind, we first discuss relevant national and international regulations before presenting an overview of institutions in and outside Barbados that collect, store, and curate artifacts from this island. We include backgrounds of and activities by both professional organizations, such as the Barbados Museum and the Nidhe Israel Museum, Barbados, and those by archaeology enthusiasts. The University of the West Indies (UWI) at Cave Hill, Barbados, also houses a private archaeology laboratory and collection. This has not been included in the following discussion.

Following this, we present and discuss past and current artifact collection, selection and deselection, storage and curation, and public stewardship and art. In so doing, we attempt to provide answers to some basic questions relating to proper storage of collected artifacts. These questions include: Who is responsible and how? What is needed? Who should pay? And which best practices or suggestions can lead to solid and feasible improvements? All of these questions are practical, yet they speak to much broader ethical issues in the field. For instance, by engaging with the practicalities of curation and archaeology, we are also asking: Who owns the Barbadian past? Who is responsible for protecting it? Who is expected to develop standards, and who or what will make such standards realistic? And how will such standards lead to best ethical practices that make the Barbadian past accessible to the public?

Rules, Regulations, and Guidelines: Heritage Law in Barbados

Answering the previous questions should start with reviewing what existing legislation in Barbados says about collecting and handling artifacts and about the responsibility for doing so.

For Barbados, Byer (2022: 9, 34, 110) and Farmer (2011) listed the following national laws relating to heritage: the Constitution of Barbados in 1966; the Museum and Historical Society Act in 1933; the National Trust Act in 1961; and the Town and Country Planning Act in 1985, which was replaced by the Planning and Development Act in 2020. Of special importance is the Barbados Preservation of Antiquities and Relics Bill, or Antiquities Bill.

According to Byer (2022: 110), the Antiquities Bill would be the first formal heritage act for Barbados, if enforced. The bill includes rules and regulations for the "preservation of places, structures and relics or other objects of archaeological, historical and cultural interest, by providing for export control of protected heritage, and licenses for archaeological excavation, to be administered and enforced by a board." According to the bill, antiquities can only be exported if allowed by the responsible minister. In addition, excavations need to be licensed and registered, and only trained and experienced researchers can be considered for excavation projects (Byer 2022: 110).

The bill thus sets important requirements for archaeological research and could thus influence the ways artifacts are being collected, selected, and preserved. However, as Byer points out, some relevant aspects of the bill have not been sufficiently highlighted. For example, there are no details about the composition of the board that is to license archaeological fieldwork, other than that members should have relevant experience. The experience required to be allowed to conduct archaeological research is not defined either (Byer 2022: 110), though with limited archaeological training on the island, the ambiguous wording would give priority to foreign researchers. The bill, designed in 2006, was rejected by the Parliament of Barbados in 2011. The failure of the bill to pass can be attributed, in part, to interest groups expressing concern that it would create problematic situations for those with private collections, as well as concerns about the relevant authorities who would be playing a role in the bill's implementation (Farmer 2011; Inniss 2019: 384–385).

Relevant laws dealing with heritage that are currently in place in Barbados include the Town and Country Planning Act in 1985, which was replaced by the Planning and Development Act in 2019 (Byer 2022: 137–138). Focus in the TCPA/PDA is on land use planning, not primarily on heritage preservation (Byer 2022: 137–138). PDA section 6 is on "Protection of the Cultural and Natural Heritage." Here, the act states that "the Minister shall cause to be compiled lists of buildings, monuments and sites of prehistoric, historic or architectural merit or interest, or may adopt, with or without modifications, any such lists compiled by the Barbados National Trust or other bodies or persons, and may amend any lists so compiled from time to time" (Parliament of Barbados 2019: part VI 53[1]). These lists, however, have not yet been compiled, although preliminary work exists in the form of the Barbados National Registry of Historic Places (2024). Existing archaeological maps, however, are known to be deficient (cf. de Waal 2019), limiting the efficiency of protection and management of archaeological artifacts, sites, and landscapes.

Barbados also has legislation relating to heritage organizations in the country. The 1933 Barbados Museum and Historical Society Act heralded the beginning of the Barbados Museum. Byer (2022: 118) describes this act as consisting of only one page, largely focusing on "liability for debts, powers of the Society including the preparation of by-laws, the recovery of fines, dispute resolution and saving rights of the Crown." In conjunction with the Planning Authority and the Barbados National Trust, the Barbados Museum is committed to heritage protection in the country.

The Barbados National Trust Act dates to 1961. Via this act, the Barbados National Trust is organized as a membership organization with a council that is responsible for its executive functions, including heritage preservation, advice and education, and company law obligations (Byer 2022: 125). The Barbados National Trust focuses on buildings and monuments of historic and architectural interest, not on precolonial sites and objects, whereas the Barbados Museum is concerned with both. In sum, Barbados does not have robust enabling legislation related to archaeology. Control and management of the nation's material heritage is decentralized, with few legal protections in place for archaeological sites and little oversight for archaeological practices or the management of public or private collections. This being the case, ethical questions concerning site and collection protection often go unresolved, resulting in site destruction or collection neglect.

Professional Organizations Collecting, Storing, and Curating Archaeological Artifacts from Barbados

Several organizations and individuals are involved in collecting, storing, and curating artifacts from Barbados. This section discusses professional organizations, such as museums and universities, inside and outside Barbados doing this work. Depending on history, mandates, facilities, funding, and trained staff, there are differences in how collections have been made, acquired, stored, and curated. A short overview of the Barbados Museum, the Nidhe Israel Museum in Barbados, and some artifact collections outside Barbados follows.[1]

Organizations in Barbados

Barbados Museum

Founded in 1933, the Barbados Museum celebrated its 90th anniversary in 2023. Although established as a historical society, and still actively functioning as such, it operates as a national museum. After a first exhibit in Queen's Park House, in 1934 the Barbados Museum opened in the old military prison at the Garrison, where it still operates today (Armstrong et al. 2019; Barbados Museum 2024a).

The museum's history cannot be seen apart from earlier museums created by the British Empire in its colonies, where the focus was on geological and natural history collections, aimed at attracting commercial interest for the islands, and on education (Cummins 2013: 11, 14–15, 33; cited in Ariese-Vandemeulebroucke 2018: 152). Today, the museum houses diverse exhibits, including the natural, historical, and cultural environment of Africa and its role in Caribbean heritage and society, fine art depictions of Barbados and the wider Caribbean, and of flora and fauna, the deep and recent past, colonial planter life, and the military history of Barbados (Barbados Museum 2024a).

The Barbados Museum is an active organization. It is not only developing and curating collections, exhibits, and publications, but it also plays a role in education (e.g., community outreach programs, internships, workshops, and heritage tours), research (e.g., by providing library and research assistance), and event planning (Barbados Museum 2024a).

Since 1933, the Barbados Museum has also been publishing its journal, with contributions about Barbados' history and heritage (Barbados Museum 2024a). The journal, which unfortunately is not open access, is available in print only.

During its first decades the Barbados Museum was often criticized regarding inclusivity and representation. From the start, it had financial and organizational government support, and there were debates about whether the museum was just the pastime of "a select group of aged, wealthy persons" and whether it was representative of Barbadian life (Cummins 2004: 225–226) or was Eurocentric (Ariese-Vandemeulebroucke 2018: 153). In the 1980s, in particular, critical reflections were being made on who should decide on representation, and how (Byer 2022: 115). In this period, the museum's mission was "to collect, preserve, and publish matter relating to the history and antiquities of Barbados, to gather and preserve appropriate articles for collections, and to promote a knowledge of Barbadian history, culture and related matters" (Whiting 1983: 33; cited in Ariese-Vandemeulebroucke 2018: 155).

Over time, the Barbados Museum changed alongside Barbadian society and the public's perception of its own past. While the majority of Barbadians have African ancestry, concerns have been expressed that the focus on African descent in the creation of a national identity risks marginalizing other groups in Barbados (Farmer 2023: 173, cited in Ariese-Vandemeulebroucke 2018: 155). In an attempt to overcome this, today's mandate of the Barbados Museum, formulated in 1990, is "to collect, document and conserve evidence of Barbados' cultural, historical and environmental heritage; and to interpret and present this evidence for *all of society*" (authors' emphasis; Barbados Museum 2024b).

Artifact storage is in Block B in the Garrison (Figure 9.2), close to the museum. This facility has a designated area with shelves where boxed artifacts can be stored. Being a late-eighteenth-century military building, it has, along with its historic charm, many challenges regarding condition and maintenance. Building deterioration has resulted at the time of writing in the migration of collections to a modern warehouse space adjacent to the cruise ship terminal outfitted to receive, hold, and make accessible the national collection.

The Barbados Museum has historically supported and facilitated a wide range of archaeological projects. It provides site numbers, guidance, resources for research, knowledge, and storage facilities for the curation and preservation of cultural resources collected by archaeological teams, and sometimes even labor for those teams.

Archaeologists from different countries and training backgrounds often arrive on island with their own systems of assemblage organization and management. As the recipient of archaeological collections (often without financial support or other resources provided by archaeological teams), the Barbados Museum has not imposed on collaborating archaeologists guidelines for collection practices, artifact care, or collection inventories. This has led to a wide variety of practices in terms of what types of artifacts are kept and in what capacity, the state of collections (whether washed, sorted, or cataloged), and how artifacts are organized and boxed for curation. Many collections are stored in low-quality Ziploc sandwich bags that rapidly degrade in a tropical climate. Provenience information, often written on the bags in permanent marker, is easily lost as well. In short, foreign researchers often prioritize excavation and the generation of archaeological knowledge over curation and long-term care for collections, thus raising ethical quandaries over assumed responsibility. In some cases, if historical archaeological projects have research questions pertaining to architecture and the sugarcane industry, this can lead to the curation of large quantities and excessive weights of bricks and other bulky artifacts like earthenware vessels used in the production of sugar. The problem highlighted here is that archaeologists abide by their own principles and practices only to expect the Barbados Museum to care for assemblages that it often had little input in collecting. Furthermore, even when permitted as budget lines by funding agencies, few archaeologists set aside funds for the curation, care, and preservation of collections at the Barbados Museum. The burden, therefore, falls on this government institution.

Over the past decade, the museum has required inventory lists and upgrades to collections materials. However, in the absence of legislation, it relies on moral suasion to compel researchers to adhere to standards. The idiosyncratic nature of site designation is unified within the collections management system of the Barbados Museum. This system has been hindered by the lack of resources and personnel but continues to operate under great constraint.

Nidhe Israel Museum

The Nidhe Israel Museum was founded in 2008. It is part of the Synagogue Historic District, an area in the center of historic Bridgetown, which also houses the Nidhe Israel synagogue, the Jewish cemetery, historic artisans' shops, and a mikvah. In 2008–2010, excavations were carried out in this area. The precolonial and historic artifacts collected were all stored in the Nidhe Israel Museum after having been processed and analyzed (Michael Stoner, personal communication 2012; Miller 2019: 233, 246).

The museum houses a suitable and neatly kept space for an archaeology lab. Excavated materials have been stored in labeled bags that are being kept in acid-free bankers' boxes, and the room is air-conditioned. Both Stoner and Miller left physical and digital inventories for the materials they collected during their excavations. The materials are safely stored, in an area that is not open to the public, but accessible for researchers after contacting the building's manager (Miller, personal communication 2023, discussing the situation as he last saw it in 2012).

Artifact Collections outside Barbados

Professional organizations outside Barbados also keep collections of archaeological materials from this island. In 2017, 17 European museums were reported to house precolonial collections from Barbados (Françozo and Strecker 2017: 457) (Table 9.1). To this number, we can add museums and universities outside Europe, such as the National Museum of the American Indian in New York, which has materials from several collections from Barbados (Smithsonian Institution 2024).

Considering Barbados's colonial past, it is not surprising that most of the listed European museums with Barbados collections are in the United Kingdom (N=8; 47.1%). Of these, the British Museum and the Museum of Archaeology and Anthropology, Cambridge, have the largest collections. These are in storage, not on display (Museum of Archaeology and Anthropology 2023; Trustees of the British Museum 2024). Several of the materials in Cambridge have been analyzed and published by Mary Hill Harris (cf. Harris 2019: 77).

A detailed catalog is also available for the Barbados artifacts in the Pitt Rivers Museum, Oxford (Hicks and Cooper 2013: 401, 403, 407). Hicks and Cooper (2013) discuss 51 artifacts from different sites in Barbados, including shell adzes and axes, a few ceramic sherds, and a stone spindle whorl, largely "collected for comparative purposes during the late 19th and early 20th centuries." It is fortunate that they were able to provide provenance information for many of the objects. In numerous collections, context information is incomplete or missing. Another challenge for museums is provide physical and digital access to these collections (Françozo and Strecker 2017: 461, 472). This is problematic, but not different from the situation of collections stored in Barbados. Collections at the Barbados Museum and the Nidhe Israel Museum are also largely in storage and not on display, and not presented in online object catalogs to researchers and the public.

Archaeological materials from excavations in Barbados are also housed in university facilities around the world. The Barbados Museum often agrees to generous loan arrangements, leaving artifacts and collections in the hands of foreign researchers. Unlike museums, universities do not make comprehensive inventories of their holdings publicly accessible. It is unclear at this time how many universities hold Barbadian collections. Without systematic assessment, unethical treatment of collections is possible as artifacts, including human remains, can be unaccounted for over long periods of time.

Researchers and Archaeology Enthusiasts Collecting, Storing, and Curating Artifacts from Barbados

Archaeology Researchers in Barbados

Archaeology legislation in Barbados is not directive. There are no strict guidelines about who is allowed to conduct archaeological research; who defines research foci and designs, and collection and sampling strategies; who decides on selection and deselection of finds after collection; and where, when, how, and by whom artifacts are being stored and curated. Such activity is affected by a de facto recognition of the Barbados Museum as the official repository of archaeological material on the island, with one caveat: contract archaeology paid for by private landowners.

Professional archaeological research is carried out by the Barbados Museum. As this organization has only one archaeologist and limited equipment, laboratory, and storage facilities, this mainly involves rescue operations. Archaeologists affiliated with universities abroad also carry out fieldwork for research and training purposes.

Fieldwork by those foreign scholars is often aimed at research questions that are relevant to their own research and that contribute to the academic output required by their (usually American or European) universities and funding agencies. Rarely, these projects are based on official, local invitations, and contacting local communities to find out what research questions are locally considered relevant. Some of these projects even transport artifacts

Table 9.1. European Museums with Precolonial Collections from Barbados

Country	Museum	Collection	Collection Period
United Kingdom	National Museum of Scotland (Edinburgh)	lithics; shell/coral	mid-19th–mid-20th C
United Kingdom	World Museum Liverpool	lithics; pottery; shell/coral	mid-19th–mid-20th C
United Kingdom	Bristol City Museum and Art Gallery	lithics; pottery; shell/coral	mid-19th–mid-20th C
United Kingdom	The Salisbury Museum	lithics; shell/coral; animal remains	mid-19th–mid-20th C
United Kingdom	Pitt Rivers Museum Oxford	human remains; lithics; pottery; shell/coral; wood/plants	mid-19th–mid-20th C
United Kingdom	Museum of Archaeology and Anthropology Cambridge	human remains; animal remains; lithics; pottery; shell/coral	mid-19th–mid-20th C
United Kingdom	British Museum (London)	human remains; animal remains; lithics; pottery; shell/coral; wood/plants	16th–early 19th C; mid-19th–mid-20th C
United Kingdom	Horniman Museum and Gardens (London)	lithics; shell/coral	mid-19th–mid-20th C
Sweden	Etnografiska Museet Stockholm	Lithics	16th–early 19th C; mid-19th–mid-20th C
Sweden	Världskulturmuseet Göteborg	lithics; pottery	mid-19th–mid-20th C
Germany	Ethnologisches Museum Berlin	human remains; animal remains; lithics; pottery; shell/coral	mid-19th–mid-20th C
Germany	Grassi Museum für Völkerkunde (Leipzig)	lithics; pottery; shell/coral; wood/plants	mid-19th–mid-20th C
Norway	Kulturhistorisk Museum Oslo	lithics; pottery	mid-19th–mid-20th C; contemporary period
Denmark	National Museum of Denmark (Copenhagen)	human remains; animal remains; lithics; pottery; shell/coral; wood/plants	mid-19th–mid-20th C
Austria	Weltmuseum Wien	lithics; pottery	16th–early 19th C; mid-19th–mid-20th C
Switzerland	Museum der Kulturen Basel	human remains; animal remains; lithics; pottery; shell/coral	mid-19th–mid-20th C
Netherlands	Wereldmuseum Leiden	not specified	mid-19th–mid-20th C

Note: Drawn from list by Mariana de Campos Françoso (NEXUS1492 n.d.).

outside Barbados. An exception was the Barbados Archaeology Survey project, carried out in the 1980s and 1990s by the late Peter and Lys Drewett (then University College London), who had reacted to a formal request by the Barbados Museum (Harris 2019: 78).

In Barbados, professional archaeology research can also be commissioned by private organizations and individual landowners. They can claim artifacts from their properties and decide to take care of storage themselves. This non-central storage, however, hinders accessibility of materials and dissemination of fieldwork results for other researchers and for the public. Examples are projects at Walkers Sand Quarry (Fitzpatrick et al. 2021), St. Nicholas Abbey plantation (Smith 2019), and the Synagogue Historic District (Miller 2019). In these projects, it is the organizations and the archaeologists in charge who set research aims and strategies for artifact collection, selection and deselection, storage, and curation. These models of collaboration are encouraging, especially since local partners play important roles in research design, but ethical considerations of collection management and accessibility persist.

Archaeology Enthusiasts in Barbados

Many artifact collections dating to the period of sole Indigenous occupation of the island and the centuries of European colonization exist not only in the Barbados Museum, but also in private collections across the island. In some cases, these include sites and attractions open to the public, like the Grenade Hall Signal Station, Harrison's Cave, and St. Nicholas Abbey. In many other instances, ad hoc collections are in the hands of private citizens at their residences. These archaeological enthusiasts might aptly be described as contemporary antiquarians, amassing ancient and more recent curiosities that reflect eras of a bygone Barbados without museum-level interest in provenance or context. Authors of this chapter have all visited such collections, which can range from a handful of Indigenous potsherds, tools, and figures to thousands of artifacts that span centuries of the Barbadian past.

Each collection has its own story. Across the island, it is not uncommon for residents to encounter finds in sugarcane fields, in gullies, along hiking trails, jutting out from coastal sands, while snorkeling or scuba diving, or within abandoned households. Other objects can be acquired as family heirlooms or purchased at estate sales.

Collectors have expressed several reasons for building their collections and for keeping them private. A general fascination with all things archaeological is a common attitude, but many collectors also express a responsibility for caring for artifacts that would otherwise decay, disappear, or be destroyed, thus indicating a moral impetus to protect the past. We have yet to encounter collectors who are unaware of the function of the Barbados Museum, but many, as is common elsewhere in the world, raised concerns about government control over valuable items, and quite a few believe in their right to private property and ownership of these vestiges of the Barbadian past. It is also not uncommon for collectors to lament the lack of resources at the disposal of the Barbados Museum, indicating that artifacts are safer in their own hands. Ethical considerations of the Barbadian past therefore encounter the economic realities of collection management.

While illicit pillaging of archaeological sites and the sale of illegally procured artifacts should be condemned, the relationship between professional archaeologists, heritage institutions like the Barbados Museum, and private collectors should be collaborative rather than adversarial. Archaeology enthusiasts do have an important role to play in the preservation of Barbadian heritage. They can be the archaeologists' eyes and ears, as it is not uncommon that they are the first to note or to be informed that archaeological materials are observed on building sites and in plowed fields. Quite a few of them are also open to making their collections accessible for public and academic study and visits.

Public Stewardship, Heritage, and Art

Related to our conversation about archaeological enthusiasts and private collectors, it is important for professional archaeologists to recognize broader public interests in material culture and archaeological practices. As Hamilakis (2011) has demonstrated in the case of Greece, everyday residents from all walks of life encounter and think about archaeological objects in their everyday lives. This includes Barbadians of past generations, like enslaved and free laborers who may have recognized artifacts as they cut cane, tended to livestock, or traversed gullies across the island. In the case of the American South, for instance, a nineteenth-century archaeologist working in Mississippi and Louisiana documented the fact that enslaved laborers regularly kept "Indian antiquities" in their homes (see Reilly 2022). The same may have been true of Barbados, meaning that archaeology can and should be a public endeavor.

Releasing the tight grasp of many international researchers on what they consider legitimate archaeology may open the door for more fruitful collaborations with Barbadian thinkers and practitioners interested in the material past. One such example is the multiyear collaboration between chapter coauthor Reilly and Barbadian visual artist Annalee Davis (Reilly and Davis 2021). Davis has been integrating archaeological information and artifacts in some of her artwork to investigate and communicate Barbados's post-plantation economies and landscapes (see Davis 2024 and volume cover).

Other Barbadian artists similarly engage with the material record. For instance, artist Cathy Cummins incorporates eighteenth- and nineteenth-century sherds of refined earthenware vessels into her work. These ceramic artifacts are ubiquitous across the island, often found on the surface along hiking trails, in fields, and in yard spaces surrounding structures. Using sherds she or family and friends collect while out and about, Cummins arranges the small pieces in stunning color schemes and shapes like that of a plate or heart (Figure 9.3). The works are then featured on social media, often accompanied by descriptions of the ceramic wares involved and some historical background information, where they can be purchased by Barbadians or international buyers. Interestingly, the works bear a striking resemblance to the Sailor's Valentine, a mosaic-like craft composed of shells of various hues that made an appearance across the Atlantic World in the nineteenth century. The tradition and the shells are said to have their origins in Barbados, with examples on display at the Barbados Museum.

The work by Cummins resembles the creative use of material heritage on other islands in the Caribbean. For instance, artists in Saint Croix have traditionally used small pieces of refined, broken earthenware, known as "chaney," to create jewelry. The ceramic sherds are largely from ceramics imported from the UK and Europe—plates, cups, and so forth, remnants of the island's colonial past. These local crafts have been interpreted as a critical intervention into the archive of colonialism. Artists such as La Vaughn Belle have popularized the form in paintings inspired by chaney, providing a narrative of empowerment to those who were enslaved and who built modern colonial economies (Johnson 2021). In Belle's case, she has actively collaborated with archaeologists from the Society of Black Archaeologists, conducting fieldwork on a former Crucian sugar estate (Flewellen et al. 2022; Priebe 2021).

These Barbadian and Crucian artistic works incorporate the discarded fragments of ceramic vessels, some of which had previously been modified by the enslaved to serve as gaming pieces. A multi-temporal engagement with material heritage is therefore at play, representing creative outlets not often

Figure 9.3. *You Give Love a Bad Name* artwork consisting of vintage sherds on 12 × 12 inch hardboard, by Cathy Cummins. Reproduced with permission of the artist.

pursued by archaeologists. At the same time, while these artifacts are in a sense preserved (on the ears and around the necks of those who wear them or on the walls of those who buy them), it should be emphasized that ceramic sherds are not a renewable cultural resource. Mining soils for these materials can result in the destruction of archaeological sites and a diminished footprint of the people who once used these everyday items. We therefore suggest more direct collaborations between artists and archaeological professionals to ensure the proper management of sites, as well as the ethical persistence of local crafts and artistic practice.

Discussion and Conclusions: Collection, Selection, Deposition, and Storage of Archaeological Materials in Barbados

Summary and Discussion

We started this chapter by asking the question "Who is responsible for proper storage of collected artifacts and how?" The answer is that this is a shared responsibility of the relevant authorities, designated heritage organizations, archaeologists, and archaeology enthusiasts. How storage is effectively organized is more complex to outline, indicating that shared responsibility is easier said than done, especially when the ethics of archaeological research and conservation are involved.

As Byer (2022: 147) notes, there usually is some friction between planning (promoting development) and heritage law (promoting conservation). Barbados is no exception to this. Even though several institutions work hard to administer and protect heritage in the island, not all legislative instruments are effective and operational yet. Some acts lack definitions, necessary listings are not being compiled or updated, and measures are rarely imposed on acts against existing heritage regulations. For archaeology researchers in Barbados, it may not be completely clear which organization to contact prior to developing fieldwork projects. Many archaeologists will reach out to the Barbados Museum, but this organization is not filing permissions or setting conditions for archaeology field research, preservation, conservation of collected materials, and publication as it is legally empowered to do so. The Barbados Museum can and does issue site numbers, but this is not a legally codified requirement for on-island research.

Storage conditions at the Barbados Museum are far from ideal, with maintenance issues for both storage space and collections, whereas storage conditions at Nidhe Israel Museum seem fairly good. For the Barbados Museum it is particularly challenging when researchers carry out excavations and only contact the museum to store the collected materials. The museum is thus burdened with responsibilities regarding the collections, but not with the funds needed to maintain them and to make them accessible to the community and researchers. Heritage professionals from Curaçao, the Dominican Republic, and Grenada indicate that this problematic situation is similar on their islands (personal communication, workshop on ethics in Caribbean archaeology, Leiden 2023). On the other hand, collections made by archaeologists working for private organizations or by archaeology enthusiasts in Barbados are not submitted to the Barbados Museum. This is also problematic, as it negatively impacts directive central data management, artifact curation, and accessibility.

The afore-mentioned organizations in Barbados have not created digital object catalogs, which limits access to the collections they do house. For some collections that are in heritage institutions outside Barbados digital catalogs exist, allowing some degree of access. As those collections were taken from Barbados in a colonial context and without consent, it is felt that these should be returned, to, for example, the Barbados Museum. This, however, must be accompanied by funding to allow adequate cultural resource management for the museum.

Suggestions for Future Collection and Conservation Strategies in Barbados

Having also considered the questions "What is needed?," "Who should pay?," and "Which best practices or suggestions can lead to solid and feasible improvements?," we conclude that enforced legislation is needed most. As the Barbados Preservation of Antiquities and Relics Bill already defines the necessary procedures, passing of this bill is essential. For this, more clarity must be provided about relevant authorities, the composition of the board that can license archaeological field research, and the expertise expected from archaeologists. More substantive community support through community involvement and consultation is also needed (cf. Byer 2022: 147–148). Calls for more community engagement in the Caribbean have had an impact in Barbados, with current projects often incorporating partnerships with island professionals (Reilly and Davis 2021) and collaborations with institutions like The University of the West Indies and the Barbados Museum.

To allow directive and central data management, artifact curation, accessibility, and monitoring, it is advisable to opt for central storage of heritage materials in one designated professional heritage institution, which could loan heritage materials to temporary or permanent exhibitions elsewhere on the island.

Therefore, we strongly encourage archaeologists to work with Barbados Museum staff during the initial phases of research design to ensure that museum professionals have a voice in determining research, collection and selection strategies, and how budgets allocate funds for curation. Whereas small archaeology projects might not be able to (greatly) contribute financially, this is something that should certainly be asked for from larger, or multiyear, projects for which considerable grants are being obtained.

Finally, as IACA has already defined prerequisites for curation and archiving (Cunningham et al. 2022a), this organization might also play a role in further dissemination of expertise regarding demands to budget, reports, documentation, transportation of materials, and storage, for example, by providing standard checklists and overviews of best practices on the organization's website.

Concluding Remarks

As strategies for collection, selection, storage, and curation influence the ways we see the past, it is crucial that professionally staffed local heritage organizations, supported by adequate legislation and financial means, set the standards for these procedures. This has massive ethical implications. Successful implementation of legislation would prioritize Barbadian researchers over outsiders, standards of site care, and curation. Furthermore, providing means for management initiatives would make collections more accessible to the Barbadian public.

This, however, is more complex than it sounds. Concrete action is needed to have the relevant legislation put in place and to acquire financial means to support ethical fieldwork and collection care. Research grants, particularly for small projects, do not allow long-term maintenance and investment in sustainable facilities. Local capacity building could therefore be part of broader reparations initiatives that could support equity in collections management and ensure the upkeep of Barbados's material heritage for generations to come.

Considering the amounts of materials stored in Caribbean heritage organizations, and the struggle to keep up these collections, the question also arises whether we should not switch to analyzing existing collections, and favoring rescue operations and nondestructive field research, instead of continuing to carry out (large-scale) excavations. Making collections accessible by means of solid databases and online catalogs might contribute to this. No matter which solutions will be chosen to ameliorate collection and storage issues, simply continuing the traditional ways of investigating sites through large-scale excavations and of storing materials is not an option. Shifting our practices to inaugurate a new, more ethical archaeological agenda in Barbados is the only way forward.

Note

1 As the focus of the Barbados National Trust is more on built heritage, this institution has not been included.

References Cited

Ariese-Vandemeulebroucke, Csilla E. 2018. *The Social Museum in the Caribbean: Grassroots Heritage Initiatives and Community Engagement.* PhD dissertation, Leiden University. Leiden: Sidestone Press.

Armstrong, Douglas V., Alissandra Cummins, Maaike S. de Waal, Kevin Farmer, Niall Finneran, and Matthew C. Reilly. 2019. "Introduction: The Past and Present of Archaeology in Barbados." In *Pre-Colonial and Post-Contact Archaeology in Barbados: Past, Present, and Future Research Directions,* edited by Maaike S. de Waal, Niall Finneran, Matthew C. Reilly, Douglas V. Armstrong, and Kevin Farmer, 15–39. Leiden: Sidestone Press.

Barbados Museum. 2024a. "History." https://barbmuse.org.bb/About/History (accessed June 27, 2024).

Barbados Museum. 2024b. "Mission and Vision." https://barbmuse.org.bb/About/Mission-Vision (accessed June 27, 2024).

Barbados National Registry of Historic Places. 2024. "About." heritagebarbados.gov.bb (accessed June 27, 2024).

Byer, Amanda. 2022. *Heritage, Landscape, and Spatial Justice: New Legal Perspectives on Heritage Protection in the Lesser Antilles.* PhD dissertation, Leiden University. Leiden: Sidestone Press.

Cummins, Alissandra. 2004. "Caribbean Museums and National Identity." *History Workshop Journal* 58: 225–245.

Cunningham, Andreana, Felicia J. Fricke, Christina Giovas, Jonathan A. Hanna, Tibisay Sankatsing Nava, John Shorter, and Amy Victorina. 2022a. "Code of Ethics." International Association for Caribbean Archaeology (IACA). https://www.jhtm.nl/excav/bibliotheek/IACA_CodeOfEthics2021.pdf (accessed June 26, 2024).

Davis, Annalee. 2024. www.annaleedavis.com (accessed June 27, 2024).

De Waal, Maaike S. 2019. "Amerindian Cultural Landscapes in Ceramic Age Barbados." In *Pre-Colonial and Post-Contact Archaeology in Barbados: Past, Present, and Future Research Directions,* edited by Maaike S. de Waal, Niall Finneran, Matthew C. Reilly, Douglas V. Armstrong, and Kevin Farmer, 99–114. Leiden: Sidestone Press.

Farmer, Kevin. 2011. "Barbados." In *Protecting Heritage in the Caribbean,* edited by Peter E. Siegel and Elizabeth Righter, 112–124. Tuscaloosa: University of Alabama Press.

Fitzpatrick, Scott M., Maaike S. de Waal, Matthew Napolitano, and Philippa Jorissen. 2021. "Results of Preliminary Archaeological Investigation at Walkers Reserve, St. Andrew, Barbados." *Journal of the Barbados Museum and Historical Society* Volume LXVII: 208–228.

Flewellen, Ayana Omilade, Alicia Odewale, Justin Dunnavant, Alexandra Jones, and William White III. 2022. "Creating Community and Engaging Community: The Foundations of the Estate Little Princess Archaeology Project in St. Croix, United States Virgin Islands." *International Journal of Historical Archaeology* 26: 147–176.

Françozo, Mariana, and Amy Strecker. 2017. "Caribbean Collections in European Museums and the Question of Returns." *International Journal of Cultural Property* 24: 451–477.

Hamilakis, Yannis. 2011. Archaeological Ethnography: A Multitemporal Meeting Ground for Archaeology and Anthropology. *Annual Review of Anthropology* 40(1): 399–414.

Harris, Mary Hill. 2019. "The Pre-Colonial Pottery of Barbados." In *Pre-Colonial and Post-Contact Archaeology in Barbados: Past, Present, and Future Research Directions,* edited by Maaike S. de Waal, Niall Finneran, Matthew C. Reilly, Douglas V. Armstrong, and Kevin Farmer, 77–97. Leiden: Sidestone Press.

Hicks, Dan, and Jago Cooper. 2013. "The Caribbean." In *World Archaeology at the Pitt Rivers Museum: A Characterization,* edited by Dan Hicks and Alice Stevenson, 401–408. Oxford: Archaeopress.

Inniss, Tara A. 2019. "Of Roots and Routes. Visioning Barbados' Cultural Heritage through Trails Development." In *Pre-Colonial and Post-Contact Archaeology in Barbados: Past, Present, and Future Research Directions,* edited by Maaike S. de Waal, Niall Finneran, Matthew C. Reilly, Douglas V. Armstrong, and Kevin Farmer, 383–394. Leiden: Sidestone Press.

Johnson, Erica L. 2021. "Comparative Counter-Archival Creativity: M. ZourbeSe Philip's *Zong!* and La Vaughn Belle's *Chaney*." *Journal of Aesthetics & Culture* 13(1). https://doi.org/10.1080/20004214.2021.1954418.

Leiden University. 2023. "Leiden Archaeologists Repatriate Human Remains to St. Eustatius." March 30, 2023. https://www.universiteitleiden.nl/en/news/2023/03/leiden -archaeologists-repatriate-human-remains-to-st.-eustatius (accessed June 27, 2024).

Miller, Derek R. 2019. "The 2009 and 2010 Synagogue Compound Excavations: An Exploration of the Material Culture of the First 100 Years of the Nidhe Israel Community." In *Pre-Colonial and Post-Contact Archaeology in Barbados: Past, Present, and Future Research Directions,* edited by Maaike S. de Waal, Niall Finneran, Matthew C. Reilly, Douglas V. Armstrong, and Kevin Farmer, 233–249. Leiden: Sidestone Press.

Müller, Lars. 2021. "Returns of Cultural Artefacts and Human Remains in a (Post) colonial Context. Mapping Claims between the Mid-19th Century and the 1970s." Working Paper Deutsches Zentrum Kulturgutverluste No. 1/2021. Deutsches Zentrum Kulturgutverluste, Magdeburg.

Museum of Archaeology and Anthropology. 2023. "Search Results: Objects." https:// collections.maa.cam.ac.uk/objects/ (accessed June 27, 2024).

NEXUS1492, n.d. "Interactive Nexus 1492." Leiden University. https://www .universiteitleiden.nl/nexus1492/about/interactive-nexus-1492 (accessed June 27, 2024).

Parliament of Barbados. 2019. "Planning and Development Act, 2019." https://www.barbadosparliament.com/uploads/bill_resolution/ 367cfdd592ad180a0d6a1c191fe41489.pdf (accessed July 10, 2023).

Priebe, Jessica. 2021. "Colonial Trash to Island Treasure: The Chaney of St. Croix." *British Art Studies* 21. https://britishartstudies.ac.uk/issues/21/colonial-trash-to-island -treasure (accessed June 8, 2025).

Reilly, Matthew C. 2022. "Archaeologies of Whiteness." *Archaeological Dialogues* 29(1): 51–66.

Reilly, Matthew C., and Annalee Davis. 2021. "An Interdisciplinary Approach to Archaeology and Art on a Caribbean Plantation." *SHA Newsletter* 54(3): 36–40.

Smith, Frederick H. 2019. "St. Nicholas Abbey: Centering People in Plantation Archaeology in Barbados in the Twenty-First Century." In *Pre-Colonial and Post-Contact Archaeology in Barbados: Past, Present, and Future Research Directions,* edited by Maaike S. de Waal, Niall Finneran, Matthew C. Reilly, Douglas V. Armstrong, and Kevin Farmer, 133–155. Leiden: Sidestone Press.

Smith, Frederick H., and Karl Watson. 2007. "Western Bridgetown and the Butchers' Shambles in the Seventeenth–Nineteenth Centuries: New Insights from the Jubilee Garden Archaeological Investigations." *Journal of the Barbados Museum and Historical Society* 53: 185–198.

Smithsonian Institution. 2024. "Collections Search: Barbados." National Museum of the American Indian. https://americanindian.si.edu/collections-search/search?edan _q=barbados (accessed June 27, 2024).

Trustees of the British Museum. 2024. "Collection Search: Barbados." https://www .britishmuseum.org/collection/search?keyword=Barbados (accessed June 27, 2024).

Welch, Christina, and Niall Finneran. 2022. "Chatoyer's Punch Ladle: A Museum Artifact that Speaks to the Hidden History of the Garifuna, An African-Caribbean People." *Journal of African Diaspora Archaeology and Heritage* 11(3): 181–204.

10

Caribbean Digital Archaeology

Ethical Challenges and Best Practices

EDUARDO HERRERA MALATESTA

This chapter presents an overview of world debates on ethics in digital archaeology and their resonance within Caribbean archaeology. Digital archaeology has seen exponential growth in the past decades as a result of the immense analytical and interpretative possibilities this field offers to the archaeological understanding of patterns in the past and to visual reconstructions. As with computer technologies in general, the rapid advance of this field has not been matched in the regulations and best practices for the various ethical issues that can arise from the uncritical or unskilled use of these technologies and methodologies. This reality spreads to Caribbean archaeology as well, and now is a perfect time to begin an open and explicit conversation on the ethical challenges of digital archaeology in the Caribbean.

To open the conversation, this chapter is divided into four sections. The section "Ethical Concerns in Digital Archaeology" first presents a discussion of the core debates on ethics in digital archaeology around the world, focusing mostly on four main points: the use and creation of codes of ethics, the fast advancement of technology, the relationship between archaeologists using digital technologies and communities, and the mostly political self-critique of ethical codes. Based on the general context from this section, as well as the general background of Caribbean archaeology as presented in the introduction to this volume by Fricke, Herrera Malatesta, and de Waal, the following section, "Ethical Challenges in the Caribbean," focuses on discussing three key challenges: digital representations and colonial history, the potential for digital neocolonialism, and involvement and representation of Indigenous and local communities. Following this, the section "Best Practices and Recommendations" proposes a series of best practices to contribute to digital Caribbean archaeology moving forward in an ethical way with the new opportunities and challenges that digital technologies can bring. The last section, "Conclusion," wraps up the discussed arguments and reflects on them for the future of ethics in Caribbean digital archaeology.

Ethical Concerns in Digital Archaeology

This section focuses on defining digital archaeology and contextualizing it within ethical debates in the discipline. First, it is relevant to clarify the use of the term "digital archaeology," which includes the field of computational archaeology. While these terms might seem synonyms, digital and computational archaeology are not the same. Digital archaeology has been defined as the application of information technology and digital media to archaeology. It includes technologies such as the use of digital photography, 3D reconstruction, virtual reality, and geographical information systems. Computational archaeology, on the other hand, refers mostly to methodological and theoretical aspects of using computer-based analysis, like, for example, spatial statistics, mathematics, and network science methods, to create models and simulations based on archaeological data (Daly and Evans 2006; Dennis 2020; Zubrow 2006). So, while all computational archaeology is digital, not all digital archaeology can be defined as computational. For the sake of simplicity in this chapter, I will use the term "digital archaeology" to refer to both digital and computational methods and technologies unless there is a need to specify them.

There are already various overviews of digital and computational archaeology available and, therefore, a full background will not be discussed here (e.g., Brughmans and Peeples 2023; Conolly and Lake 2006; Daly and Evans 2006; Gillings et al. 2020; Grosman 2016; McCoy 2017; Romanowska et al. 2021). Digital archaeology has been formally used and discussed in archaeology since the 1970s (e.g., Hodder 1999; Hodder and Orton 1976; Lock 2003; Zubrow 2006). However, the discussion on ethical challenges raised by this field is quite recent. Ethics have become an important aspect to address within digital archaeology as archaeology is increasingly dealing with large databases and big data, fast technological developments, high costs for advanced technologies and tools, and open-access needs. This produces challenges in terms of data sovereignty, data privacy and security, black box methodologies, data/model transparency and research, academic asymmetries, engagement of stakeholders, and educational plans for local communities and researchers (e.g., Chase et al. 2020; Cohen et al. 2020; Dennis 2020; Floridi and Taddeo 2016; Morgan 2022; Richardson 2018; Tenzer et al. 2024). As Huggett (2015) proposed, archaeology needs to reflect critically on the open access of archaeological data. Colley (2015) argued, for example, that granting access to information in some cases is ethical, yet in others, where the shared data is sensitive material of a person or a community or the sharing of a particular information might be harmful, then it will be unethical to share it (see also Nägele, Benn Torres, and Nieves-Colón, this volume).

The literature on ethics in digital archaeology has been focused on two overarching aspects that have several points of interrelation. On the one hand, there are issues directly related to the digitalization of data, open access and stakeholders, black box methodologies, and digital outputs. On the other hand, there are issues directly related to power asymmetries, sovereignty, and a critique of places of enunciation, that is, who decides what is good and bad? For ease of argument, in this paper, I will refer to the first issues as "scientific ethical challenges" and the second as "political ethical challenges."

Scientific Ethical Challenges

The European Commission (2021) created a document to provide an ethical guide for researchers working in the fields of social science and humanities. While it does not directly address digital data, it does focus on the use of the internet and social media in research. Its primary focus is on calling attention to the fact that digitization of data involves, in one way or another, the processing of human information. Therefore, researchers must be aware of this to minimize any potential impact on local communities or stakeholders. In archaeology, data collection always involves contact with people and communities. When archaeologists are in the field collecting and registering materials and sites, they are also collecting information about contemporary people. A site location is usually within the terrain of a local farmer or within a national park that is protected under regional or national laws. When researchers publish this information or make it open access, they might be putting individuals or communities (human or animal) at risk by identifying or exposing their territories as relevant for, for example, looters. As Floridi and Taddeo (2016: 3) have argued, "in a few decades, we have come to understand that it is not a specific technology (computers, tablets, mobile phones, online platforms, cloud computing and so forth), but what any digital technology manipulates that represents the correct focus of our ethical strategies. The shift from information ethics to data ethics is probably more semantic than conceptual, but it does highlight the need to concentrate on what is being handled as the true invariant of our concerns." This is a key point in relation to the collection and open access of digital data. As mentioned before, satellite imagery or a GPS point does not only represent the location or area of a site, but it shows the location of the house or terrain of actual people whose lives could be affected by opening those datasets to the public. The data could be providing more information than intended, and therefore, trust and transparency are crucial aspects of ethics for digital data and archaeology in general.

Chase et al. (2020) have made a similar argument in the context of Lidar studies in Mesoamerica. They argue that while open data carries several benefits for archaeological research, it might bring issues of national security and site protection, which can create friction between researchers and regional and national governments. Furthermore, this creates conflicts of interest between funding agencies (e.g., Horizon Europe, National Science Foundation) and national governments, as the former requires of researchers that all data has to become open access, while the latter might argue that open data could be a risk to security and sovereignty. Another argument raised by Chase et al. (2020) is related to stakeholders. In the case of Lidar data, as well as other types of data, such as point locations or digital reconstructions, several stakeholders could benefit from data and models created by archaeologists using digital and computational methods; for example, regional governments, the military, private companies, and organizations could benefit from these digital outputs to advance in hydrological studies, tourism, resource management, military planning, public outreach, and education. However, on the other hand, other organizations or individuals could take benefits that will not necessarily support local communities or educational programs and that could potentially destroy or limit access to the archaeological heritage. Therefore, while the collection and digitization of archaeological evidence and its posterior analysis and modeling need to be revised to protect local communities, the sharing of data through open access is also in need of review to protect local and national communities.

The discussion on using digital technologies to preserve archaeological heritage is an important one, as among the core aims in the humanities and social science is the ethical significance of protecting heritage to avoid its destruction or loss (Colley 2015). Yet, safeguarding heritage is not always the most ethical action (e.g., Labadi 2022). Similarly, while making research data open access is a positive ethical matter, the standardization of best practices could risk the prevalence of certain research designs over others, particularly academic projects led by the traditional centers of power in the United States and Europe, which in turn will affect the local development of archaeological theories and practices. This raises the ethical challenge that ethical codes and best practices should be written together with local communities and researchers and not solely by the academic centers that usually provide or have the funding for research.

Another key point to discuss is the ethical challenge related to black box methodologies and the relation between data, methods, and analyses. Floridi and Taddeo (2016) stress the importance of understanding that there can be different moral dimensions in different types of data. For example, there is data that is directly used for analyses and other data that is just considered to contextualize or aid in the decision-making process. In this sense, the focus should be on the nature of the computational analysis and not only on the digital technologies that enable them. As Tenzer et al. (2024) have also shown for the case of artificial intelligence (AI) and machine learning (ML), researchers need to be aware of what is happening when they input data into software that has such complex capabilities. Computational analyses should continue to involve human actors and not be left alone for an automatic process, particularly considering that the results of these analyses will be used to create narratives about the past that will be publicly disseminated as the "truth" of archaeological research. Black box methodologies obscure the possibility of addressing ethical issues properly and "by its very nature, if a system cannot be understood by its user, then its user cannot ensure that a formalized ethical compliance is being met, let alone if an aspirational ethical standard is being met" (Dennis 2020: 213).

In this sense, archaeological research designs that aim at using digital technologies must consider, before starting the project, the real need to use certain technologies and how those technologies and methodologies will contribute to answering questions in a better way than without using them. Dennis (2020) has identified two related aspects for which failing to address potential black boxes explicitly could harm the research and the discipline. The first relates to how researchers choose digital methodologies and tools, and the second to how digital archaeology meets the ethical obligations it has with local, marginalized, and/or Indigenous communities. For example, Tenzer et al. (2024: 3) argued that "AI algorithms in analyzing archaeological data could inadvertently lead to biased interpretations of historical events or the reinforcement of existing power structures if the models used are not designed with these ethical considerations in mind." Applying AI and ML methods without an understanding of the computational process behind or using datasets that have not been properly curated or are not representative could lead to the creation of narratives that represent the past from biased and inaccurate perspectives.

In general terms, current literature in digital archaeology and its ethical implications support the creation of codes of ethics and best practices to allow researchers to interact better with digital technologies, avoid black-box methodologies, and improve the interaction between researchers, digital data, and stakeholders. However, there have also been critiques of the general notion and framework of the code of ethics. For example, Colley (2015) argues that a code of ethics creates asymmetrical relations and exclusion and perpetuates single-side perspectives. A similar critique is presented by Dennis (2020) who consider that codes of conduct are among the failures of digital archaeology. The current "Ethics Policy of the Computer Applications and Quantitative Methods in Archaeology (CAA)" organization (Brughmans et al. 2018) includes within its statements the need for diverse perspectives, condemning discrimination, considering accountability, and encouraging outreach activities as a responsibility of all digital archaeologists. However, the critique from several digital and non-digital archaeologists remains: Who is deciding what is good and bad? How do the codes really materialize symmetrical relations? And how do they bring accountability? (e.g., Gnecco 2015; González-Ruibal 2018; Haber and Shepherd 2015). The next section will revise these questions.

Political Ethical Challenges

Beyond the previously discussed aspects lies the implicit notion that the main critique of the codes of ethics is based on the fact that they have been written from what Fernández (2015) has called "mainstream Western archaeology." This perspective assumes that there is a universal notion of ethics and that all archaeologists have the same cultural background and values to be bound together. Therefore, a universal definition of ethics and a universal code of ethics will suffice for a homogeneous discipline. As Fernández (2015) proposed, while the universality in the code of ethics has brought its greatest merits, that is, a guideline for best practices in archaeology, the code of ethics has also reduced society to a standardized entity. Similarly, Tarlow (2006) argued that as long as ethical arguments keep depending on a frame based on shared cultural beliefs, there will continue to be friction among groups as each has their own agendas, as well as beliefs and notions of right and wrong. She goes on to propose that "codes of ethics promote conservatism and conformity, reinforce the power of hegemonic institutions and pre-empt ethical debate." (Tarlow 2006: 245). In this line, several authors have argued that one of the problems with codes of ethics and ethical approaches, in general, is that they have instrumentalized and depoliticized ethics (Hamilakis 2007). According to Hamilakis (2018) this is a result of considering ethics only as a way to regulate professional archaeology. Furthermore, this disciplinary regulation has created profound asymmetrical relations between "disciplinary knowledge in archaeology and local, indigenous and subaltern knowledge" (Haber and Shepherd 2015: 5; see also Richardson 2018). In a similar line, Gnecco (2015: 3) argued that the "other" has become contained within the ethical code as a result of the lack of a "thorough discussion about power, capitalism, multiculturalism, and inequalities, that is, about contextual conditions." In this way, certain ethical approaches can perpetuate coloniality, as the voices and standards coming only from the perspective of the global political, economic, academic centers. Archaeologists must ask themselves, how are we dealing with the fact that right and wrong are dependent on cultural and historical contexts? In the matter of digital technologies, the set of ethical values is based on what is important and appropriate for the European Union and United States and not on what is important for the people in the rural areas or the Indigenous communities outside these regions. As Dennis (2020: 213) proposed, "No widespread study on how indigenous groups view their rights in digitally mediated archaeology has been undertaken within archaeology itself." A key point in this critique is that for several researchers, the code of ethics has frozen reflexivity as they seek to standardize and universalize practices and knowledge (González-Ruibal 2018; Haber and Shepherd 2015; Hamilakis 2007; Tarlow 2006). However, ethics is not an absolute term; it entails historical conditions and moral thinking of diverse societies at different times in their histories (Gnecco 2015).

Finally, it is important to acknowledge the fact that most ethical discussions have been framed within the idea of multivocality and multiculturalism. Curtoni (2015) explains that there are current demands in specialized congresses (such as the TAAS[1] or the World Archaeological Congress) from Indigenous people to participate and be involved in the archaeological research process. A main force behind this is that the notion of multivocality often comes from an uncritical application of the term in Anglo-Saxon academic circles. Multivocality does not imply the assumption that we are all equal or that there should not be criticism. As Morgan (2022) highlighted, while ethical discussions in digital and computational archaeology are increasing, engagement with the political and ethical challenges in these subfields are only scratching the surface. A debate and discussion about ethics in digital archaeology, and archaeology in general, should consider the larger political ramifications. For example, it should openly debate issues of state, institutional, and individual power and the consequent asymmetrical relations, privileged positions, and equal access to digital resources and technologies. These topics will be discussed in the next section.

Ethical Challenges in the Caribbean

Based on the above discussion of the contemporary challenges that digital archaeology faces in the world, this chapter will present the mentioned aspects that are particularly relevant when thinking of digital archaeology in the Caribbean. These are (1) digital representations and colonial history, (2) the potential for digital neocolonialism, and (3) the involvement and representation of Indigenous and local communities.

Digital Representations and Colonial History

The colonization of the Caribbean and the American continent was a process that has impacted the lives of millions of people in the past and in the present (e.g., González-Tennant 2014; Hauser and Hicks 2007; Hofman et al. 2018; Pagán-Jiménez and Rodríguez Ramos 2008). The representations done of the Indigenous people by the early colonizers, both in written and graphical accounts, created the idea of the "Indian" back in the past and the legacy of the "Indigenous" in the present (Hauser 2022; Herrera Malatesta 2022; Ulloa Hung 2016). The Indigenous history that Caribbeans learn in school settings is strongly biased by these early representations to the point that people will defend the colonial Indigenous image even when presented with less biased and less colonial alternatives (e.g., Fricke and Hoerman 2022; Herrera Malatesta and Sony Jean 2023; see also Antczak et al. this volume). However, local communities are not to blame for this, as the perpetuation of colonialist biases in the Caribbean has been the result of early and late historical accounts and the perpetuation of colonialist categories in archaeological research.[2] There has been plenty of debate regarding the colonialist role of archaeology and its influence in perpetuating narratives of exclusion and discrimination by maintaining control over the classification and management of peoples, objects, stories, and histories (e.g., Benavides 2010; Curtoni 2015; Gnecco and Langebaek 2006a; Jofré Luna 2015; Pagán-Jiménez 2004).

Within this frame, digital representations of past people in the Caribbean carry the risk of perpetuating hegemonic archaeology and its traditional categories of classifying and organizing past cultures and societies (e.g., Gnecco and Langebaek 2006b). Furthermore, they threaten to implicitly contribute to the political and ideological system on which archaeology was built, that is, capitalism and mercantilism (Hamilakis 2007). The wide possibilities of digital archaeology in terms of open-access data, visual representations, and interoperability of archaeological models in social media, while tools for positive change and decolonization of knowledge, could also be used to maintain the globalization of Western perspectives and monocultural knowledge, which ultimately diminishes and excludes the worldviews of non-Western societies (Curtoni 2015). As Herrera Malatesta and Pellini (forthcoming) have stated for northern South America, while in the present, archaeology seeks to study past Indigenous people, at the same time, the discipline and society exclude the contemporary descendants of those peoples. Ethical approaches in digital and computational Caribbean archaeology should not be distracted by the potential of technological advances. They should not forget to be aware of the risks of perpetuating coloniality and silencing voices. Therefore, by thoughtlessly implementing ethical aspects coming from European and US digital archaeologies, one might risk implicitly employing asymmetrical and power-oriented "best practices."

The Potential for Digital Neocolonialism

Digital neocolonialism refers to "the use of information technology and the internet by hegemonic powers as a means of indirect control or influences over a marginalized group or country" (Adam 2019: 370). There are various manifestations of digital neocolonialism. The most relevant ones for Caribbean archaeology, to be discussed in the following paragraphs, are data colonialism and algorithmic coloniality.

Data colonialism refers to the appropriation of data as a material resource for economic profit (e.g., Mouton and Burns 2021; Zembylas 2023). Digital information is one driver of the global economy and in the contemporary world, several regions from the Global South are facing developmental stagnation (e.g., Menon 2023). Within this point, there are some aspects that need mentioning in relation to Caribbean archaeology, such as advanced technologies and training and education. Local Caribbean institutions and researchers often lack the necessary funds to get advanced technologies such as Lidar, which means that these are often only possible to be used with foreign funds. However, Chase et al. (2020) mentioned that relying on external funds to pay for these technologies means that foreign data policies have to be followed, which often generates friction with national or regional governments. Enforcing digital policies in relation to archaeological data generated in a Caribbean nation represents a breach of their sovereignty. Furthermore, data gathered under a project financed with foreign funding might be under a different set of rules or even a different set of standardized parameters in relation to data configuration, metadata, and open access. For example, Colley (2015) warned about the risks of metadata standardization as it enables what Curtoni (2015) referred to as monocultural knowledge. Additionally, while open access has several advantages for countries with reduced access to research funds, it also opens up the possibility, as mentioned before, for sensitive data to be accessed by anyone. Regarding training and education, most Caribbean nations, particularly within the social sciences and humanities, lack the infrastructure and specialized staff to develop programs on digital technologies. A solution for students and researchers, although not necessarily for government officials, has been enrolling in platforms that offer low-cost, Massive Open Online Courses (MOOC). However, as Adam (2019) has highlighted, while MOOCs bring connectivity and optimism for the democratization of knowledge, they also carry the risk of maintaining historical inequalities and normalizing the Western way of knowledge as the only option for understanding the world.[3]

The second aspect, algorithmic coloniality, denotes the ways in which algorithms perpetuate colonial biases (Menon 2023). For example, the algorithms and parameters by which AI is created are based on Western ontology and epistemology. This inherently carries along all their existing biases and discriminations. As Tenzer et al. (2024) have argued, AI can greatly help archaeology overcome several existing challenges, such as dealing with the data deluge (e.g., Bevan 2015), improving text analysis, and assisting in the identification of personally identifiable information and potential copyright infringements. However, as the authors pointed out, there are concerns regarding the transparency of the procedures as they "have been shown to perpetuate social inequalities (Casilli, 2019), propagate misinformation (Wilner, 2018), and compromise privacy (Véliz, 2023). Furthermore, the use of AI technologies has been linked to instances of racial discrimination (Raji et al., 2020), the endangerment of natural resources, and the exploitation of human labor (Crawford, 2021)" (Tenzer et al. 2024: 3). These authors also warn about the dangers of using AI to create narratives about the past as all these biases might inadvertently produce altered histories. In Caribbean archaeology, researchers should be careful about how new technologies such as AI will be used to create narratives about past Indigenous and African people.

Involvement and Representation of Indigenous and Local Communities

As previously discussed, academic and funding organizations in the European Union and United States request that all data be submitted to open-access repositories. Yet, who will ultimately have access to those datasets? How are archaeological research projects considering the needs of the local and Indigenous communities in terms of open access and ethical practices? As previously discussed, open data is based on the idea that everyone can access the data; however, as stated by Chase et al. (2020), while the large majority of people in Europe and the United States have high-speed internet and access to computer hardware, the average person in the Latin American and Caribbean countryside does not. Open-access data does not open information to everyone but favors those specialists who have the knowledge and equipment to access and do something with that data. To avoid perpetuating the "digital divide" between richer and poorer countries and between highly educated people and the public, research projects should aim beyond making the data open access to create knowledgeable access to data (Bezuidenhout et al. 2017; Heeks 2022). For local and international research projects in the Caribbean, it is important to keep the questions proposed by Chase et al. (2020) in mind, that is, who benefits from the open-access data, and does having an open-access dataset deprive the local government of its sovereignty? Furthermore, it is important to consider that digital technologies are expensive, and even when they have become standard, usually projects in wealthier countries are the ones that can afford them.

To avoid deepening asymmetries and divisions between academia and the public and between richer and poorer countries, archaeological research projects need to consider the direct involvement and representation of Indigenous and local communities. References in a code of ethics are not enough, as first, they tend to be quite ambiguous on how digital archaeologists should specifically act, and second, there is no actual repercussion for not acting according to the code (Dennis 2020). Furthermore, codes of ethics tend to be apolitical guidelines that risk perpetuating global neocolonial logic (Curtoni 2015). So, the challenge is how to involve local and Indigenous communities within the research project and the posterior access to the data and results. This, in essence, follows the debate on how digital archaeology can be multicultural and multivocal without falling into the dangers of reproducing relations of knowledge-power and naïve narratives about the "other."

Best Practices and Recommendations

Based on the previous discussions, this section will present some recommendations for best practices that could contribute to seeking a more ethically oriented digital Caribbean archaeology.

Guidelines for Responsible Data Collection, Storage, and Sharing

Digital technologies and methodologies need to be explicitly considered by researchers when designing archaeological projects. Researchers need to be clear on which digital tools and methods will be used, which questions these methods will answer, what the limitations of these methods are, and what potential impacts these technologies and methodologies could have on the data and the local population. Besides this, all archaeological projects in the Caribbean should share with regional/national organizations and local communities what type of data will be collected, how and where it will be stored, the platforms and ways it will be shared, and indicate who can access the data. Extra attention should be paid to the type of personal information that can inadvertently be passed on to digital databases, for example, naming archaeological sites after the landowners. Providing landowner's names to archaeological sites is a common tradition in Caribbean and world archaeology, yet how are we certain that we are not sharing more than what is intended? How can we control it after the research is finished? Sites and material culture distributions should receive codes for their naming and classification, and no link to contemporary people should be placed on digital databases. Archaeological projects need to pay attention to how the creation and storage of databases could expose vulnerable populations and/ or perpetuate historical asymmetries. Even when people agree for their data to be used in research, they are usually agreeing for a particular researcher, whom they trust, to use their information. They do not know and cannot foresee who else will use their information. If informed of the full extent of potential uses, they might not want their names, opinions, and information to be openly available to anyone. This brings two important considerations. First, provision of sufficient information to informants and collaborators on how their data will be used. Second, online repositories should have layers of open access, where people could have access to certain data but not to all metadata unless they directly contact the creator(s) or institution(s).

Sharing archaeological data in open-access repositories is done out of good faith that everyone who will access and use the data will behave according to a general standard of ethical scientific behavior. Yet, this might not always be the case, and usually there will be no controlling or enforcing mechanisms in place. European and US-based funding organizations must be aware that open access might bring external prejudices to local communities and might even affect national sovereignty. For example, the European Commission's "Ethics in Social Science and Humanities" document recognizes that "some research involves materials, methods or technologies or generates knowledge that could be used for unethical ends. Although such research is usually carried out with benign intentions, it has the potential to harm humans, animals or the environment, or society" (European Commission 2021). However, they refer to professional codes to remind scientists of ethically correct procedures and do not offer any advice on how to manage communications between the commission and local or national agencies. In this case, the researcher holds all responsibilities regarding how to collect and store the data, but also regarding all potential uses after the data is openly available. This cannot in practice be the procedure as, on the one hand, researchers constantly interact with local organizations, and, on the other, how can they be held responsible for the future use of a database when they have no control over how the repositories work? A general proposal could be that repositories provide a more personalized service, including (1) some of the information is open access but not all; (2) full access is only available by application to the repository; (3) the data creators will always be contacted when someone wants to download their data, and in the case that they are not available anymore, then the institutions where they worked will be contacted instead; (4) platforms where the open data is stored can be easily accessed by local communities; (5) local communities and individuals can have a direct line of communication with the researchers; and (6) researchers upload a presentation where they talk about what is being shared and the conclusions they reached by working with the data. In this way, information could be openly available while taking care that no misuse will happen, as well as that it will be accessible and understandable by local communities.

Involving Local and Indigenous Communities in Digital Archaeology Projects

Even before the beginning of the project and of the data collection, local communities should be informed about the archaeological project and its impact. Consultation is the first ethical aspect of involving local and Indigenous communities in digital and non-digital archaeological projects. Consulting, however, is not the same as informing. Informing people means they know that something will happen, which is, of course, important in archaeology. However, consulting implies that the community gets involved in the project from the start and is able to make decisions and have an impact on the project itself. Consultation is a way of avoiding the colonial underlying component of archaeological hegemonic position in relation to local and Indigenous communities. As previously discussed, multiculturalism and multivocality can be used to maintain coloniality when considered passively. An active approach considers the community's opinions, even though they might affect the direction of the project and/or which data can be digitized; however, it does this in a way that will ultimately benefit the people and the research as a whole. Furthermore, presentations of the research and its resulting digital data and models to the community should take place at regular and preset intervals during the period of the project, as well as activities for educational content and training regarding the use of digital technologies and data.

Training and Education

This section has two aspects: on one side, the education of archaeologists and, on the other, the education of the public. Regarding archaeologists, in the Caribbean, not every country has an official program for studying archaeology, and people often study related disciplines and later formalize their studies in the United States or Europe. While higher education in Europe and the United States has more specializations and opportunities in digital archaeology, few programs have an explicit approach to dealing with ethical issues (Dennis 2020), and even fewer programs focus on ethical challenges for specific regions. Nonetheless, the advances in digital education around the world have brought the possibility for students to train themselves via online courses and degrees, such as the MOOCs provided by different platforms and universities. Yet, it is a point for attention that getting training and education on the tools and methodologies is not enough for students to be ethically aware of the potential impacts of their research in the Caribbean or elsewhere. As mentioned before, these massive online open courses might come with a one-sided perspective of the world—the Western one—that might have negative or distorted connotations for students in Indigenous or rural communities and thereby reinforce traditional historical inequalities and colonialist ideals.

Regarding local and Indigenous communities, training and education should not relate to the teaching of archaeological digital methods unless that is what the community wants. Other strategies can also be implemented to help their members gain a formal education in archaeology. Rather, training and education refers to teaching local communities what archaeologists do, the type of data they register and how it is used, and the impact digital archaeology projects can have on the lives of people today. As suggested by the code of ethics of the CAA (Brughmans et al. 2018), digital archaeologists need to help communities understand the benefits and risks of digital technologies for their autonomy, histories, and culture. The diverse and multidisciplinary background digital archaeologists have could play an important role in connecting digital and non-digital archaeology with communities, governments, and organizations by presenting transparent research designs, and the uses and abuses of digital models. The wide range of tools and visual aids resulting from digital archaeology places these subfields in a privileged position to educate the public and train local museum staff about diverse methodologies, multiple digital epistemologies, the power of networks, advanced audiovisual representations, archaeo-gaming, and the advantages of hard sciences in the study and interpretation of the past. Without diminishing the importance of non-digital educational material, digital representations have the potential to store and disseminate information for longer and to make it easily accessible by anyone who has access to digital hardware and software. Of course, this is an advantage only as long as professional educational programs explicitly teach ethics and ethical challenges in digital Caribbean archaeology. As Gnecco (2015: 14) stated, "A relational ethics, an ethics of multiple perspectives, moves beyond critique and reflexivity and tackles the issue of (un) communication." Digital archaeologists need to ask themselves, for example, how do we connect digital data with traditional histories and stories? How does digital data represent and enable a dialogue with local communities? If right and wrong are contextual and historical categories, and if archaeology as a discipline perpetuates colonialist ideas and power asymmetries, how can we set up boundaries for accountability and the integration of local voices?

Collaborative International Efforts

While this chapter has presented a standpoint in relation to US and European hegemonic archaeology, it does not imply that relations should be cut off; rather, it aims to reflect on how we can foster partnerships while respecting local autonomy. Besides the previously discussed topics regarding open data, information, consent, education, training, and communication, there are some aspects that can promote better and more symmetrical communication channels. For example, the recent Local Voices initiative (Jean and Herrera Malatesta 2024) seeks to create a platform for local Caribbean archaeologists to communicate, establish collaborations, provide and get training and education, and interact with other local colleagues and agencies without the mediation or coordination of US or European (senior) academics. Another example is the Caribbean Digital Scholarship Collective, which provides training in digital technologies and methodologies, as well as digital cultural activities that enhance the local Caribbean histories. Collaborations with international colleagues or agencies are encouraged, particularly if they seek to develop projects where non-colonialist perspectives, symmetrical relationships, equal responsibilities, and ethical approaches are the core.

Based on the previous discussions and on the recommendations provided by Richardson (2018: 70), some key points for future directions for ethical digital archaeology in the Caribbean are that archaeologists should lobby governmental and professional organizations to ensure that robust ethical statements on digital forms of archaeology are created and included within their codes of ethics. For example, as Fricke, Giovas, Hanna, Shorter, and Victorina (this volume) have mentioned, the newly created code of ethics of the International Association of Caribbean Archaeology still needs a section on digital and computational archaeology. Considering the advantages of digital technologies, well-defined strategies for citizen science and fair and transparent relationships with local people should be embedded in project design. Archaeologists should be clear about how digital data is collected, stored, and shared. The communication between local researchers, institutions, and international collaborators should always be direct and transparent and follow local regulations. Finally, local Caribbean archaeologists need to work toward the development of a way to hold local and international researchers accountable for unethical behaviors.

Conclusion

This chapter aimed to provide the general context of ethical discussions and considerations in world digital archaeology and how this can be used in the Caribbean. It is a first attempt to open the debate on ethical challenges in Caribbean digital archaeology. As the chapter presented, the main challenges for ethical considerations in digital archaeology are the issues with data creation, use, and storage, particularly those related to open-access databases, rights to reuse datasets, and concerns regarding potential negative exposure and vulnerability of local communities in open-access metadata. Also, questions are raised regarding the ethical dimensions of advanced digital technologies such as AI and ML and how those can perpetuate traditional asymmetries and colonialist representations. Finally, there is a big debate in digital and non-digital archaeology on the use of codes of ethics, as they can spread monoculture perspectives and hegemonic discourses about the past. It is relevant that archaeologists recognize that the concepts of right and wrong are historically and contextually dependent. Digital archaeological projects in the Caribbean must produce transparent research designs that inform local and Indigenous communities and obtain their consent. Additionally, research projects should aim to educate and train the local public.

Overall, this chapter calls for ongoing ethical reflections and community involvement in Caribbean digital archaeology. Archaeological research does not finish when analysis and narratives are written; it continues through the museums and platforms where materials and digital data are stored and from where new stories can be created. The archaeological process contributes to the social, economic, and cultural capitals of communities and individuals who could develop new skills and knowledge to be used in their lives—this is part of archaeology's potential to provide social justice. A digital archaeological ethical perspective that seeks social justice will open possibilities for the local and Indigenous communities of the past and the present to have their voices heard.

Notes

1 The Teoría Arqueológica en América del Sur (TAAS) is the only subcontinental conference in South America that deals with archaeological theories and practices. It started in 1998 and since then it has run every two years in different Latin American countries (Herrera Malatesta n.d.).

2 For example, see the debate about the use of early colonial maps in archaeological research on the island today shared by the Dominican Republic and Haiti in Herrera Malatesta and Jean (2023). Or the debate about the term "encounter" in González-Ruibal (2008).

3 Two groups that offer training and activities for Caribbean people in digital humanities and archaeology are the Caribbean Digital Scholarship Collective (https://cdscollective.org/) and the Computer Applications and Quantitative Methods in Archaeology chapter for Latin America and the Caribbean (CAA LAC, https://lac.caa-international.org/).

References Cited

Adam, Taskeen. 2019. "Digital Neocolonialism and Massive Open Online Courses (MOOCs): Colonial Pasts and Neoliberal Futures." *Learning, Media and Technology* 44(3): 365–380.

Benavides, Oswaldo Hugo. 2010. "Lo indígena en el pasado arqueológico: Reflejos espectrales de la posmodernidad en el Ecuador." In *Pueblos indígenas y arqueología en América Latina,* edited by Cristóbal Gnecco and Patricia Ayala Rocabado, 417–437. Bogotá: Fundación de Investigaciones Arqueológicas Nacionales, Banco de la República.

Bevan, Andrew. 2015. "The Data Deluge." *Antiquity* 89(348): 1473–1484.

Bezuidenhout, Louise M., Sabina Leonelli, Ann H. Kelly, and Brian Rappert. 2017. "Beyond the Digital Divide: Towards a Situated Approach to Open Data." *Science and Public Policy* 44(4): 464–475.

Brughmans, Tom, Hugh Corley, L. Meghan Dennis, Kate Ellenberger, Penelope Foreman, César González-Pérez, Vivian S. James, Rachel Opitz, Hanna Marie Pageau, Sara Perry, Lorna-Jane Richardson, Doug Rocks-Macqueen, and Arianna Traviglia. 2018. "Ethics Policy of the Computer Applications and Quantitative Methods in Archaeology (CAA)." Computer Applications and Quantitative Methods in Archaeology. https://caa-international.org/about/policies/ethics-policy/ (accessed June 27, 2024).

Brughmans, Tom, and Matthew A. Peeples. 2023. *Network Science in Archaeology.* Cambridge: Cambridge University Press.

Casilli, Antonio A. 2019. *En attendant les robots: Enquête sur le travail du clic.* Paris: Editions du Seuil, Paris.

Chase, Adrian S. Z., Diane Chase, and Arlen Chase. 2020. "Ethics, New Colonialism, and Lidar Data: A Decade of Lidar in Maya Archaeology." *Journal of Computer Applications in Archaeology* 3(1): 51–62.

Cohen, Anna, Sarah Klassen, and Damian Evans. 2020. "Ethics in Archaeological Lidar." *Journal of Computer Applications in Archaeology* 3(1): 76–91.

Colley, Sarah. 2015. "Ethics and Digital Heritage." In *The Ethics of Cultural Heritage,* edited by Tracy Ireland and John Schofield, 13–32. New York: Springer. https://doi.org/10.1007/978-1-4939-1649-8_2.

Conolly, James, and Mark Lake. 2006. *Geographical Information Systems in Archaeology.* Cambridge: Cambridge University Press.

Crawford, Kate. 2021. *The Atlas of AI: Power, Politics, and the Planetary Costs of Artificial Intelligence.* New Haven, Connecticut: Yale University Press. https://doi.org/doi:10.12987/9780300252392 (accessed June 27, 2024).

Curtoni, Rafael Pedro. 2015. "Against Global Archaeological Ethics: Critical Views from South America." In *Ethics and Archaeological Praxis,* edited by Cristóbal Gnecco and Dorothy Lippert, 41–47. New York: Springer.

Daly, Patrick, and Thomas L. Evans, eds. 2006. *Digital Archaeology: Bridging Method and Theory.* London: Routledge.

Dennis, L. Meghan. 2020. "Digital Archaeological Ethics: Successes and Failures in Disciplinary Attention." *Journal of Computer Applications in Archaeology* 3(1): 210–218.

European Commission. 2021. "Ethics in Social Science and Humanities." https://ec.europa.eu/info/funding-tenders/opportunities/docs/2021-2027/horizon/guidance/ethics-in-social-science-and-humanities_he_en.pdf (accessed June 27, 2024).

Fernández, Víctor M. 2015. "Europe: Beyond the Canon." In *Ethics and Archaeological Praxis*, edited by Cristóbal Gnecco and Dorothy Lippert, 61–68. New York: Springer.

Floridi, Luciano, and Mariarosaria Taddeo. 2016. "What Is Data Ethics?" *Philosophical Transactions of the Royal Society A: Mathematical, Physical and Engineering Sciences* 374(2083), 20160360.

Fricke, Felicia, and Rachel Hoerman. 2022. "Archaeology and Social Justice in Island Worlds." *World Archaeology* 54(3): 484–489.

Gillings, Mark, Piraye Hacıgüzeller, and Gary Lock. 2020. *Archaeological Spatial Analysis: A Methodological Guide*. London: Routledge.

Gnecco, Cristóbal. 2015. "An Entanglement of Sorts: Archaeology, Ethics, Praxis, Multiculturalism." In *Ethics and Archaeological Praxis*, edited by Cristóbal Gnecco and Dorothy Lippert, 1–17. New York: Springer.

Gnecco, Cristóbal, and Carl Henrik Langebaek. 2006a. Contra la tiranía del pensamiento tipológico. In *Contra la tiranía tipológica en arqueología: Una Visión desde Suramérica*, edited by Cristóbal Gnecco, ix–xiv. Bogotá: Universidad de Los Andes, Facultad de Ciencias Sociales, CESO.

Gnecco, Cristóbal, and Carl Henrik Langebaek, eds. 2006b. *Contra la tiranía tipológica en arqueología: Una visión desde Suramérica*. Bogotá: Universidad de Los Andes, Facultad de Ciencias Sociales, CESO.

González-Ruibal, Alfredo. 2008. "Postpolitical Colonialism." *Journal of Mediterranean Archaeology* 21(2): 285.

González-Ruibal, Alfredo. 2018. "Ethics of Archaeology." *Annual Review of Anthropology* 47: 345–360.

González-Tennant, Edward. 2014. "The 'Color' of Heritage: Decolonizing Collaborative Archaeology in the Caribbean." *Journal of African Diaspora Archaeology and Heritage* 3(1): 26–50.

Grosman, Leore. 2016. "Reaching the Point of No Return: The Computational Revolution in Archaeology." *Annual Review of Anthropology* 45: 129–145.

Haber, Alejandro, and Nick Shepherd. 2015. "After Ethics: Ancestral Voices and Post-Disciplinary Worlds in Archaeology: An Introduction." In *After Ethics: Ancestral Voices and Post-Disciplinary Worlds in Archaeology*, edited by Alejandro Haber and Nick Shepherd, 1–10. New York: Springer.

Hamilakis, Yannis. 2007. "From Ethics to Politics." In *Archaeology and Capitalism: From Ethics to Politics*, edited by Yannis Hamilakis and Philip Duke, 15–40. London: Routledge.

Hamilakis, Yannis. 2018. "Decolonial Archaeology as Social Justice." *Antiquity* 92(362): 518–520.

Hauser, Mark, and Dan Hicks. 2007. "Colonialism and Landscape: Power, Materiality and Scales of Analysis in Caribbean Historical Archaeology." In *Envisioning Landscape: Situations and Standpoints in Archaeology and Heritage*, edited by Dan Hicks, Laura McAtackney, and Graham Fairclough, 251–274. London: Routledge.

Hauser, Mark W. 2022. "The Work of Boundaries: Critical Cartographies and the Archaeological Record of the Relatively Recent Past." *Annual Review of Anthropology* 51: 509–526.

Heeks, R. 2022. "Digital Inequality beyond the Digital Divide: Conceptualizing Adverse Digital Incorporation in the Global South." *Information Technology for Development* 28(4): 688–704.

Herrera Malatesta, Eduardo. n.d. La Reunión de Teoría Arqueológica en América del Sur. In *Arqueologías de cuerpos, políticas y memorias: Reflexiones teóricas desde América del Sur,* edited by Eduardo Herrera Malatesta. Book manuscript in peer-review.

Herrera Malatesta, Eduardo. 2022. "The Transformation of Indigenous Landscape in the First Colonized Region of the Caribbean." *Land* 11(4): 509.

Herrera Malatesta, Eduardo, and José R. Pellini. Forthcoming. "The Professionalization of Archaeology and the Study of the Past: Brazil, Colombia, and Venezuela." In *The Oxford Handbook of South American Archaeology,* edited by M. Aldenderfer, M. Sepulveda, and E. Goes Neves. Oxford: Oxford University Press.

Herrera Malatesta, Eduardo, and Joseph Sony Jean. 2023. "Colonization, Indigenous Resilience, and Social Justice in Caribbean Archaeology." In *The Oxford Handbook of Global Indigenous Archaeologies,* edited by C. Smith, K. Pollard, A. Kumar Kanungo, S. K. May, S. L. López Varela, and J. Watkins. Oxford: Oxford University Press.

Hodder, Ian. 1999. *The Archaeological Process: An Introduction.* Oxford: Blackwell.

Hodder, Ian, and Clive Orton. (1976). *Spatial Analysis in Archaeology.* Cambridge University Press.

Hofman, Corinne L., Jorge Ulloa Hung, Eduardo Herrera Malatesta, Joseph S. Jean, Till F. Sonnemann, and Menno L. P. Hoogland, 2018. "Indigenous Caribbean Perspectives: Archaeologies and Legacies of the First Colonised Region in the New World." *Antiquity* 92(361): 200–216.

Huggett, Jeremy. 2015. "2 Digital Haystacks: Open Data and the Transformation of Archaeological Knowledge." In *Open Source Archaeology,* edited by Andrew T. Wilson and Ben Edwards, 6–29. Warsaw: De Gruyter Open.

Jean, Joseph Sony, and Eduardo Herrera Malatesta. 2024. *Local Voices, Global Debates: The Uses of Archaeological Heritage in the Caribbean.* Leiden: Brill.

Jofré Luna, Ivana Carina. 2015. "The Mark of the Indian Still Inhabits Our Body: On Ethics and Disciplining in South American Archaeology." In *After Ethics: Ancestral Voices and Post-Disciplinary Worlds in Archaeology,* edited by Alejandro Haber and Nick Shepherd, 55–78. New York: Springer.

Labadi, Sophia. 2022. *Rethinking Heritage for Sustainable Development.* London: UCL Press.

Lock, Gary. 2003. *Using Computers in Archaeology: Towards Virtual Pasts.* London: Routledge.

McCoy, Mark D. 2017. "Geospatial Big Data and Archaeology: Prospects and Problems too Great to Ignore." *Journal of Archaeological Science* 84: 74–94.

Menon, Sunita. 2023. "Postcolonial Differentials in Algorithmic Bias: Challenging Digital Neo-Colonialism in Africa." *SCRIPTed: A Journal of Law, Technology & Society* 20(2): 383–399.

Morgan, Colleen. 2022. "Current Digital Archaeology." *Annual Review of Anthropology* 51: 213–231.

Mouton, Morgan, and Ryan Burns. 2021. "(Digital) Neo-Colonialism in the Smart City." *Regional Studies* 55(12): 1890–1901.

Pagán-Jiménez, Jaime R., and Reniel Rodríguez Ramos. 2008. "Sobre arqueologías de liberación en una 'colonia postcolonial' (Puerto Rico)." *Revista de Ciencias Sociales* 19: 8–41.

Pagán-Jiménez, Jaime R. 2004. "Is All Archaeology at Present a Postcolonial One? Constructive Answers from an Eccentric Point of View." *Journal of Social Archaeology* 4(2): 200–213.

Raji, Inioluwa Deborah, Timnit Gebru, Margaret Mitchell, Joy Buolamwini, Joonseok Lee, and Emily Denton. 2020. "Saving Face: Investigating the Ethical Concerns of Facial Recognition Auditing." *Proceedings of the AAAI/ACM Conference on AI, Ethics, and Society,* New York, NY, USA.

Richardson, Lorna-Jane. 2018. "Ethical Challenges in Digital Public Archaeology." *Journal of Computer Applications in Archaeology* 1(1): 64–73.

Romanowska, Iza, Colin D. Wren, and Stefani A. Crabtree. 2021. *Agent-Based Modeling for Archaeology: Simulating the Complexity of Societies.* Santa Fe: Santa Fe Institute Press.

Tarlow, Sarah. 2006. "Archaeological Ethics and the People of the Past." In *The Ethics of Archaeology: Philosophical Perspectives on Archaeological Practice,* edited by Chris Scarre and Geoffrey Scarre, 199–216. Cambridge: Cambridge University Press.

Tenzer, Martina, Giada Pistilli, Alex Brandsen, and Alex Shenfield. 2024. "Debating AI in Archaeology: Applications, Implications, and Ethical Considerations." *Internet Archaeology* 67.

Ulloa Hung, Jorge. 2016. "Colonialismo, Indigenismo y Arqueología en la República Dominicana: Silencios confusos y encubrimientos diversos." In *Indígenas e Indios en el Caribe: Presencia, legado y studio,* edited by Jorge Ulloa Hung and Roberto Valcárcel, 203–246. Santo Domingo, Dominican Republic: Instituto Tecnológico de Santo Domingo.

Véliz, Carissa. 2023. *Privacy Is Power: Why and How You Should Take Back Control of Your Data.* London: Bantam Press.

Wilner, Alex S. 2018. "Cybersecurity and Its Discontents: Artificial Intelligence, the Internet of Things, and Digital Misinformation." *International Journal* 73(2): 308–316.

Zembylas, Michalinos. 2023. "A Decolonial Approach to AI in Higher Education Teaching and Learning: Strategies for Undoing the Ethics of Digital Neocolonialism." *Learning, Media and Technology* 48(1): 25–37.

Zubrow, Ezra B. W. 2006. "Digital Archaeology: A Historical Context." *Digital Archaeology: Bridging Method and Theory,* edited by Patrick Daly and Thomas L. Evans, 10–31. London: Routledge.

Conclusion

Acknowledgment, Deference, Awareness, Politics, and Action

Five Keywords for a Brighter Ethical Future in Caribbean Archaeology

Jaime R. Pagán-Jiménez and Reniel Rodríguez Ramos

It has been clearly shown in this volume that the concept "ethics" is not a single universal construct, although its use is commonplace in modern academic scenarios and in many other instances of our daily lives. Most of the elements historically signified by this concept have been, and still are, typically articulated from an Eurocentric ethos. This fact is not surprising. Ethics has been an important aspect of Western academic philosophy, from which it has sought to understand and subjectively categorize human behavior mainly from binomial concepts such as good and bad, right and wrong, beneficial and harmful, and so on. There is not, and there will hardly be, a universal consensus by which a single definition of this concept, or rather of the scaffolding of its internal structure, can be conceived so that it can be accepted and unanimously suited for gauging our actions in the diversity of contexts of human endeavor. We must accept that globally there are too many different contextually bound perspectives to be able to articulate a completely balanced, aseptic, or neutral definition of this concept that satisfies us all.

However, throughout the world, the different political, commercial, professional, and religious organizations and collectivities that exist in the supranational and local spheres tend to adhere to various standards mostly derived from Western definitions of "ethics" that have been negotiated and developed by their members to satisfy very specific needs or goals. The so-called codes of ethics, sometimes equated to "rules of thumb," generally serve to give shape and cohesion to countless agendas, projects, and plans that require clear guidelines for action in order to achieve their objectives in a "correct" manner. In this sense, those of us who today embrace the elusive concept of ethics from the fields situated under the umbrella of cultural heritage studies acknowledge the great limitations, but also the vast opportunities, that are tied to any effort to establish balanced and fair principles to perform our actions ethically between and betwixt our fields or our places in life.

As some contributors of this book have shown, there is already one supra-national code of ethics built for Caribbean archaeology, and there are also new collectives such as the Coalition for Caribbean Archaeological Heritage (CoCAH) that are setting the stage for furthering awareness for the need of ethical and inclusive practices in the management of our cultural heritage that integrally incorporate other fields and local stakeholders that are attached to the study and management of our pasts. For this reason, rather than try-ing to assess what ethics and its different iterations are or should be in the context of this book, we wish to highlight some key issues that depart from the contributions of our colleagues. We will be briefly doing this from a local Caribbean prism that is irremediably nuanced by our particular perspective from Puerto Rico, an island that still lives under colonial rule.

This contribution is not intended to be a review of the works included in this volume, but instead a reflection on what aspects must be still thought about and emphasized more deeply to reach goals that can directly benefit the peoples that configure our multifaceted Caribbean. Our reflection is structured on the basis of the discussion of some key elements that should accompany any ethical practice regarding the management of our Caribbean cultural patrimonies.

1. Acknowledgment

In the Caribbean region, archaeology practitioners and any other parties dealing with our archaeological/cultural heritage must be aware of and acknowledge local researchers and their contributions. Before starting ar-chaeological and cultural heritage work anywhere in the islands, researchers must first identify (not in just their own language, but considering all the languages used in the islands), appraise, analyze, and give proper credit to previously produced information by local practitioners. The practice in Caribbean archaeology of mostly citing articles produced by scholars from the academic centers (Pagán-Jiménez 2000; Pagán-Jiménez 2004), while not recognizing the works made by local researchers in their own language, is obviously connected to the colonialist origins of archaeology. It is not fair at all, from any point of view, to disregard or recolonize the knowledge and methodologies that local people have already produced on their cultural heritage and its different action frameworks. This makes local contributions, sometimes groundbreaking in their time and even now, invisible because we believe we now have more advanced ways of dealing with topics that we deem relevant to our disciplines. Many Caribbean thinkers in different areas of knowledge such as philosophy, political science, history, critical theory, anthropology, and archaeology have already experienced this injustice too many times to have to experience it again, but this time launched from ethical or social awareness perspectives. This type of practice is too commonplace in Caribbeanist archaeology, and it is time to acknowledge it and put an end to it.

2. Deference

Acknowledging the existence of different local stakeholders implies not only identifying them but also understanding their social, cultural, religious, and political motivations, and knowing everything they have produced and worked on regarding certain key aspects of the archaeological topic that is to be addressed. Working in the archaeology of the Caribbean from an inclusive and horizontal perspective requires a deep knowledge of the political, economic, and sociocultural scenario in which local research has been developed. Although it is completely acceptable not to agree with all the positions that the various local practitioners of the islands may take, we must learn, sometimes along with them, what their paths and directions have been, seeking to find common ground, or even totally the opposite. Respecting the interests of stakeholders, especially if they are local, means dialoguing, knowing, and uniting when we can reach consensus on the issues or actions that we wish to carry out.

3. Awareness

In our archipelago, most local professional archaeologists and people from other disciplines who deal with this kind of work are also members of local communities. We have to be careful when making the common differentiation in our fields between professional archaeologists and local communities. In most cases, when islander archaeologists have managed to obtain a professional degree in the field, they have not ceased to be members of their local communities. On the contrary, they are usually seen by their island peers as local members who also managed to enter a professional guild. Therefore, the work and knowledge produced by local professional archaeologists must also be seen as a triumph for local communities because they have contributed one of their members to the field of professional archaeology/history/geography. This assertion has serious and profound implications for the Caribbean since these local archaeologists integrate into the professional world of archaeology without abandoning their community matrix or their local traditional knowledge, which contributes to their particular way of engaging with their cultural patrimony.

4. Politics

We strongly believe that working from an ethical standpoint in our disciplines necessarily entails assuming concrete political positions, particularly when disciplinary and social performance occurs in environments still impregnated with colonial histories in which patrimonial practices are led by social and political subjects who are heirs of imperial power (Pagán-Jiménez 2004). The uses of (cultural) heritage are almost infinite, and its transformative or overwhelming power in the construction of official pasts has been widely recognized and discussed elsewhere (Jean and Herrera Malatesta 2024; Smith 2007). Often in our islands, the heirs of colonial power today are those who occupy the administrative and political action spaces, attempting to perpetuate colonial practices that are sometimes almost imperceptible to the most experienced scholar on this topic. Assuming political positions against colonialism in the Caribbean and against all its past and current consequences cannot be just another fashionable narrative in centrist discursive performance; decolonial practices must induce disciplinary and concerted action between academia and society in concrete terms. Therefore, our work as scholars of the past must strive not only to discover, interpret, conserve, and disseminate but also to energize those new pasts together with those who have the right to enjoy it: local or regional communities.

5. Action

As the readers of this volume are possibly practitioners of archaeology who have already been exposed, at least theoretically, to the ideas we have hereby discussed, what remains is a call to go beyond mere politically correct discourse and to engage in concrete actions toward ethical practices in Caribbean archaeology. We, as local professional archaeologists, since 2006 have chosen to conceive and put into practice (in books and on the streets) what we have previously called "archaeologies of liberation" (Pagán-Jiménez and Rodríguez Ramos 2008), precisely to deal with the existing disconnection between our discipline and our communities and also as a way of empowering our discipline and our society in search of a future for a truly decolonized archaeology. In our case, our emancipatory project has been and continues to be an extremely complex task, especially because we live in the bowels of the colonial monster. Our work has hardly received economic or academic support and incentives, since it is inconceivable for local institutions or those of our dominant entity (the United States) to support an openly anti-colonial scientific and social project. The operationalization of some of the aspects discussed here, through venues such as the Coalición Puertorriqueña de Arqueología (2024), has had important repercussions not only in the dissemination of newly generated archaeological knowledge but also in raising awareness of the need to protect our cultural heritage for future generations.

Archaeological practice in the Caribbean has been moving in this direction, making evident the need to, first, decolonize archaeological practice in the region, and second, to promote practices that will allow both foreign and local agents to engage ethically with our cultural patrimony. The newly founded Coalition for Caribbean Archaeological Heritage (CoCAH) is and will be open enough to help and participate with us in our academic and social endeavors, but without ceasing to cover other equally diverse and complex regional and local objectives. By being part of CoCAH, other colleagues and members of our societies who decide to carry out archaeological projects of a socially and politically complex nature should not feel alienated. They will now be able to count on the profound experiences and dynamism of this diverse group of peers who will strengthen any initiative that requires ethical positions to safeguard our archaeological heritage, the people who work for it, and the people it serves.

This book exemplifies the diversity of topics and voices, many of them politically and socially transversal, that also echo in our Caribbean societies. Almost all of these authors, with such clear ways of thinking in archaeology, cultural heritage, and community engagement, are our partners in CoCAH, demonstrating that this new organization can positively influence local issues and matters of global interest which affect the management and production of knowledge about our cultural heritage. In sum, CoCAH aims to create a brighter ethical present and future for our cultural heritage and the people to whom it belongs.

Acknowledgment

We are thankful to the editors of this book for their kind invitation to critically reflect on the central axis of the work.

References Cited

Coalición Puertorriqueña de Arqueología. 2024. "Coalición Puertorriqueña de Arqueología." Digital repository. https://cparqueo.blogspot.com/2009/04/que-es-la-coalicion-puertorriquena-de_18.html (accessed August 16, 2024).

Jean, Joseph Sony, and Eduardo Herrera Malatesta, eds. 2024. *Local Voices, Global Debates: The Uses of Archaeological Heritage in the Caribbean.* Leiden: Brill.

Pagán-Jiménez, Jaime R. 2000. "La Antropología en Puerto Rico: Dicotomía de Centro-Periferia." *Boletín de Antropologia Americana* 36: 193–202.

Pagán-Jiménez, Jaime R. 2004. "Is All Archaeology at Present a Postcolonial One? Constructive Answers from an Eccentric Point of View." *Journal of Social Archaeology* 4(2): 200–213.

Pagán-Jiménez, Jaime R., and Reniel Rodríguez Ramos. 2008. "Toward the Liberation of Archaeological Praxis in a 'Postcolonial Colony': The Case of Puerto Rico." In *Archaeology and the Postcolonial Critique,* edited by Matthew Liebmann and Uzma Rizvi, 53–71. Lanham, Maryland: AltaMira Press.

Smith, Laurajane. 2007. *Uses of Heritage.* Oxford: Routledge.

CONTRIBUTORS

Lauriane Ammerlaan is president of Bonaire Archaeological Institute (BONAI).

Oliver Antczak is teaching associate in heritage studies at the University of Cambridge. He is the coeditor of *Rethinking the Archaeology Heritage Divide.*

Anne I. Bancroft is the head of Conservation and Collection Care at the Barbados Museum.

Jada Benn Torres is an associate professor and director of the Genetic Anthropology and Biocultural Studies Laboratory at Vanderbilt University.

Daniel Antonio Brito-Pacheco is a master's student in computer science at Universidad Autónoma de Yucatán.

Oriana Chiappa is a joint PhD candidate between Ghent University and Vrije Universiteit Brussel, focusing on funerary rituals and mobility patterns of cremated human remains from the Balearic Islands.

Andreana S. Cunningham is an assistant professor of anthropology, archaeology, and African American and Black diaspora studies at Boston University.

Kevin Farmer is deputy director of the Barbados Museum and Historical Society.

Felicia J. Fricke is an archaeologist, osteologist, and historian, and assistant professor at the University of Copenhagen. She is author of the book *Slaafgemaakt: Rethinking Enslavement in the Dutch Caribbean.*

Christina M. Giovas is an associate professor of archaeology at Simon Fraser University. She is coeditor of *Zooarchaeology in Practice: Case Studies in Methodology and Interpretation in Archaeofaunal Analysis.*

Jonathan A. Hanna is a project archaeologist at Richard Grubb & Associates and former curator at the Grenada National Museum. He is coeditor of *Real, Recent, or Replica: Precolumbian Caribbean Heritage as Art, Commodity, and Inspiration.*

Eduardo Herrera Malatesta is a landscape and computational archaeologist currently holding an Alexander von Humboldt senior postdoctoral researcher position at the University of Bonn. He is the editor of *Archaeological Perspectives on Contested and Political Landscapes* and coeditor of *Local Voices: The Uses of Archaeological Heritage in the Caribbean.*

Joseph Sony Jean is a postdoctoral researcher at the Institute for History at Leiden University and the Royal Netherlands Institute of Southeast Asian and Caribbean Studies (KITLV). He is coeditor of *Local Voices, Global Debates: The Uses of Archaeological Heritage in the Caribbean.*

marjolijn kok is an independent researcher at her own company, Bureau Archeologie en Toekomst.

Nelda Issa Marengo Camacho is the executive director at Boundary End Archaeology Research Center. She is coeditor of *When East Meets West: Chichen Itza, Tula, and the Postclassic Mesoamerican World.*

John Angus Martin, an independent researcher, is a historian, archivist, and museum curator specializing in Grenada's history and culture. He is the author/coauthor/editor of several books, including *A to Z of Grenada Heritage* and *Island Caribs and French Settlers in Grenada, 1498–1763.*

Ashleigh John Morris is a PhD candidate at Leiden University and is a heritage preservation and research officer at the National Trust of Trinidad and Tobago.

Kathrin Nägele is a group leader at the Max Planck Institute for Evolutionary Anthropology in Leipzig, Germany.

Maria A. Nieves-Colón is assistant professor of anthropology and principal investigator of the Anthropological Genetics Laboratories at the University of Minnesota Twin Cities.

Jaime R. Pagán-Jiménez is a research professor and director of the Center for Social Research's Laboratory of Ethnoecology and Human Paleoenvironments at the University of Puerto Rico in Río Piedras.

Matthew C. Reilly is an associate professor of anthropology and interdisciplinary programs at the City College of New York and the CUNY Graduate Center. He is the author of *Archaeology below the Cliff: Race, Class, and Redlegs in Barbadian Sugar Society*.

Reniel Rodríguez Ramos is a professor in the social sciences program of the Universidad de Puerto Rico in Utuado. He is the author of *Rethinking Puerto Rican Precolonial History* and coeditor of *The Oxford Handbook of Caribbean Archaeology*.

Fidel Rodríguez Velásquez is Faperj Postdoctoral fellow at department of history, Pontificia Universidade Católica do Rio de Janeiro (PUC-Rio), Brazil. He is the coeditor of Mundos del Trabajo: Sociabilidad, resistencias y vidas en movimiento.

Eleni Seferidou is a PhD candidate at the Max Planck Institute for Evolutionary Anthropology (MPI-EVA), focusing on ancient DNA in the Caribbean region.

John Shorter is a public history graduate student at the University of the West Indies (Mona) in the Department of History and Archaeology. He is a coauthor of *Appleton Estate: From the Dickinson Family to the Campari Group, a Short History*.

Amy A. Victorina is an archaeologist at the National Archaeological-Anthropological Memory Management (NAAM, Curaçao).

Maaike S. de Waal is assistant professor and head of the Field Research and Education Centre at the Leiden University Faculty of Archaeology.

William A. White III is an associate professor of anthropology at the University of California, Berkeley. He is the author of *Segregation Made Them Neighbors: An Archaeology of Racialization in Boise, Idaho*.

INDEX

www.ingramcontent.com/pod-product-compliance
Lightning Source LLC
Chambersburg PA
CBHW031124270326
41929CB00011B/1485